THE ROMANTIC QUEST

THE ROMANTIC QUEST

BY
HOXIE NEALE FAIRCHILD

NEW YORK
RUSSELL & RUSSELL · INC
1965

PRINTED IN THE UNITED STATES OF AMERICA

ONULP

TO

THE MEMORY OF

MY DAUGHTER

PREFACE

The Romantic Quest is a book for students of some intellectual maturity, who, having already a bowing acquaintance with the writers of the age of Wordsworth, desire an interpretative analysis and synthesis of the chief tendencies of that period. If the reader possesses adequate preliminary knowledge, he may equally well be a college upper classman, a candidate for a graduate degree, or a private student beyond academic walls. Although most of my facts will be familiar to the specialist, the interpretation of those facts is not without elements of originality; and I have some hope that experts who open this book to estimate its suitability for their students will pause to read at least portions of it for themselves. They may feel, indeed, that the book is sometimes too subjective and opinionated for purposes of instruction. But in the present divided state of opinion, a personal interpretation of the subject is inevitable. The student must form his own views by comparing them with the views of others. Here, then, is only one of several interpretations with which he should become familiar.

Both in form and content, this book closely follows a course which I gave in the Columbia University Summer Session of 1929 to a class of graduate students most of whom had recently entered upon candidacy for the master's degree. The expansion of my lecture notes into written chapters naturally made many changes either necessary or desirable. But even in revising I have tried to preserve the quality of direct address to the reader, for I wished him to feel that he was not so much reading a book as taking a lecture course in the romantic period. I might have done more to balance the proportions of the original hasty sketch and render it more nearly complete. Such revision, however, would have drawn me toward a full-dress history of the English romantic movement, an undertaking for which I do not yet feel prepared. It seemed best to present these lectures as what they were originally intended to be, and then to return to my studies.

The Summer Session course included reading assignments and bibliographical suggestions. The former have here been omitted entirely, and the latter have been preserved only when they formed part of the actual text of a lecture. To add to the already abundant bibliographical aids to the study of this period would be a wasteful duplication of labor.

In preparing some of the original lectures on the naturalistic aspect of romanticism, I found it convenient to draw upon material contained in my dissertation, *The Noble Savage: A Study in Romantic Naturalism*; and at various points in the course I read to the class passages from that book. With the generous permission of the publishers, the Columbia University Press, some of those passages have been incorporated in the text of the present volume.

H. N. F.

Barnard College
Columbia University

CONTENTS

I

NATURE

Since the purpose of this course is to show how the romantic spirit manifests itself in the main tendencies of the age of Wordsworth, we might logically begin with a definition of romanticism. It will be better, however, to proceed inductively rather than deductively until we reach a point beyond which we cannot advance without defining. I adopt this method not only because it seems educationally desirable but because my conception of romanticism is one which if declared at the outset might confuse or antagonize. I prefer to introduce it to you gradually and by implication until you are prepared for an explicit statement of it. Obviously we need some hypothetical description of romanticism to hold in our minds as we set out, but at present almost any of the definitions which have been given you in the past will serve if it is not too narrow and fussy. We can probably all agree, for example, that romanticism is charaterized by the predmominance of emotion and imagination, and that it is partly a reaction against a view of life which produced a literature comparatively deficient in those qualities.

Whatever romanticism may be, it is probably too late to protest against the habit of referring to the age of Wordsworth as the romantic period. Resigning ourselves to this practice, indeed, we may say that if romanticism is anything at all it is some element which pervades and animates the chief intellectual tendencies of that period. The

age is full of the most perplexing currents and cross currents, but three streams of tendency are especially full and
strong. These are naturalism, medievalism, and transcendentalism. To the first, which I am now about to discuss,
almost half of the course will be devoted. The naturalistic
aspect of the romantic movement is in itself a complex
and extensive subject. Any one of several parts of this
field might furnish a starting point, but it seems best to
begin with the relation of the French Revolution to
naturalistic thought in England.

At the outset we are confronted by the fact that, at the
time of the Revolution, naturalism, political liberalism,
social idealism, and humanitarianism were the exclusive
property neither of romanticism nor of forces hostile to
romanticism. In English courses, you have probably been
told that these *isms* were watchwords of the romantic
movement. On the whole, that is true. In history courses,
you have probably been told that the French Revolution
represents the invasion of the sphere of practical politics
by the spirit of eighteenth century rationalism. On the
whole, that is true. And you have probably been told or
have read or inferred for yourselves that rationalism and
romanticism are hostile to each other. On the whole, that
also is true. But if political liberalism is an important
aspect both of rationalism and of romanticism, and if
rationalism and romanticism are essentially opposed, our
craving to simplify the past receives a rather serious
check. It is almost unwise to try too hard to clarify this
matter. The late eighteenth century itself was confused
about it, so that in being confused we are at least faithful
to the facts of intellectual history. Both in France and
England, the period of the French Revolution was a mix-

ture of rationalistic and romantic tendencies. Often they are mixed in a single writer — witness Rousseau. Now "nature" in one sense was a shibboleth of rationalism, while "nature" in another sense was a shibboleth of romanticism. Hence just as rationalism and romanticism are perplexingly mingled, so the two senses of "nature" are perplexingly mingled. Rousseau again would provide plenty of examples.

But it is making matters excessively simple to say that "nature" had two meanings. Professor Lovejoy, whose acute feeling for distinctions we shall elsewhere have occasion to admire, has discovered many different shades of meaning for this term in the eighteenth century. That, after all, is hardly surprising, for "nature" has always been primarily a loose kind of synonym for "things in general as I suppose them to be"; and since every man lives in a universe of his own, every man might be found to have his own private conception of nature if only he could express himself with sufficient clarity.

These individual conceptions of nature, however, subject themselves fairly well to classification. One cannot play the game of intellectual historiography without generalizing and simplifying. If we generalize and simplify hard enough, we may say that the ruling philosophy from about the middle of the seventeenth century to about the middle of the eighteenth was rationalistic. It believed in a simple, orderly, workmanlike universe based upon general principles like the axioms of Euclid. Human reason could understand those principles and could by more or less geometrical methods evolve from them all the specific facts that a sensible man should desire to know. Paley was to compare this universe to a watch. When the average man of the age of Pope talked about "nature," he generally meant this watch — the neat, common sense, readily comprehensible principles that made the universe tick. When Pope says,

> Learn hence for ancient rules a just esteem;
> To copy Nature is to copy them,

he has in mind this rationalistic conception of nature. He means that the ancients have discovered a body of critical axioms so exact and useful that they form part of the mechanism of the universal watch.

You may feel that this description of the "nature" of the age of Pope does not take sufficient account of the development of experimental science. But as a matter of fact experimental science, except as regards its immediate practical applications, was the handmaid of rationalistic philosophy and deductive logic until at least the middle of the eighteenth century. There are, of course, striking exceptions to this statement, but I must confine myself to the broad outlines. On the whole, seventeenth century philosophy was like medieval scholasticism in its habit of reasoning from the general to the particular. It used Euclidean mathematics where scholasticism had used Aristotelian syllogisms, but it was still essentially deductive. Its method was established, not by the experimental-minded Bacon, but by the mathematical-minded Descartes, who appealed to intuitively apprehended geometrical axioms rather than to the testimony of the senses. The seventeenth century, to be sure, made tremendous strides in physics and chemistry. But when men attempted to formulate experimentally observed facts into laws; the Cartesian influence long had the upper hand. The only way of establishing a scientific law was to show that it illustrated some proposition of the universal *a priori* deductive system. Even the experimenters of the Royal Society followed Descartes rather than Bacon. Their prime aim was to relate the processes of nature to the established laws of mathematics.

The discoveries of Newton, to be sure, tended to make scientific speculation physico-mathematical rather than merely mathematical. But although Newton himself was a genuine scientist who emphasized the necessity of experimental verification, he inherited the geometrical philosophy of Descartes. He found a way of describing mechanics in terms of mathematics, and he applied that method to the universe. He seemed therefore to have reconciled experiment and geometry, the inductive and the deductive, the Baconian and the Cartesian, the genuinely naturalistic and the rationalistic. To him the world was a great machine every operation of which could be deduced from the basic mathematical laws of that machine. In several respects, of course, Newton had been anticipated by Thomas Hobbes, but the influence of Hobbes' philosophy had been limited because of its cynicism and scepticism. Newton, on the other hand, might almost be called the father of our modern "no conflict between religion and science" attitude.

The Newtonian physico-mathematical conception of nature is the dominant philosophy of the 1690-1730 period. It coincides almost exactly, you will observe, with the dominance of literary pseudoclassicism. But while Newton's results were eagerly seized upon, the deductive and geometrical aspect of his philosophy was more acceptable to his age than the inductive and experimental aspect.

Even after a century of scientific research, the old idea
that speculation was more dignified and noble than direct
observation of nature was deeply rooted in the minds of
men. Experiment was desirable for purposes of verification, but Newton's discoveries had left little to be verified.
That little would soon be disposed of, the universe would
be completely understood, and men of intellect could
dispense with the vulgar necessity of handling pulleys and
test tubes. Any hitherto unobserved fact which might
appear could at once be related to one of the established
physico-mathematical laws.

This philosophy applied no less to man than to mechanics. Nature was a universal system, and man was
completely included in it. But to the spiritual, moral,
esthetic, and institutional life of man — fields in which
experimentation was either impossible or had not been
developed — the inductive aspect of Newton's thought
was largely inapplicable, and what remained was an
essentially Cartesian deductive rationalism expressing
itself to some extent in the jargon of science. Religion,
ethics, government, law, art — all were included in the
rationalistic conception of nature, and "laws of nature"
were fabricated to justify the prevalent ideas on those
subjects. These laws were to be apprehended by the reason, which was itself a part of nature. As John Herman
Randall, Jr., says in *The Making of the Modern Mind*:

Nature was through and through rational; hence what was
natural was easily identified with what was rational, and conversely, whatever, particularly in human society, seemed to an
intelligent man reasonable, was regarded as natural, as somehow
rooted in the very nature of things. So Nature and the Natural
easily became the ideal of man and of human society, and were
interpreted as Reason and the Reasonable.

This standard had hardly reached its full development before it began to decay. The term "decay" is used with intent. There undoubtedly was a certain amount of conscious rebellion against official rationalism, but on the whole we have to deal with a gradual, mainly unconscious, breaking down of old tendencies and an equally gradual and unconscious formation of new ones. The unraveling of this transitional medley is the major problem of eighteenth century scholarship, and it is far from being solved. Even if we had six years at our disposal instead of six weeks, we should still be baffled by it.

We may, however, observe several developments which contributed to the breakdown of rationalism. One is the gradual growth of an inductive and scientific spirit which by about the middle of the eighteenth century had given genuine observation and experiment a prestige equal to that of mathematical physics. This movement was initiated at the end of the seventeenth century by John Locke, the father of English empiricism. Locke analyzed Descartes' geometrical axioms into the thin air of which they were composed, and showed that the only valid basis of knowledge is observation of the facts of experience. But despite the wide popularity won by certain aspects of Locke's philosophy, eighteenth century thought as a whole never adopts a thoroughgoing empiricism. The natural sciences become more and more scientific, but the social sciences, with theology and philosophy, are much slower to abandon geometrical deduction. This cleavage between a deductive conception of man and an inductive conception of the rest of nature is perhaps the chief curse of modern thought. We must not suppose, of course, that the attempts now being made to bridge this gap are novel except in details. In the eighteenth century, genuine scientific method does increasingly invade the citadel of *a priori* assumptions about man and his relation to the universe. This extension of experiment and of the experimental attitude contributed greatly to the advance of knowledge, and freed the human mind from many bonds of tradition. Frequently, however, it produced a sophomoric cocksureness, a glib assumption of certitude in fields where no certitude existed.

A quite opposite result of the influence of scientific method is the discrediting of the validity of intellect as a means of arriving at truth. Locke, as I have said, grounded his philosophy upon observation of the facts of experience. But when, as a psychologist, he attempted critically to study the interaction of the mind and the external world, he found himself confronted by an insoluble mystery. If the facts of experience consist merely of internal impressions of sight, sound, smell, touch, and taste, what proof have we that the elaborate subjective creations of the mind are anything but a figment of imagination? This exposure of the dubiety of reason in the interests of reason was carried by Hume to the verge of an almost nihilistic scepticism. Santayana says of Locke and his followers:

The principle of their reasoning, where they chose to apply it, was always this, that ideas whose materials could all be accounted for in consciousness and referred to sense or to the operations of mind were thereby exhausted and deprived of further validity. Only the unaccountable, or rather the uncriticized, could be true. Consequently the advance of philosophy meant, in this school, the retreat of reason; for as one notion after another was clarified and reduced to its elements, it was *ipso facto* deprived of its function. It became impossible to be at once quite serious and quite intelligent; for to use reason was to indulge in subjective fiction, while conscientiously to abstain from using it was to sink back upon inarticulate and brutish instinct. In Hume this sophistication was frankly avowed. Philosophy discredited itself; but a man of parts, who loved intellectual games even better than backgammon, might take a hand with the wits and historians of his day, until the clock struck twelve and the party was over.

Except perhaps as regards Hume, Santayana rather overemphasizes the sophisticatedly malicious element in this self-destructive psychology. On the whole, eighteenth century psychology involved itself in the epistemological dilemma with sincerity and sobriety. Starting out in the rationalistic faith that the truth about mind could be discovered by the mind, it seemed at last to discover a truth about mind which discredited the same rationalistic faith which had motivated its quest. Thus in the long run this application of scientific method gave encouragement to those who desired to believe in the truth of the unaccountable and the uncriticized. The experimental attitude, then, caused a cleavage not only between the natural and the social sciences, but also between the external world and the inner visions of humanity.

Borrowing Santayana's words, I have just spoken of those who desired to believe in the truth of the unaccountable and the uncriticized. This desire, never absent from the heart of man, contributed to the decay of the official eighteenth century philosophy. The rationalistic universe was unable to satisfy man's craving for wonder and glamor. It was too cold, systematic, and mechanical. It either gave no answers to the deep mysteries of the heart, or gave answers which deprived those mysteries of their beauty. The development of empirical science, though it exposed the futility of deductive rationalism, gave even less support to man's impulse to dream the world of his desires. And the scepticism generated by science, until it was turned upside down and converted into transcendental faith, was even more soul-cramping than the assumptions of Cartesian rationalism. Descartes had at least dreamed of an angel who came to his bedside and assured him that he was perfectly right. And so in many minds the "nature" of the eighteenth century, while it retained its old claims to be a universal system, slowly became less like a watch than like a tree. It thrust roots into the soil, but lifted its head into the skies. It was at once vast and intimate. It had room for love, beauty, and religion, for all the warm stirrings of emotion. It was free, plastic, and expansive, rather than determined, final, and restrictive.

Rationalism had never been able to destroy a conception of nature which the Renaissance had drawn from the ancients, especially from the Stoics, and had passed on to the seventeenth century. This is the "nature" of the Golden Age tradition, a primitivistic and sentimental view of nature as a primeval standard of goodness and simplicity from which man has been sundered by the corruptions of civilization. This is what Montaigne means by "nature" when he writes in his essay *Of the Cannibals*: "There is no reason, art should gain the point of honor of our great and puissant mother Nature. . . . All our endeavour or wit cannot so much as reach to represent the nest of the least birdlet, its contexture, beauty, profit and use, no nor the web of a seely spider." The primitivistic and sentimental conception of nature never disappears even in the age of rationalism and pseudo-classicism. Men never cease to speak of nature in connection with words

like "simple," "free," "innocent," "uncorrupted," "spontaneous," "instinctive." And although on the whole this
sort of nature is relegated to polite literature, it is by no
means absent from serious philosophical works. Even so
hard-headed a person as Locke regards his social contract
as necessitated by the corruption which has followed man's
departure from that state of nature, the Golden Age.
If Pope can use the rationalistic conception of nature in
the passage just quoted from the *Essay on Criticism*, he
can sometimes use the primitivistic and sentimental conception of nature even in his avowedly philosophical poem,
the *Essay on Man*. In Epistle III, for example, he writes:

> Reason, however able, cool at best,
> Cares not for service, or but serves when pressed,
> Stays till we call, and then not often near;
> But honest instinct comes a volunteer,
> Sure never to o'er-shoot, but just to hit;
> While still too wide or short is human Wit;
> Sure by quick Nature happiness to gain,
> Which heavier Reason labours at in vain.
> This too serves always, Reason never long;
> One must go right, the other may go wrong.
> See then the acting and comparing powers
> One in their nature, which are two in ours;
> And Reason raise o'er Instinct as you can,
> In this 'tis God directs, in that 'tis man.

The fact that Rousseau would subscribe to every word in
these lines should warn us not to make sweeping generalizations.

The view of nature as "things as they exist prior to or
apart from human control" was adjusted in various ways
to that satisfaction with common sense and material pro-

gress which characterized the earlier part of the eighteenth century. Sometimes nature was regarded as a wild
and "Gothic" mass of matter to be curbed and regulated
by man's reason. Sometimes it was more tenderly, though
still somewhat superciliously, regarded as if it were a
moving but disorderly Elizabethan play suitable for gentle
and admiring revision by judicious wits. But sometimes it
was regarded as a state of primeval goodness which contrasted very sharply with the régime of Robert Walpole;
and this feeling grew in seriousness as the eighteenth century lost confidence in the ideals on which its civilization
had been based.

In short, when the rationalistic conception of nature
gradually decayed with the philosophy which had fostered
it, the primitivistic and sentimental conception of nature
grew stronger and stronger, until it became, with certain
changes and additions, an important aspect of the romantic movement. Since the romantic conception of nature
will keep us busy for the next month, this preliminary
sketch will not grapple with its details. An idea of its
general spirit has already been given you.

One more point, however, calls for attention. In the
passage which I have just read from the *Essay on Man*,
Pope opposes reason and instinct to the advantage of the
latter. This attitude becomes increasingly prevalent as the
eighteen century phase of the romantic movement
gathers headway. A more subtle and interesting development, however, is an alteration within reason itself — not
so much an open strife between reason and instinct as the
gradual transformation of the former into something like
the latter. Nature and reason are so inextricably bound
together in eighteenth century thought that one changes

as the other changes. The geometrical and deductive character of the official rationalism glorified reason, but glorified it in such a way as to relegate it from the top of life to the bottom of life. If nature is a universal system, the reason which is its essence must be a universal possession of mankind. This transformation was aided by the tendency, so commonly associated with literary classicism, to deal with highest common denominators of thought and feeling. The universe of rationalism was ruled by a few broad, simple principles like the axioms of geometry. Now one requirement of an axiom is that anybody can understand it; and if anybody can understand the principles which regulate the universe, then reason is the possession of the child, the peasant, and the savage no less than of the philosopher. Reason, in other words, becomes common sense. Then with the growth of primitivism and anti-intellectualism during the eighteenth century, the links between logic and common sense become weaker and weaker, until at last common sense is often indistinguishable from mystical intuition.

The developments which I have been summarizing are anything but regular or systematic. At the outbreak of the French Revolution, we find various stages and combinations of them mingled in the thought of various writers. In his monograph on Thelwall, Charles Cestre attempts to distinguish three main currents of revolutionary philosophy in France. There was Montesquieu, with his not very radical and very "English" *a priori* science of government. There was Rousseau, with his identification of the natural and civil rights of man. And finally there were the Encyclopedists — Diderot, d'Alembert, Helvétius and Holbach — with their doctrine of mechanical utilitarian-ism. Although this classification is no doubt allowable, it is much neater than the tangled skein of tendencies which it attempts to unravel. One can understand that the old régime might be opposed because it was not reasonable enough, or because it was too reasonable. But the balance of the foregoing sentence tumbles into a chaos in which rationalism and romanticism seem inextricably confused when one remembers that "reason" may mean geometrical deduction, scientific method, cool common sense, warm common sense, the promptings of sensibility, mystical intuition, or any blend of these conceptions. Philosophy, at the height of her pride in intellect, is about to topple over into emotionalism. There is no genuine contrast between two things the former of which is in process of becoming the latter.

Similarly, any generalizations which we may feel disposed to make about the prevalence in the revolutionary period of theories concerning "nature," "natural rights," "natural man," and so forth, need to be controlled by the fact that the term "nature" bears no one set of implications for the age. "Our call to liberty is ordained by nature!" cries the Abbé Fauchet in a typical address. But what does he mean by "nature"? The neat mathematical system formed in the brains of the *philosophes*, or the life of instinct as preached by those who thought they understood Rousseau? It would not be merely frivolous to conjecture that while Fauchet may have meant either kind of nature, he very likely meant both at the same time. In this period the "wild virtuous spontaneity" idea is never wholly absent from the mental content of the rationalist who speaks of "nature," and the "universal system" idea is never wholly absent from the mental content of the romanticist who uses that term.

What has been said today proves merely that the subject is exceedingly complex. One errs equally in regarding the French Revolution as essentially romantic, and in regarding rationalism and romanticism as two clearly antipodal tendencies of the age. A genuinely rationalistic mind might oppose the Revolution because of its underlying emotionalism; a genuinely romantic mind might oppose it because of its parade of rationalism; the typical confused mind of the period would either support or oppose it for a mixture of both reasons. Perhaps all this will be clearer as we approach it from other angles. At present I cannot suppose that it is clear at all. For a brief and elementary but thoroughly sound survey of seventeenth and eighteenth century thought see Book III of *The Making of the Modern Mind*, by John Herman Randall, Jr. Leslie Stephen's *History of English Thought in the Eighteenth Century* is the classical treatment of the subject. The relations between French and English philosophy are so important that Daniel Mornet's *French Thought in the Eighteenth Century* should also be recommended. An adequate translation by L. M. Levin has recently (1929) been published.

II

BURKE AND GODWIN

Abandoning the generalizations of the preceding lecture, let us take the solid fact that the Bastille fell on July 14, 1789, and observe some of the ripples made by this stone in the waters of English literature. First, however, we must remind ourselves that the collapse of the North government in 1782 made possible the rise of two groups, both of which offered a liberal program: the Reformed Whigs, under Charles James Fox; and the New Tories, under William Pitt the younger. The victory of the New Tories in the 1784 elections brought in Pitt as Prime Minister. Under him, much progress was achieved along liberal lines. Nor did all this come to a sudden stop in 1789. The first response of the majority of Englishmen to the outbreak of the Revolution was one of approval and sympathy. Four years before, even the mild, rabbit-loving recluse William Cowper had written of the Bastille in these words:

> Then shame to manhood, and opprobrious more
> To France than all her losses and defeats,
> Old or of later date, by sea or land,
> Her house of bondage, worse than that of old
> Which God aveng'd on Pharaoh — the Bastile!
> Ye horrid tow'rs, th' abode of broken hearts;
> Ye dungeons and ye cages of despair,
> That monarchs have supplied from age to age
> With music such as suits their sov'reign ears —

The sighs and groans of miserable men!
There's not an English heart that would not leap
To hear that ye were fall'n at last; to know
That ev'n our enemies, so oft employ'd
In forging chains for us, themselves were free.
                    (*The Task*, V, 379 ff.)

The images of the French Revolution which first arise in our minds are associated with the Reign of Terror — heads plopping into baskets or reeking on the ends of pikes. We must remember, however, that Louis was not beheaded until January 21, 1793, and that the actual Reign of Terror, under the so-called Committee of Public Safety, did not begin until the following summer, four years after the fall of the Bastille. At first the revolutionary leaders wished merely to change the practically absolute monarchy into a limited monarchy with a constitutional form of government. England, who had herself fought to obtain such a government, could hardly object to that aim. Her attitude toward the Revolution did not become panicky or hostile until 1792, when the National Convention declared France a Republic.

From the first, however, Edmund Burke had felt that the Revolution constituted a menace to England. He found a good many who agreed with him, and as the radical proletarian side of the revolt grew stronger his influence became very great. His chief antirevolutionary work, *Reflections on the Revolution in France*, should be read by everyone who wishes to understand the thought of the period. To us the book is especially interesting because it combines three elements which were glanced at in the last lecture: empiricism, rationalism, and romanticism.

Burke's empiricism is that of a practical politician. For a student on this side of the Atlantic, it may be difficult to understand why Burke, who enjoyed a reputation as a political liberal and had defended the colonies in the days of the American Revolution, should so bitterly oppose the uprising in France. But the American colonists, when Burke came to their defense, were Englishmen, demanding in a dogged English way certain immemorial English rights. The French, on the contrary, were not talking about the traditional rights of Frenchmen: they were talking about the Rights of Man. Largely under the influence of abstract philosophy, they were manufacturing a social creed out of whole cloth. As a man experienced in the machinery of statecraft, Burke insists that governments cannot be constructed upon a basis of *a priori* reasoning. They are the outcome of gradual growth. The rightness or wrongness of a proposed political measure is a question of expediency.

I cannot stand forward, and give praise or blame to any thing which relates to human actions, and human concerns, on a simple view of the subject as it stands stripped of every relation, in all the nakedness and solitude of metaphysical abstraction. Circumstances (which with some gentlemen pass for nothing) give in reality to every political principle its distinguishing colour, and discriminating effect.

Knowing that the constitution of England has grown like an oak, Burke distrusts the sort of constitution that is suddenly assembled like a Ford car. He hates the meddling of philosophers. "The pretended rights of these theorists are all extremes; and in proportion as they are metaphysically true, they are morally and politically false." For in government there is no such thing as an invariable and absolute right to anything: "The moment you abate anything from the full rights of men, each to govern himself, and suffer any artificial positive limitation upon those rights, from that moment the whole organization of government becomes a consideration of convenience."

The strain of deductive rationalism in Burke is less evident than his empiricism. One catches a hint of it from the words, "Men have no right to what is not reasonable, and to what is not for their benefit." Burke would say that his conceptions of the reasonable and the beneficial were derived from the recorded experience of mankind, but they are derived to an almost equal extent from a number of assumptions which themselves go back to the basic axiom that the British government is an approximately perfect reflection of the will of God. For all his emphasis on the practical, Burke often resorts to *a priori* reasoning.

Burke's appeals both to experience and to general principles find an essentially romantic source in his almost mystical love of tradition. To him, nature is not a watch-like mechanism: it is the beautiful and authoritative past majestically unfolding into the present. English liberties, he says, are an inheritance from the past. We have attained them, not by reasoning, like the French, but by trusting our instincts and letting our necessarily artificial institutions conform as closely as possible to the processes of nature.

We are afraid to put men to live and trade each on his own private stock of reason; because we suspect that this stock in each man is small. . . . Many of our men of speculation, instead of exploding ancient prejudices, employ their sagacity to discover the latent wisdom which prevails in them. . . . We have not lost the generosity and dignity of thinking of the fourteenth century; nor as yet have we subtilized ourselves into savages. We are not the converts of Rousseau; we are not the disciples of Voltaire; Helvetius has made no progress amongst us. Atheists are not our preachers; madmen are not our lawgivers. We know that *we* have made no discoveries; and we know that no discoveries are to be made, in morality; nor many in the great principles of government, nor in the ideas of liberty, which were understood before we were born.

This rather disturbing elevation of traditional prejudices into sublime "natural" virtues is accompanied by a strain of sentiment, if not of sentimentality. Burke hates the revolutionary philosophy not merely because it is impractical, but because it is cold, raw, unlovely, and impersonal. He is shocked to see France, the "sweet enemy" of Sir Philip Sidney, breaking away from her graceful and majestic past, revolted by the rudeness with which Louis has been haled from Versailles to Paris by the noisy mob. To him, the very core of the great tradition in government is the loyalty of the people, expressed through persons of quality, to a sovereign. Take that away, and all else crumbles.

> "O Richard! O mon roi!
> L'univers t'abandonne!"

He sees Marie Antoinette as the focus of those chivalric sentiments which the revolutionary philosophy has cast aside:

It is now sixteen or seventeen years since I saw the queen of France, then the dauphiness, at Versailles; and surely never lighted on this orb, which she hardly seemed to touch, a more delightful vision. . . . Little did I dream that I should have lived to see such disasters fallen upon her in a nation of gallant men, in a nation of men of honour and of cavaliers. I thought ten thousand swords must have leaped from their scabbards to avenge even a look that threatened her with insult. — But the age of chivalry is gone. That of sophisters, œconomists and calculators has succeeded; and the glory of Europe is extinguished for ever. Never, never more, shall we behold that generous loyalty to rank and sex, that proud submission, that dignified obedience, that subordination of the heart, which kept alive, even in servitude itself, the spirit of an exalted freedom. The unbought grace of life, the cheap defence of nations, the nurse of manly sentiment and heroic enterprize, is gone! It is gone, that sensibility of principle, that chastity of honour, which felt a stain like a wound, which inspired courage whilst it mitigated ferocity, which ennobled whatever it touched, and under which vice lost half its evil, by losing all its grossness.

This is the quality in the *Reflections* which enabled the reformer John Thelwall to refer mockingly to "Burke's sentimental romance of Antoinetta, the falling star of chivalry, or royalty in the suds."

A detailed examination of Burke's political philosophy cannot here be attempted. For our purposes his chief importance lies in showing that sympathy with the Revolution is not a sure touchstone of romanticism. There can be a conservative romanticism just as easily as there can be a rationalistic radicalism. Burke is not alone in this. Walter Scott is a conservative romanticist. Wordsworth, Coleridge, and Southey gradually turn conservative, and their later political ideas are largely based upon those of Burke. That love of the past which underlies the romantic revival of interest in medieval literature appears also in political theory.

William Lisle Bowles, the minor poet whose sonnets exerted so powerful an influence over Wordsworth, Coleridge, Southey, Lamb, and others, will provide an example of the rather numerous appearances of Burke's attitude in poetry. He is almost paraphrasing the *Reflections* when, in *To the Right Honourable Edmund Burke*, he writes:

> No, Burke! thy heart, by juster feelings led,
> Mourns for the spirit of high Honour fled;
> Mourns that philosophy, abstract and cold,
> Withering should smite life's fancy-flowered mould;
> And many a smiling sympathy depart,
> That graced the sternness of the manly heart.

Of course the French invasion of Switzerland gives Bowles a good opportunity to show the consequences of the revolutionary philosophy. In *The Sorrows of Switzerland* he bids the French gaze upon the fruits of their adherence to what he supposes to be the doctrines of Rousseau. Then he imagines the spirit of that great Swiss as brooding remorsefully over the havoc he has brought upon his native land:

> And ye who, all enlightened, all sublime,
> Pant in indignant thraldom till the time
> When man, bursting his fetters, proud and free,
> The wildest savage of the wilds shall be;
> Artful instructors of our feeble kind,
> Illumined leaders of the lost and blind,
> Behold the destined glories of your reign!
>
> .   .   .   .
>
> Methought, Rousseau, thy troubled spirit passed;
> His ravaged country his dim eyes survey.
> Are these the fruits, he said, or seemed to say,
> Of those high energies of raptured thought,
> That proud philosophy my precepts taught?

Burke's ideas, however, would obviously be detestable to the reformers of his day. His almost cynical insistence

on expediency aroused the wrath of the warmly sentimental; his romantic loyalty to tradition aroused the
wrath of the coldly rationalistic. He was answered in
Parliament by Fox and Sheridan. Scores of attacks in the
form of books and pamphlets were written by English
sympathizers with the Revolution: William Godwin,
Mary Wollstonecraft, John Thelwall, Horne Tooke,
Capell Lofft, Tom Paine, James Mackintosh, Richard
Price, Joseph Priestley, and many others. As the Jacobin
party came to the fore in France, the term "Jacobin" was
more and more frequently applied to those Englishmen
who approved of the Revolution. We ourselves may find
the term convenient if we remember that there were many
different shades of English pro-revolutionary opinion.

John Thelwall is so fully representative of the contemporary state of mind that Charles Cestre's study of him
is a good introduction to the whole period. A few years
later, he was to become the friend of Wordsworth and
Coleridge. His principal work, *The Peripatetic*, helped
to provide the plan for Wordsworth's *Excursion*. Thelwall attacked Burke's *Reflections* and his other antirevolutionary writings such as the *Letter to a Noble Lord* in
several addresses which were also printed as pamphlets.
The Rights of Nature is typical. Burke has said that the
"natural representative" of the people is the person of
leisure, education, and means. At this Thelwall breaks
out:

O insulted and degraded Nature! O awful aggregate of existence! How is thy venerable name blasphemed by these pious, cant-
ing, juggling politicians! By what right does this base renegade
doom to political annihilation nine-tenths of the adult inhabitants
of a nation?

Thelwall has his own conception of nature:

> Mr. Burke's *nature* and mine are widely different. With him everything is natural that has the hoar of ancient prejudice upon it; and novelty is the test of crime. In my humble estimate, nothing is natural, but what is fit and true, and can endure the test of reason.

Joseph Priestley, another of Burke's assailants, is now best known as the discoverer of oxygen; but besides being an eminent chemist, he was a Unitarian minister, a theologian, a philosopher, and an educator. His *Letters to the Right Honourable Edmund Burke* (1791) contain a passage which will serve to show the enthusiasm with which reformers greeted the advent of the Revolution:

> I cannot conclude these *Letters*, without congratulating . . . the French nation, and the world; I mean the liberal, the rational, and the virtuous part of the world, on the great revolution that has taken place in France, as well as on that which some time ago took place in America. . . . These great events . . . mark a totally new era in the history of mankind. It is . . . a change from darkness to light, from superstition to sound knowledge, and from a most debasing servitude to a state of the most exalted freedom. It is a liberating of all the powers of man. . . . So that, in comparison with what has been, now only can we expect to see what men really are, and what they can do.

Priestley's confidence in the future progress of liberated mankind provides a logical transition to the great apostle of perfectibility, William Godwin. Every student of the period should be well acquainted with his work. He had a profound influence on the Lake poets, and later on Shelley, who of course became his son-in-law. It should be added that his influence, though strong, is transitory. One sure sign that a romantic writer is growing up is his repudiation of Godwin.

My inclusion of Godwin among those who wrote hostile rejoinders to Burke was not strictly accurate, for although his chief work, *An Enquiry Concerning Political Justice and Its Influence on Morals and Happiness*, is an assault upon everything that Burke holds dear, it did not appear until 1793, three years after the publication of the *Reflections*, and is only indirectly related to the turmoil aroused by that work. Godwin, in fact, generally held himself aloof from contemporary clamor. His ardor for reform was abstract and theoretical. The ministry, although by 1793 it had begun to persecute the English Jacobins, let Godwin alone; for Pitt did not believe that a long, difficult book priced at three guineas could be dangerous. Nevertheless, *Political Justice* was widely read.

Godwin is the chief English representative of the revolutionary thought of the French encyclopedist school. He stands for the cool rationalism of Helvétius rather than for the emotional fervor of Rousseau. To Rousseau's *Social Contract*, however, his political theories are much indebted. The habit of contrasting Rousseau's influence upon the romantic poets with that of Godwin may lead us into difficulties unless we pause here to make certain reservations.

Rousseau was very different from Voltaire, but he was not by any means the antithesis of Voltaire. With all his sentimentality and primitivism and anti-intellectualism, he had plenty of the eighteenth century scientific spirit, and plenty of the eighteenth century fondness for geometrical system-building. Everything said about Rousseau requires to be qualified. For our present purposes, however, a crude simplification must suffice. He was a mixture of rationalism and romanticism. In the second half of the eighteenth century, when Rousseau's influence began to be felt in England, the tendencies which we think of as constituting the early symptoms of romanticism had already made great progress — the heart as opposed to the head, preference of country to town, sensibility, sentimental primitivism, humanitarianism, interest in medieval literature, and so on. In fact early English romanticism, as we may learn from Joseph Texte's *Jean-Jacques Rousseau et le cosmopolitisme littéraire*, had exerted a considerable influence upon Rousseau himself. England, in short, was prepared to accept Rousseau's romantic aspect rather than his rationalistic aspect. On the English side of the Channel he was thought of chiefly in connection with sensibility, virtuous eroticism, highly emotionalized and unorthodox religion, "natural" education, and the back-to-the-woods philosophy. I have been leading up to the statement that Godwin's *Political Justice* was by no means antithetical to the doctrines of the real Rousseau, but that it was opposed to those doctrines as they had been selected and refracted by the English thought of the period. If you considered yourself a Rousseauist, you talked about nature and the heart; if you were a Godwinian, you talked about reason and the perfectibility of the species. The divergence between *Political Justice* and the current English conception of Rousseau shows that the contemporary radicalism, like the contemporary conservatism, can be either rationalistic or romantic.

Godwin declares his belief in "the desirableness of a government in the utmost degree simple." To all intents and purposes, he is an anarchist. Anarchy, however, is not for him an immediate prospect. He merely looks forward to a time when man will become so reasonable, and hence so virtuous, that he will require no political control. But

Godwin has none of the primitivism which the young Rousseau had expressed in his clever, immature, consciously paradoxical, discourses *On the Moral Effect of the Sciences and Arts* and *On the Origins of Inequality among Men.* In his maturer works, *Émile* and *The Social Contract*, Rousseau has little of this primitivism; but England never got over thinking of him as the man who wanted everyone to go back to the state of nature and live like a savage. Godwin, on the contrary, believes in a high though simple state of civilization, with plenty of learning and culture. He attacks the prevalent "back to nature" gush which had become associated with Rousseau:

> Innocence is not virtue. Virtue demands the active employment of an ardent mind in the promotion of the general good. . . . Individuals of exquisite feeling . . . have recurred in imagination to the forests of Norway, or the bleak and uncomfortable Highlands of Scotland in search of a purer race of mankind. This imagination has been the offspring of disappointment, not the dictate of reason and philosophy.

He insists that the injunction, "follow nature," is meaningless. Man cannot help following nature: however he acts, he must act by nature's laws. Glancing at Burke, he declares that those who use this maxim generally make it an excuse for perpetuating ancient prejudices.

This writer is opposed to the Rousseauistic reliance on instinct, intuition, and feeling, as guides to truth. He hates all sorts of warm, primary impulses; cold, hard reason is his ideal. "The perfection of the human character consists in approaching as nearly as possible to the perfectly voluntary state. We ought to be, upon all occasions, prepared to render a reason for our actions." When human feeling conflicts with logic, Godwin sides with logic. "It is of no consequence," he writes, "that I am the parent of a child, when it has once been determined that the child will live with greater benefit under the superintendence of a stranger." The Socratic identification of reason and virtue is essential in Godwin's theory. To be good is to be wise; vice is simply ignorance. Moreover, "reason depends for its clearness and strength upon the cultivation of knowledge." His attitude on this point is worth noting, for we shall find that several writers of the period are inclined to say that knowledge too often stifles man's natural ability to reason. Rousseau's first discourse, in fact, makes much of this idea.

Godwin's name is always associated with the doctrine known as "perfectibility." The doctrine of perfectibility was rather common in the eighteenth century; but it was held on various grounds, and it does not mean the same thing every time it appears. In other words, there were various ways in which man could perfect himself. In his two early discourses, Rousseau said that man had deteriorated because civilization had cut him off from the state of nature, and hence from his natural heritage of equality, reason, and benevolence. Hence Rousseau was then generally identified, and is still often identified, with deteriorationism — just the opposite of perfectibilitarianism. These two attitudes run throughout our period. When a romanticist is discouraged, he is a deteriorationist; when he has had a good dinner, he is a perfectibilitarian.

In his later works, Rousseau worked out his own theory of perfectibility. The goal was to be approximated, not by returning to the forest — a solution which he had never proposed but which had been attributed to him by

many readers — but by instituting a system of education
(*Émile*) and a form of government (*Social Contract*)
which would make it possible for us to regain and then to
build upon our natural inheritance. But this harmonizing
of deteriorationism and perfectibilitarianism was not understood by many Englishmen. Wordsworth has some
grasp of it, and Shelley, in his mature work, possesses it
completely. In her notes to *Prometheus Unbound,* Mrs.
Shelley says that Prometheus "used knowledge as a weapon to defeat evil, by leading mankind beyond the state
wherein they are sinless through ignorance to that state
in which they are virtuous through wisdom." This noble
remark could equally well be applied to the final aims of
Rousseau.

Godwin, on the contrary, casts no backward glances at
"the state wherein men are sinless through ignorance."
For him, a state of ignorance is tantamount to a state of
sin. His theory of perfectibility is based upon the following chain of propositions:

Reason depends for its clearness and strength upon the cultivation of knowledge. The extent of our progress in the cultivation
of knowledge is unlimited. Hence it follows, that human inventions, and the modes of social existence, are susceptible of perpetual improvement.

This illustrates the extreme shallowness which often characterizes late eighteenth century rationalism. The whole
structure collapses as soon as we test it by experience.
Reason does *not* depend for its clearness and strength
upon the cultivation of knowledge: there are too many
learned fools in the world to enable us to believe that. As
every weary teacher knows, the extent of our progress in
the cultivation of knowledge is *not* unlimited. Hence so

far as this particular syllogism is concerned it certainly does *not* follow that human inventions and so on are susceptible of perpetual improvement. Minds like Godwin's are but playing an elaborate game.

The citation just given, however, should warn us not to ascribe to Godwin the notion that absolute perfection will ever be attained. He simply believes that the race will go on improving indefinitely once it learns to live in the light of reason. "Perpetual improvability" would be a more accurate term for his theory than perfectibility, but the latter has become too firmly fixed in usage to justify a change.

Godwin's name is associated not only with perfectibility but with what we now call "mechanical determinism." In the eighteenth century it was called the "doctrine of necessity." According to this theory, the universe is a machine in which we are helpless cogs. At any given time, it is impossible for us to act otherwise than as we are acting. The doctrine of necessity appealed so strongly to the reason of several of the young romanticists, and yet was so repugnant to their emotions, that they had difficulty in digesting it. Transcendentalism, as we shall see later, provided the solvent. Perfectibilitarianism and necessitarianism are not inconsistent if we assume that through the operation of necessity man is automatically becoming more and more reasonable and is therefore continually improving. But in order to achieve this mechanistic optimism we must deprive reason of that voluntary character which Godwin frequently insists upon as essential. This tangle in his thought is never quite unraveled.

The extreme complexity of the intellectual currrents of this period is shown by the fact that even Godwin's

rationalism is less throughgoing than it appears to be.
Although he clings to it for polemic purposes, it is probable that his private conception of reason had, even by
1793, become somewhat romanticized. Soon after the
publication of *Political Justice*, at any rate, we find him
saying in a letter to John Thelwall:

To quote authorities is a vulgar business; every soulless hypo-
crite can do that. To quote authorities is a cold business, it excites
no responsive sentiments and produces no heart-felt conviction. . . .
Appeal to that eternal law which the heart of every man of com-
mon-sense recognizes immediately.

Rousseau might well have written this; in fact, he very
nearly did. It seems to imply a conception of reason different from that found in *Political Justice*, where Godwin
says that "reason depends for its clearness and strength
upon the cultivation of knowledge." Here reason is not
the product of learning or of logic, but a warm glow of
intuitive insight. That is what I meant by saying in the
last lecture that in the revolutionary period philosophy,
at the height of her pride in cold reason, is about to topple
over into the warmest emotionalism. It is interesting to
see that common sense has become a natural faculty of the
heart by which eternal law can be recognized.

In later years, when writing on philosophy or political
economy, Godwin continues to repeat his old formulas;
but in his imaginative writings he is much more hospitable
to what we usually regard as romantic tendencies. As one
would expect, his best-known novel, *Caleb Williams*
(1794), reflects the philosophy of *Political Justice*. In the
later novel *St. Leon* (1799), however, he begins to waver,
and in *Fleetwood* (1805) he writes as if he had become
a thoroughgoing anti-intellectualist and a worshipper of

nature in its most romantic sense. The subtitle of *Fleet-wood*, "the new Man of Feeling," is significant. Perhaps Godwin, hard pressed by his creditors, is merely trying to meet the changing demands of the literary market; but Hazlitt, who had a passion for intellectual honesty, gives him credit for complete sincerity. More probably we may see in Godwin a conflict, not uncharacteristic of the period, between head and heart.

The later Godwin even possesses a sort of religion, which, he declares, was derived from Coleridge. That poet begins as an admirer of Godwin's system, though always with reservations. Soon, however, he rejects the system and expresses dislike of Godwin's character. But in 1800 he becomes fairly intimate with Godwin and forms a better opinion of him as a man, though not as a philosopher. It is during this intercourse that the formerly atheistic Godwin acquires what he terms "my theism, if such I may be permitted to call it, . . . a reverent and soothing contemplation of all that is grand or mysterious in the system of the universe." In 1820 he writes to a friend:

The religious man, I apprehend, is, as Tom Warton phrases it in the title of one of his poems, "an enthusiastic or a lover of nature." I am an admirer of nature. I should pine to death if I did not live in the midst of so majestic a structure as I behold on every side. I am never weary of admiring and reverencing it. All that I see, the earth, the sea, the rivers, . . . and, most of all, man, fills me with love and astonishment. My soul is full to bursting with the mystery of all this, and I love it for its mysteriousness. . . . This is what I call religion.

We are later to see more of this sort of religion.

Plainly, the author of *Political Justice* traveled a long

and winding road before he wrote that letter. When in reading works about the romantic period you come upon the statement that Wordsworth, Coleridge, and Southey threw off the influence of Godwin and turned to nature, you should remember that these poets were abandoning a position which Godwin himself was abandoning at about the same time. He represents a fixed point no more than any other man of this fluid age.

III

JACOBINS AND ANTI-JACOBINS

Today I shall deal briefly with a few examples of English Jacobinism and of opposition to English Jacobinism. Let me remind you that here and elsewhere I am merely sketching the general outline of topics which you must investigate for yourselves.

One of the numerous answers to Burke was *A Vindication of the Rights of Men* (1790), by Mary Wollstonecraft, the noble woman who became Godwin's consort and later his wife. Her ideas as expressed in this book are similar to Godwin's, but have a stronger emotional and Rousseauistic strain. Two years later she published *A Vindication of the Rights of Woman*, which gives her fame as the earliest important English feminist. Her thesis is that woman is naturally the equal of man, and can regain that equality through education. Her *Historical and Moral View of the Origin and Progress of the French Revolution*, which appeared in 1794 when the Terror was in full swing, blames the horrors of the Revolution upon the fact that human nature, though naturally good, had become corrupted under the old régime, and could not purify itself fast enough to take advantage of its new opportunities. But she is still a true perfectibilitarian, and has high hopes for the future.

The fiction of the 1790's often reflects the revolutionary turmoil. There are a good many pro-revolutionary novels, and a still larger number of antirevolutionary ones. For a fuller account of this subject I must refer you to Allene Gregory's *The French Revolution and the English Novel*.

Godwin's *Caleb Williams* (1794) is a mystery story, and a rather good one, but it manages to bring in a great deal of reform propaganda. Its original title, indeed, was *Things As They Are*. The book implies an answer to Burke in that Falkland's character is ruined by his adherence to the ideals of the age of chivalry. The fact that this rich murderer can turn the law against Caleb Williams, a poor man of humble birth, provides good chances for a criticism of society. Particularly interesting is the attack on prison conditions. Of course the great reformer John Howard had published his *State of the Prisons* in 1777, and exposures of the horrors of English jails go back at least as far as Geffray Mynshul's *Essayes and Characters of a Prison and Prisoners*, 1618, but in Godwin the theme is related to a broader and more definitely radical social indignation.

"Thank God," exclaims the Englishman, "we have no Bastille!" Unthinking wretch! Is that a country of liberty, where thousands languish in dungeons and fetters? Go, go, ignorant fool, and visit the scenes of our prisons! Witness their unwholesomeness, their filth, the tyranny of their governors, the misery of their inmates! After that, show me the man shameless enough to triumph, and say, England has no Bastille! . . . I have felt the iron of slavery grating upon my soul. I looked round upon my walls and forward upon the premature death I had too much reason to expect and I said, "This is society. This is the object, the distribution of justice, which is the end of human reason. For this sages have toiled, and midnight oil has been wasted. This!"

In connection with this attack on prisons, we might note

that Godwin's *Fleetwood* (1805) contains a protest against child labor.

After escaping from prison, Williams falls in with a band of thieves. They are portrayed rather sympathetically, and one is given to understand that the criminal is merely the victim of society. This idea is to become extremely common. Indeed, the modern theory that no individual is ever to blame for anything seems to find its immediate source in the sentimentalized necessitarianism of the revolutionary period. When, by the way, we find in English romantic literature a virtuous, moody, melancholy, philosophical brigand, he usually represents the influence of Karl Moor, the hero of Schiller's early play, *Die Räuber*.

Have you noticed the more or less fixed types assumed by the interesting young men of various literary periods? In the romantic period proper we have the greatly blighted Byronic hero. He gives place to the earnest young Victorian of the John Sterling or Arthur Hallam type. He gives place to the young esthete. He gives place to the "flaming youth." He gives place either to the bright young debunker or to the futilitarian — it is too early to tell which. Now the 1790's had their own type of interesting youth — the Young Jacobin. The fact is of some importance because for a short period Wordsworth, Coleridge, and Southey approach this norm rather closely. Moreover, although Hazlitt, Leigh Hunt, and Shelley appear somewhat later, they represent the type as young men because of their attempt to preserve or revive the Jacobin attitude.

The Young Jacobin is himself the outgrowth of a mid-eighteenth century type, the Man of Feeling. The Man of

Feeling has the sensibility of Sterne, but in a particularly virtuous, serious, and purposive form. The type really appears earlier than Mackenzie's famous novel of 1771. Disregarding its occurrences in sentimental comedy, we see something like it in Henry Brooke's *The Fool of Quality* (1766). At the age of twelve, Brooke's hero always takes the side of the geese in the game of "fox and geese." When a lady asks for an explanation, he replies, "Because, madam, I always wish that simplicity should get the better of fraud and cunning." As he grows to young manhood, he becomes more and more benevolent and sententious. After listening to his modest explanation of how he has spent fifty thousand pounds in hospitals and prisons, one of the less virtuous characters exclaims: "Let me go, let me go from this place! This boy will absolutely kill me if I stay any longer. He overpowers, he suffocates me with the weight of his sentiments!"

When the French Revolution broke out, the Man of Feeling was transformed into the Young Jacobin by finding an outlet for his overpowering sentiments. His vague philanthropy became more sharply focused by contemporary events, and his sensibility took on a thin veneer of Godwinian rationalism. The Young Jacobin had advanced literary tastes — felt that Pope was coldly artificial, and admired the sonnets of Bowles hardly less than the syllogisms of *Political Justice*. In his own writing he cultivated a melancholy either gently pensive or more violently Gothic. On every page he displayed his sensibility and love of scenery. Through his most fervent outbursts, however, ran a strain of solemn didacticism. He was a reformer, a propagandist, whose poems and novels, to say nothing of his pamphlets, were *Tendenzstücke*. In the same breath he could be frigidly romantic and torridly rationalistic. He yearned for a system of society unhindered by priests and kings. Hence the Revolution appeared to him as a great upheaval of nature from beneath the smothering burdens imposed upon it by organized society. He often advocated, though he seldom even vaguely plotted for, an English Revolution. Among other peculiarities of the Young Jacobin may be mentioned religious radicalism. To him, formal religious organizations were agencies of oppression. His own beliefs were earnest but uncertain. Emotional deism, nature worship, and Unitarianism attracted him strongly. He was seldom an out-and-out atheist: he had too much heart for that. If to literary, political, and religious heterodoxy we add opposition to the convention of marriage and a warm interest in prison reform, the anti-slavery movement, and perhaps in vegetarianism, we shall have a fairly accurate cross section of the average Young Jacobin mind.

For one of many possible glimpses of the Young Jacobin in the literature of the period, we may turn to Thomas Holcroft's *Anna St. Ives* (1792). Frank Henley, the hero, is the son of a baronet's gardener, but he does not therefore hesitate to fall in love with his master's daughter. "Pshaw! What is a baronet? Away with such insolent, such ridiculous distinctions." That remark typifies his character. He is very severe with the nobility, sneers at laws, and disbelieves in private property. Frank's life is one series of remarkable deeds. He rescues Anna from a highwayman, then rescues the highwayman from jail and reforms him (a particularly characteristic touch). He is constantly relieving the poor or saving the lives of his enemies. Nor can he understand why his nobility

should be admired. He simply has a system, and follows it
consistently. That system is what distinguishes him from
a mere Fool of Quality or Man of Feeling. He is benevolent "by the book," and his sensibility is but the soft fruit
of severely rational principles.

Fortunately Anna St. Ives shares the opinions of her
lover. This pair have acquired the complete Godwinian
doctrine of perfectibility a year before the appearance of
Political Justice. Godwin, indeed, derived much from
Holcroft, who was his close friend at this time. But the
love of Frank and Anna, if the term can be applied to
their calm mutual esteem, is thwarted by Coke Clifton, a
lively young aristocrat whom the baronet regards as a
more suitable claimant for his daughter's hand.

Clifton is represented as a clever youth whose natural
goodness has been spoiled by selfishness and frivolity.
In every respect he is Frank's opposite, and he amusingly
expresses his opinion of his rival:

> I scarcely know what to make of him; except that he seems to
> have quite conceit enough of himself. Every other sentence is a
> contradiction of what the last speaker advanced. This is the first
> time he ever ventured to cross his father's threshold, and yet he
> talks as familiarly of kingdoms, governments, nations, manners,
> and other high sounding phrases, as if he had been secretary of
> state to King Minos. . . . He is the Great Mogul of politicians!
> And as for letters, science, and talents, he holds them all by patent
> right.

Clifton later comes to understand that Frank's self-
confidence arises not from conceit, but from philosophy.
The knowledge to which he lays claim has nothing to do
with worldly experience: it is acquired simply by follow-

ing the dictates of natural reason — that reason which provides the common denominator of all mankind.

He is one of your levellers! Marry! His superior! Who is he? On what proud eminence can he be found? . . . Dispute his prerogative who dare! He derives from Adam; what time the world was all "hail fellow well met!" The savage, the wild man of the woods, is his true liberty boy; and the ourang-outang, his first cousin. A lord is a merry Andrew, a duke a jack-pudding, and a king a tom-fool; his name is man!

Clifton's vivacity suggests that Holcroft does not wholly admire the prig whom he has selected for a hero. Some of his own feeling must enter into Clifton's remark that there is nothing "so nauseous as an overdose of wisdom; mixed up, according to the modern practice, with a quantum sufficit of virtue, and a large double handful of the good of the whole." But Frank Henley, despite even his creator's limited enthusiasm for him, rises from pinnacle to pinnacle of virtue until at last he wins Anna, while Clifton becomes more and more a thwarted Richardsonian villain.

So far we have regarded the Young Jacobin from a somewhat quizzical angle. Let us now forget his absurdities in order to remind ourselves that he is often a figure no less noble than absurd. These were days when the young men beheld visions. Though we may smile at them, we must not sneer unless we are prepared to sneer at every sort of generous, idealistic ardor. The loftier, less doctrinaire side of revolutionary feeling is beautifully expressed by Wordsworth in lines 105-141 of Book XI of *The Prelude* — the passage which was separately published in *The Friend*, 1809, under the title *French Revo-*

*lution as It Appeared to Enthusiasts at Its Commence-
ment*:

> O pleasant exercise of hope and joy!
> For mighty were the auxiliars which then stood
> Upon our side, us who were strong in love!
> Bliss was it in that dawn to be alive,
> But to be young was very heaven! O times,
> In which the meagre, stale, forbidding ways
> Of custom, law, and statute, took at once
> The attraction of a country in romance!
> When Reason seemed the most to assert her rights
> When most intent on making of herself
> A prime enchantress — to assist the work,
> Which then was going forward in her name!
> Not favored spots alone, but the whole Earth,
> The beauty wore of promise — that which sets
> (As at some moments might not be unfelt
> Among the bowers of Paradise itself)
> The budding rose above the rose full blown.
> What temper at the prospect did not wake
> To happiness unthought of? The inert
> Were roused, and lively natures rapt away!
> They who had fed their childhood upon dreams,
> The play-fellows of fancy, who had made
> All powers of swiftness, subtilty, and strength
> Their ministers, — who in lordly wise had stirred
> Among the grandest objects of the sense,
> And dealt with whatsoever they found there
> As if they had within some lurking right
> To wield it; — they, too, who of gentle mood
> Had watched all gentle motions, and to these
> Had fitted their own thoughts, schemers more mild,
> And in the region of their peaceful selves; —
> Now was it that *both* found, the meek and lofty

Did both find, helpers to their hearts desire,
And stuff at hand, plastic as they could wish;
Were called upon to exercise their skill,
Not in Utopia, — subterranean fields, —
Or some secreted island, Heaven knows where!
But in the very world, which is the world
Of all of us, — the place where, in the end,
We find our happiness, or not at all!

That passage may serve to balance Coke Clifton's jibes at Frank Henley. It also illustrates that element in revolutionary thought which best deserves to be called romantic. As has already been suggested, a great deal of the reforming spirit of the age must be associated with eighteenth century rationalism. Romanticism enters when the Young Jacobin, like Wordsworth in these lines, feels that the actual lives of men have at last identified themselves with an ideal world of beauty and goodness called Nature, that a lovely romance has come true, that Utopia lies all around us, and that the chasm between the waking and the dreaming states has been bridged.

The English Jacobins of course had plenty of enemies. In 1797 and 1798 a spirited attack was made upon them by a conservative journal, *The Anti-Jacobin*. William Gifford, its chief, is remembered as an editor of Jonson, Massinger, and Ford, as a translator of Juvenal, and as a heavy-handed satirist who had earlier done the world a good service by crushing the absurd Della Cruscan coterie. His work for *The Anti-Jacobin*, however, is less important than that of his three associates: George Ellis, George Canning, and John Hookham Frere. Ellis, a man of forty-four, had already made a reputation as a writer of political satire. In the 1780's he had been a member of

the Esto Perpetua Club, which through the *Rolliad* and
other satires took delight in lampooning Pitt's ministry.
Now the Revolution had brought him over to Pitt's side.
We may note in passing that he was associated with
Walter Scott in his medieval studies. Canning and Frere
were recent university graduates — Canning of Oxford
and Frere of Cambridge, but they had been schoolmates
at Eton. Canning, of course, was to become a famous
English statesman whose connection with the formulation
of the Monroe Doctrine is familiar to everyone. Frere
is known as one of the greatest masters of parody and
light verse in English literature. Like most good par-
odists he was also an accomplished translator, and his
translations from Aristophanes are admirable. Under
the pseudonym Whistlecraft, moreover, he wrote *The
Monks and the Giants* (1817), a mock romance in the
Italian manner and in the difficult *ottava rima* stanza,
which encouraged Byron to use the same form and style in
Don Juan.

These writers contributed to *The Anti-Jacobin* a series
of brilliant satires and burlesques which have outlived the
prose portions of that journal. The parody of Southey's
Sapphics in *The Friend of Humanity and the Knife-
Grinder* is perhaps the most generally known. Amusing
also are these rippling revolutionary dactyls, another
thrust at Southey:

> Come, little drummer-boy, lay down your knapsack here:
> I am the soldiers's friend — here are some books for you;
> Nice clever books by Tom Paine the philanthropist.
> Here's half-a-crown for you, here are some handbills too;
> Run to the barracks and give all the soldiers some;
> Tell them the sailors are all in a mutiny.

It is almost worth the labor of reading Erasmus Darwin's *Loves of the Plants* in order to be able to appreciate *The Loves of the Triangles*, in which Euclid is treated with a fantastically Linnæan eroticism and Darwin's liberal opinions, as well as his botany, are burlesqued. *The Rovers* parodies Schiller's *Die Räuber* in particular, with side glances at Goethe's *Stella*. The Young Jacobins were admirers of German romantic drama.

The Progress of Man is a parody on R. P. Knight's *The Progress of Civil Society*, but the authors kill two birds with one stone by pretending that it has been written by a Mr. Higgins, who seems to represent William Godwin. Using the old journalistic trick of the mock correspondent, they have him submit to *The Anti-Jacobin* a description of his great work, with copious extracts. It is interesting to see that the ideas of Higgins combine the philosophy of *Political Justice* with the current English interpretation of the philosophy of Rousseau. The mixture does not hit off Godwin very accurately, but it is quite true to the medley of tendencies which enter into revolutionary thought in general. "What you call the new principles," Higgins is made to say, "are, in fact, nothing less than new. They are the principles of primeval nature, the system of original and unadulterated man." His aim is "to restore this first and pure simplicity; to rescue and recover the interesting nakedness of human nature, by ridding her of the cumbrous establishments which the folly, pride, and self-interest of the worst part of our species have heaped upon her." This is not only excellent as parody, but is a useful reminder of the connection between sentimental primitivism and revolutionary rationalism. Higgins continues:

Our first principle is, then, the reverse of the trite and dull maxim of Pope — "Whatever is, is right." We contend that, "Whatever is, is wrong;": that institutions, civil and religious, that social order (as it is called in your cant) and regular government and law, and I know not what other fantastic inventions, are but . . . so many badges of his degradation from the primal purity and excellence of his nature.

So much for Rousseauistic deteriorationism; now for Godwinian perfectibilitarianism:

Our second principle is "the eternal and absolute perfectibility of man." We contend that if, as is demonstrable, we have risen from a level with the cabbages of the field to our present comparatively intelligent and dignified state by the mere exertion of our own energies, we should, if these energies were not repressed and subdued by the operations of prejudice and folly, by kingcraft and priestcraft, and the other evils incident to what is called Civilized Society, continue to exert and expand ourselves in a proportion infinitely greater than anything of which we have any notion . . . but which would in time raise man from his present biped state to a rank more worthy of his endowments and aspirations; to a rank in which he would be, as it were, all mind; would enjoy unclouded perspicacity, and perpetual vitality; feed on oxygen; and never die but by his own consent.

By all means read the specimens of the work in which these ambitious hopes are embodied; they rank high among the delights of our humorous literature.

The poetry of *The Anti-Jacobin* was not confined to parody. *The New Morality*, a direct satire written chiefly by Canning, is essentially a rendering in verse of the ideas of Burke. The poem lumps together as Jacobins the following rather mixed collection: Coleridge, Southey, Lloyd, Lamb, Priestley, Thelwall, Paine, Williams, Godwin, and Holcroft. Charles Lamb and Tom Paine look

especially queer in the same list; but although Lamb could
never be called a Jacobin, he was a friend of Godwin,
and, at this time, very liberal in his sentiments. The first
number of *The Anti-Jacobin*, by the way, contained a car-
toon by Gilray representing Rousseau as a naked savage
surrounded by various English admirers, including Coleridge and Southey with asses' heads. Charles Lloyd,
Coleridge's friend, appears as a toad, and Lamb as a
frog.

Perhaps the most powerful passage in *The New
Morality* thrusts at the Jacobin fusion of sensibility with
revolutionary enthusiasm:

> Next comes a gentler virtue. Ah, beware
> Lest the rough verse her shrinking softness scare.
> Visit her not too roughly; the warm sigh
> Breathes on her lips; the tear-drop gems her eye.
> Sweet Sensibility, who dwells enshrined
> In the fine foldings of the feeling mind;
> With delicate Mimosa's sense endued,
> Who shrinks, instinctive, from a hand too rude;
> Or, like the anagallia, prescient flower,
> Shuts her soft petals at the approaching shower.
> Sweet child of sickly Fancy! — her of yore
> From her loved France Rousseau to exile bore;
> And, while 'midst lakes and mountains wild he ran,
> Full of himself, and shunned the haunts of man,
> Taught her o'er each lone vale and Alpine steep
> To lisp the story of his wrongs, and weep;
> Taught her to cherish still in either eye
> Of tender tears a plentiful supply,
> And pour them in the brooks that babbled by.
>
> · · · ·
>
> Mark her fair votaries, prodigal of grief,

With cureless pangs, and woes that mock relief,
Droop in soft sorrow o'er a foolish flower;
O'er a dead jackass pour the pearly shower;
But hear, unmoved, of Loire's ensanguined flood
Choked up with slain; — of Lyons drenched in blood;

. . . .

Of savage cruelties that scare the mind,
The rage of madness with hell's lusts combined —
Of hearts torn reeking from the bleeding breast, —
They hear — and hope, that all is for the best.

Unfortunately, opposition to the Jacobins was not restricted to literary expression. The government and various groups of unofficial hundred-per-centers actively persecuted the English reformers. Severe acts against sedition and sympathetic correspondence with France were promulgated. Innocent idealists were imprisoned or sent to Botany Bay for long terms; legal and orderly meetings were dispersed with violence; books were burned and newspapers censored or suppressed. It was all very like the anti-Bolshevist activities of Attorney-General Palmer just after the World War. The ministry, the upper classes and the mob were conservative; the lower middle class and the young intellectuals sided with the Revolution.

A famous instance of intolerance is the Birmingham Riots. In July, 1791, the Constitutional Society of Birmingham held a dinner to celebrate the anniversary of the fall of the Bastille. A riot ensued in which the violence of the mob was directed chiefly against the persons and homes of the dissenters, who were numerous in Birmingham and whose sympathies were generally liberal. Joseph Priestley was not active in connection with the dinner, but since he was a noted reformer his house was sacked and his chapel burned. Priestley left Birmingham and lived in London and its suburbs until 1794. He then emigrated to Northumberland, Pennsylvania, on the banks of the Sus- quehanna — an action which encouraged the pantisocratic dream of Coleridge and Southey. In Number III of his *Sonnets on Eminent Characters* (1794), Coleridge repre- sents Nature as lifting her "matron veil" in the Pennsyl- vanian wilderness "to smile with fondness on her gazing son," Dr. Priestley. Merely to show how differently the same event could be regarded by two thoughtful men of the same period, let me quote from Cobbett's *Observa- tions on the Emigration of Dr. Joseph Priestley*:

Dear bought experience has at last taught him, that an Utopia never existed anywhere but in a delirious brain. He thought, like too many others, to find a Terrestrial Paradise . . . but alas; he is now convinced, I believe, that those who cultivate the fertile Lesowes of Warwickshire . . . have little reason to envy him his rocks and his swamps, the music of his bull frogs and the stings of his musquitoes.

The antirevolutionary hysteria reached its height in 1794, the year of the Terror. In that year Thomas Hardy, Horne Tooke, John Thelwall, Thomas Holcroft and eight less important reformers were indicted for high treason on flimsy and fabricated evidence. Pitt vaguely charged the London Corresponding Society, of which the honest shoemaker Hardy was founder and secretary, with being at the bottom of a terrible plot. Whether the government was sincerely alarmed or merely wished by fair means or foul to arouse feeling against the radicals is a doubtful question. At all events the case involved more than the lives of the accused: it is said that a large number of signed warrants for other reformers were held ready in case a conviction should be obtained. But the good English jury, its sense of fairness outraged, acquitted Hardy, Tooke, and Thelwall, and the remaining defendants were released without trial. Holcroft was somewhat chagrined at being deprived of the opportunity to deliver a fiery speech which he had prepared.

After this, active persecution of liberals abated, although Coleridge tells in *Biographia Literaria* that he and Wordsworth were shadowed by a government agent in 1797. The agent reported that they kept talking about a certain "spy nosey." The pun on Spinoza was not impossible in an age when "Pamela" could be pronounced "Pameely."

The dying down of anti-liberal activity does not imply that liberalism flourished. By the end of the century, practically no pro-revolutionary sentiment was left to persecute. Even in 1797 and 1798, *The Anti-Jacobin* was beating a dead snake. The war with France and the rise of Napoleon caused a conservative reaction which affected all but a few minds, and which lasted until the collapse of Napoleon in 1814. Then a new wave of liberalism began to gain force and swept on to the Reform Bill of 1832.

We are now ready to ask how all this revolutionary ferment is related to the work of the Lake Poets. Wordsworth is chronologically the earliest of the group, but it will be more convenient to begin with Southey and Coleridge.

IV

THE PANTISOCRATIC PHASE

Since Southey was born in 1774, he was only a lad of fifteen when the Bastille fell; and we have no record of his immediate response to the outbreak of the Revolution. Years later, however, he wrote to Caroline Bowles of those stirring days: "A visionary world seemed to open upon those who were just entering it. Old things seemed passing away, and nothing was dreamt of but the regeneration of the human race." Evidently his feelings had been much like those of Wordsworth.

But when we see Southey in 1793 as a student at Balliol College, Oxford, we see a young man who is already rather discouraged about the Revolution. Wordsworth will provide another instance of the same reaction. The Reign of Terror has begun, and England has declared war against France. The ardent young men, shocked by these circumstances, are becoming disillusioned. Young Southey wears his own hair, and for this and less superficial reasons is considered a radical. But he is a tired radical, writing self-consciously melancholy letters to friends like Grosvenor Bedford. "O," he cries, "for emancipation from these useless forms, this useless life, these haunts of intolerance, vice, and folly!" Here he is rather accurately describing the Oxford of his day, but he would not object to having his words applied to the world in general. He dreams of founding an ideal city, or of migrating to America: "I should be pleased to reside in a country where man was considered as more valuable than money; and where I could till the earth, and provide by honest industry the meat which my wife would dress with pleasing care." But he knows that this is an idle dream: "There is no place for virtue. Seneca was a visionary philosopher; even in the deserts of Arabia, the strongest will be the happiest, and the same rule holds good in Europe and Abyssinia." In this gloomy state of mind, he looks to Rousseau as his guiding star.

But Southey had the faculty of being able to observe his own character and bend it in the way in which he wanted it to grow. Even while he is mournfully pouring out his sensibility, he is cultivating a more controlled and stoical view of life. In 1799, when William Taylor of Norwich accuses him of having too much sensibility, he replies: "Once indeed I had a mimosa sensibility, but it has long ago been rooted out. Five years ago I counteracted Rousseau by dieting upon Godwin and Epictetus." In 1794, then, Southey is a Young Jacobin who has been disillusioned into a state of pseudo-Rousseauistic deteriorationism, and who is trying to keep a stiff upper lip by reading Epictetus and Godwin.

It was in the Spring of 1794 that Samuel Taylor Coleridge came from Cambridge to Oxford to see his old schoolmate, Robert Allen, and met Southey in the course of the visit. Coleridge was a dreamy, learned, poetic youth of twenty-two, two years older than Southey and much more precocious. He was already widely read, not only in pure literature, but in strange, out-of-the-way aspects of philosophy and theology. How early these studies had begun we learn from Lamb's essay, *Christ's Hospital Five-and-Thirty Years Ago*.

Coleridge had certainly been much inflamed by the

Revolution. Allusions to events which took place in November, 1792, indicate that the present text of his *Destruction of the Bastile* is a revision of earlier work, but the following stanza breathes the vaguely confident enthusiasm which the outbreak of the Revolution aroused in so many idealistic young Englishmen:

Heard'st thou yon universal cry,
    And dost thou linger still on Gallia's shore?
Go, Tyranny! beneath some barbarous sky
    Thy terrors lost and ruined power deplore!
        What tho' through many a groaning age
        Was felt thy keen suspicious rage,
        Yet Freedom roused by fierce Disdain
        Has wildly broke thy triple chain,
And like the storm which Earth's deep entrails hide,
At length has burst its way and spread its ruins wide.

Yet although Coleridge wrote in this vein when poetically stimulated by an exciting event, he was not at any time a complete Jacobin. He was never at any time much like anybody else in the world. He was strongly influenced by both Rousseau and Godwin, but he never swallowed either of them whole. In 1794, however, his strange individuality had by no means assumed its final form. During their first meetings, he and Southey must have felt that they had much in common. Both were disillusioned lovers of freedom; both thought Bowles' sonnets the last word in poetry; both were Unitarians and admirers of Priestley; both, with some reservations on Coleridge's part, were disciples of Godwin. Together, then, they evolved the plan of pantisocracy — "a scheme," as old Joseph Cottle says, "perfectly harmless in itself, but obnoxious to insuperable objections." With a group of friends, they were to emigrate to America and found a little communistic society on the banks of the Susquehanna.

In this they illustrate to some extent Oscar Wilde's paradox that life imitates art. For Frank Henley, the hero of Holcroft's *Anna St Ives*, in a moment of discouragement writes to a friend: "I have studied to divine in what land or among what people, whether savage or such as we call polished, the energies of mind might be most productive of good. . . . I think of sailing for America, where I may aid the struggles of liberty . . . and at the same time form a society of savages, who seem in consequence of their very ignorance to be less liable to repel truth than those whose information is more multifarious." This recoil of the perfectibilitarian has the same psychological basis as the pantisocracy of Coleridge and Southey. Robert Bage's *Man As He Is Not, or Hermsprong* is of the same general school as Holcroft's novel. Not having been published until 1796, it provides no evidence for Oscar Wilde, but we may notice that its hero also thinks of migrating to America. "I have," says Hermsprong, "sixty acres of uncleared land upon the Potowmac. . . . I have imagined a society of friends within a two mile ring; and I have imagined a mode of making it happy." Again and again we shall have occasion to note the close relation between the literature of this period and the actual circumstances of the authors' lives. Often it is impossible to say which parodies the other.

Whether Coleridge or Southey first proposed the plan is not certain. Southey, as we know, was already dreaming of peace and freedom in America. One may conjecture that he told Coleridge of his dreams and that Coleridge said "Why not?" and immediately began to speculate. Coleridge, who always regarded reality as coincident with the scope of his imagination, was to be a lover of impossibilities all his life. It was certainly Coleridge who elaborated the theoretical side of the scheme, and his own statement of the plan in the eleventh issue of *The Friend* should therefore be quoted:

What I dared not expect from constitutions of governments and whole nations I hoped from religion and a small company of chosen individuals, and formed a plan, as harmless as it was extravagant, of trying the experiment of human perfectibility on the banks of the Susquehannah; where our little society, in its second generation, was to have combined the innocence of the Patriarchal Age with the knowledge and general refinements of European culture; and where I dreamed that in the sober evening of my life I should behold the cottages of independence in the undivided dale of industry.

The tradition that Coleridge selected the Susquehanna merely because of its mellifluous name should be discarded. Joseph Priestley, whom the pantisocrats greatly admired, was just settling on the banks of that river, and there was a vague hope of getting him to join them. The same region was being made the scene of another social experiment, for a group of moderate-liberal Frenchmen, all of them wealthy and some of them nobles, had there set up a little community. The noblemen had abandoned their titles, and all was to be peace and equality.

The influence of an early American "realtor" should also be recognized. Coleridge writes to Southey from London:

Every night I meet a most intelligent young man, who has spent the last five years of his life in America, and is lately come from there as an agent to sell land. . . . He says that 2000 pounds will do; that he doubts not that we can contract for our passage under 400 pounds; that we shall buy the land a great deal cheaper when we arrive at America than we could do in England; "or why," he adds, "am I sent over here?" That twelve men may *easily* clear 400 acres in four or five months, and that, for 600 dollars, a thousand acres may be cleared, and houses built on them. He recommends the Susquehanna, from its excessive beauty, and its security from hostile Indians. Every possible assistance will be given us: we may get credit for the land for ten years or more, as we settle upon it. That literary characters make *money* there, etc., etc. He never saw a bison in his life, but has heard of them; they are quite backward. The musquitoes are not so bad as our gnats; and after you have been there a little while, they don't trouble you much.

William Haller's *Early Life of Robert Southey* will give you the facts about the movement: how Coleridge and Southey corresponded and argued over the scheme with a gradually growing sense of its futility; how the idea of emigrating to America simmered down to a vague notion of buying a farm in Wales; and how the whole plan collapsed in November, 1795, with a quarrel between the two leaders which was made up after Southey's return from Lisbon. Far from having enough money to finance a transatlantic settlement, the pantisocrats had barely enough to live on in England. Poor Southey remained in Bristol, whence they intended to sail, trying to work out the practical details of the project; while Coleridge roamed about, prated of the "book of pantisocracy" — one of his many never-to-be-written opuses — and in his lofty philosophical way reproached Southey for suggesting that any difficulties existed.

As we have seen, the pantisocrats expected the real

fruits of their experiment to appear in the second generation of settlers rather than in themselves. In order that
there should be a second generation, Coleridge, Southey,
and their friend Robert Lovell, with that rather cold-
blooded idealism characteristic of the age, married three
Fricker sisters of Bristol. These ladies very sensibly began
to worry about the details of life in the wilds of Pennsylvania. Southey passed on their doubts and fears to
Coleridge, who, alarmed at last, responded in a set of
"queries" which are very typical of his curious nature. In
order to understand them we need also to remember that
marriage to the Fricker sisters entailed the entrance into
the experiment of a number of relations both young and
old. Coleridge writes:

Quaere: should not all who mean to become members of our
community be incessantly meliorating their temper and elevating
their understanding? Qu.: whether a very respectable quantity of
acquired knowledge . . . be not a prerequisite to the improvement
of the head and heart? Qu.: whether our Women have not been
taught by us habitually to contemplate the littleness of individual
comforts and a passion for the *novelty* of the scheme rather than a
generous enthusiasm of benevolence? . . . These questions are
meant merely as motives to you, Southey, to the strengthening the
minds of the Women, and stimulating them to literary acquire-
ments. But, Southey, there are *children* going with us. . . . These
children, — the little Frickers, for instance, and your brothers, —
are they not already deeply tinged with the prejudices and errors
of society? . . . How are we to prevent them from infecting the
minds of *our* children? By reforming their judgments? At so early
an age, *can* they have *felt* the ill consequence of their errors in a
manner sufficiently vivid to make their reformation practicable? . . .
I have told you, Southey, that I will accompany you on an *imperfect* system. But must our system be thus necessarily imperfect? I

ask the question that I may know whether or not I should write the Book of Pantisocracy.

We shall not be wrong in inferring from this that behind the ideals of pantisocracy lay a somewhat disillusioned view of human nature. In another letter to Southey, for instance, Coleridge writes: "Wherever men *can* be vicious, some *will* be. The leading idea of Pantisocracy is to make men *necessarily* virtuous by removing all incentives to evil." This should put us on our guard against the rather common practice of referring to pantisocracy as purely Rousseauistic. These young men thought of themselves primarily as Godwinians. The *Memoirs of Thomas Holcroft* contain a letter written to Holcroft on December 11, 1794, by the pantisocrat Robert Lovell, describing the plan and asking him to consult Godwin about it and to give the group their advice. Theoretically at least, emigration to the banks of the Susquehanna was not a return to Rousseau's state of nature, where the native goodness of man could flourish unchecked by civilization. It was rather the application of Godwin's idea of perfectibility through reason to a selected group of people in an environment that had the negative advantage of shutting out opportunities for evil. The events of the Revolution had shown the pantisocrats that man as a whole was not yet ready to become virtuous through wisdom. But "a small company of chosen individuals" might succeed where whole nations had failed.

Yet although the abstract theory of pantisocracy is chiefly Godwinian, the feelings of Coleridge and Southey at this time are tinged with the atmosphere of the back-to-nature cult. Doubtless they felt that the benign influence of the Pennsylvanian forest would assist their efforts to

reason themselves into a state of perfection. How strong
this influence might be can be seen in Thomas Campbell's
Gertrude of Wyoming. The pantisocrats were certainly
influenced by such books as Bartram's *Travels* and
Crèvecœur's *Letters from an American Farmer*. To all
young lovers of liberty, America was then a land of
promise, and in their minds the romantic love of scenery
was blended with the romantic love of freedom as they
thought of the American wilderness. "There," sings
James Montgomery of Sheffield in *The Wanderer of
Switzerland*,

> There, in glens and caverns rude,
> Silent since the world began,
> Dwells the virgin Solitude,
> Unbetrayed by faithless man;
> Where a tyrant never trod,
> Where a slave was never known,
> But where Nature worships God,
> In the wilderness, alone.

Hence although pantisocracy is on the whole Godwinian,
it mingles Godwin and Rousseau, rationalism and emotionalism, deteriorationism and perfectibilitarianism, in a
way thoroughly representative of the thought of the
period.

Let us now consider some of the poems which Southey
and Coleridge were writing between 1793, when they got
into the state of mind which underlies pantisocracy, and
1795, when the plan was abandoned. The lesser poet may
be dealt with first.

At this time Southey was at work on his epic, *Joan of
Arc*. She appears in1796 as a kind of Mary Wollstonecraft, or, as Coleridge said in his conservative later days,

"a Tom Paine in petticoats." This first version of the poem is much less significant for us than the second version, published in 1798, which will be dealt with in another connection. *Wat Tyler*, in which Southey uses the historic uprising as modern reform propaganda, was written in 1794. "A good critic," says Saintsbury, "might take it for a deliberate and very happy parody of the cruder and more innocent utterances of sentimental republicanism." Among other poems of 1794, the *Botany Bay Eclogues* deserve mention. These are little sketches and stories of the lives of the victims of an unjust society. It was bold of Southey to give this twist to the old respectable eclogue tradition. In *Elinor*, the first of the series, we see the exile calling out in gratitude to the trackless woods, silent save for "the kangaroo's sad note":

> Welcome, wilderness,
> Nature's domain! for here, as yet unknown
> The comforts and the crimes of polished life,
> Nature benignly gives to all enough,
> Denies to all a superfluity.

Perhaps the feeling here expressed colored Southey's dreams of pantisocracy, so that he sometimes pictured himself on the banks of the Susquehanna crying "Welcome!" to the wilderness.

In 1794, also, Southey collaborated with Coleridge in a revolutionary drama, *The Fall of Robespierre*. (Robert Lovell was to be a third collaborator, but dropped out.) Robespierre, not having received the coat of whitewash which some modern historians have given him, was loathed as a bloodthirsty monster by English lovers of freedom. When he was guillotined in July, 1794, the hopes of English idealists, as we may see from Book X

of Wordsworth's *Prelude*, once more rose high. But of
course what then happened in France was not a renewal
of the Golden Age but a return to conservative bourgeois
control, with one last proletarian uprising in October,
1795, which a young Corsican artillery officer helped to
put down.

What was Coleridge writing in the years of the pantisocratic vision? In 1794 he published in the *Morning Chron-
icle* a group of *Sonnets on Eminent Characters*, praising
reformers like Godwin and Priestley (I have already
quoted the sonnet on Priestley) and condemning conservatives like Burke and Pitt. His views on Burke and Pitt
represent the feelings of most romantic liberals. Burke
was a genius, he had defended the Americans, he had
written a treatise *On the Sublime and Beautiful*, and he
could quote Milton at meetings of the Royal Academy.
Hazlitt was not alone in being torn between adoration of
Burke's style and detestation of his politics. Hence it is
not surprising that Coleridge makes the personified spirit
of Freedom rebuke Burke in the words:

> Great son of Genius! sweet to me thy name,
> Ere in an evil hour with altered voice
> Thou badst Oppression's hireling crew rejoice,
> Blasting with wizard spell my laurell'd fame.

But the practical politician Pitt, with his cold, cautious,
money-loving heart, is assailed in a way equally typical
of the romanticists as a

> dark Scowler . . .
> Who with proud words of dear-loved freedom came —
> More blasting than the mildew from the south!
> And kissed his country with Iscariot mouth.

To 1794 also belong several poetic footnotes to Coleridge's unwritten Book of Pantisocracy. They are full of
a sentimentality that shows how thin was the layer of
Godwinian rationalism which had temporarily been
spread over the emotions of this group. These lines from
Pantisocracy are a fair sample:

> No more my visionary soul shall dwell
> On joys that were; no more endure to weigh
> The shame and anguish of the evil day,
> Wisely forgetful! O'er the ocean swell,
> Sublime of hope, I seek the cottag'd dell,
> Where Virtue calm with careless steps may stray,
> And dancing to the midnight roundelay,
> The wizard Passions weave an holy spell.

But of course the most famous of these pantisocratic lays
is *To a Young Ass*:

> Innocent foal, thou poor despised forlorn!
> I hail thee *Brother* — spite of the fool's scorn;
> And fain would take thee with me, in the Dell
> Of Peace and mild Equality to dwell.

It is not necessary to regard these lines as wholly serious.
That Coleridge was quite capable of poking fun at him-
self is pleasantly shown in his *Sonnets Attempted in the
Manner of Contemporary Writers*.

After the scheme of pantisocracy collapses, what ensues
in the minds of Southey and Coleridge? Briefly, their
veneer of rationalism and their belief in Godwinian perfectibility disappear almost completely; and they become
much more frankly emotional and "romantic" in the ordinary loose meaning of that term. The most essential
fact in their development, however, is a return to nature

in the Wordsworthian sense — that is, a return to the peace and quiet of rustic life and to the joys that the beauty of external nature can give. This falling back upon natural simplicity is not, as under the pantisocratic theory, an initial step toward perfectibility through reason. It is at first merely a retreat to "the cot" in order to heal a sick and disappointed soul. Later, largely thanks to Wordsworth's influence, nature offers them not only refuge, but positive guidance and inspiration. Out of the negation of retreat gradually comes the happy affirmation of the poet who responds to the impulses from the vernal wood.

This development in Southey and Coleridge takes place between 1795 and 1797. Their state of mind will be clearer after we have considered Wordsworth. Southey's return to nature can best be studied in his *Hymn to the Penates*, in the series of blank verse *Inscriptions*, and in the second (1798) version of *Joan of Arc*. But we must pass on to two poems by Coleridge, the *Ode to the Departing Year* and *France: an Ode*. Their importance justifies a rather full analysis.

Ode to the Departing Year was composed December 24, 25, and 26, 1796, and published on the last day of that year. Coleridge says in his Argument,

The ode commences with an address to the Divine Providence that regulates into one vast harmony all the events of time, however calamitous some of them may appear to mortals. The second Strophe calls on men to suspend their private joys and sorrows, and devote them for a while to the cause of human nature in general. The first Epode speaks of the Empress of Russia, who died of an apoplexy on the 17th of November, 1796; having just concluded a subsidiary treaty with the kings combined against France. The first and second antistrophe describe the Image of the Departing Year, as in a vision. The second Epode prophesies, in anguish of spirit, the downfall of this country.

It is the second Epode which more particularly concerns us. From the horrors of war the poet turns to the beauty of free Britain:

> Not yet enslaved, not wholly vile,
> O Albion! O my mother Isle!
> Thy valleys, fair as Eden's bowers,
> Glitter green with sunny showers;
> The grassy upland's gentle swells
>   Echo to the bleat of flocks;
> (Those grassy hills, those glittering dells
>   Proudly ramparted with rocks)
> And Ocean mid his uproar wild
> Speaks safety to his Island-child!
> Hence for many a fearless age
> Has social Quiet loved thy shore;
> Nor ever proud invader's rage
> Or sacked thy towers, or stained thy fields with gore.

Then, to quote Coleridge's note, "the poet, from having considered the peculiar advantages which this country has enjoyed, passes in rapid transition to the uses which we have made of those advantages." Like all his fellow liberals, Coleridge is indignant at England for making war against France:

> Abandoned of Heaven! mad Avarice thy guide,
> At cowardly distance, yet kindling with pride —
> Mid thy herds and thy corn-fields secure thou hast stood,
> And joined the wild yelling of Famine and Blood!

But Coleridge no longer feels any impulse to right those wrongs or even to try the experiment of progress on a limited scale in some special environment. He merely wants to get away from the vileness of the world, earn his living as best he can, and cultivate a pastoral mood of "meek self-content":

> Away, my soul, away!
> In vain, in vain the birds of warning sing —
> And hark! I hear the famished brood of prey
> Flap their lank pennons on the groaning wind!
> Away, my soul, away!
> I, unpartaking of the evil thing,
> With daily prayer and daily toil
> Soliciting for food my scanty soil,
> Have wailed my country with a loud lament.
> Now I recentre my immortal mind
> In the deep Sabbath of meek self-content;
> Cleansed from the vaporous passions that bedim
> God's image, sister of the seraphim.

France: an Ode was written in February, 1798, and published in April of that year. Its original title, *The Recantation: an Ode*, is more appropriate than the final one, for here Coleridge is recanting all his faith in the Revolution. Since the composition of *Ode to the Departing Year*, France had invaded Switzerland. Now Switzerland occupied a favored place in the heart of every young romanticist. Her scenery, the simple virtues of her mountaineers, her traditional love of freedom, would have made her the ideal romantic land even without the influence of Rousseau. We may imagine, then, how Coleridge and his contemporaries felt when this ideal romantic land was oppressed by France, the supposed champion of the rights of man. It is this circumstance which motivates Coleridge's "recantation."

The poem is divided into sections each of which represents a phase of Coleridge's changing attitude toward the Revolution. These phases, on the whole, represent the experience of his contemporaries as well as his own. You should compare them with those more fully described in Wordsworth's *Prelude*.

My analysis of Coleridge's ode will follow the Argument. Stanza I: "An invocation to those objects in Nature the contemplation of which had inspired the Poet with a devotional love of liberty."

> Ye Woods! that listen to the night-birds singing,
>   Midway the smooth and perilous slope reclined,
> Save when your own imperious branches swinging,
>   Have made a solemn music of the wind!
> Where, like a man beloved of God,
> Through glooms, which never woodman trod,
>   How oft, pursuing fancies holy,
> My moonlight way o'er flowering weeds I wound,
>   Inspired, beyond the guess of folly,
> By each rude shape and wild unconquerable sound!
> O ye loud Waves! and O ye Forests high!
>   And O ye Clouds that far above me soared!
> Thou rising Sun! thou blue rejoicing Sky!
>   Yea, every thing that is and will be free!
>   Bear witness for me, wheresoe'er ye be,
>   With what deep worship I have still adored
>   The spirit of divinest Liberty.

Before the Revolution, then, the untrammeled beauty and majesty of nature had prepared Coleridge to be a lover of liberty. That, we shall find, is exactly Wordsworth's thought, and probably Coleridge's expression of it reflects the influence of the other poet. Wordsworth and Coleridge had met in September, 1795, and by 1797 they were close friends. Each had much to give the other. Though from the first neither was lacking in appreciation of external nature or in intellectual force, on the whole Wordsworth opened Coleridge's eyes to what nature could do for man; while Coleridge, with his metaphysical mind, stimulated Wordsworth to make a kind of philosophy out of his feeling for nature. At this point, therefore, the autobiographic value of *France* is perhaps less than that of *To a Young Lady, With a Poem on the French Revolution.* In these lines, written in 1794, Coleridge pictures himself as having been, before the Revolution, not a particularly ardent worshipper of scenery, but a young Man of Feeling, fond of walking among "echoing cloisters pale . . . amid the pensive twilight gloom" and shedding the tear of sensibility. But to return to the *Ode.*

Stanza II: "The exultation of the Poet at the commencement of the French Revolution, and his unqualified abhorrence of the alliance against the republic."

> When France in wrath her giant-limbs upreared,
>   And with that oath, which smote air, earth, and sea,
>   Stamped her strong foot and said she would be free,
> Bear witness for me, how I hoped and feared!
> With what a joy my lofty gratulation
>   Unawed I sang, amid a slavish band:
> And when to whelm the disenchanted nation,
>   Like fiends embattled by a wizard's wand,
>   The Monarchs marched in evil day,
>   And Britain joined the dire array;
>   Though dear her shores and circling ocean,
> Though many friendships, many youthful loves
>   Had swoln the patriot emotion
> And flung a magic light o'er all her hills and groves;
> Yet still my voice, unaltered, sang defeat

To all that braved the tyrant-quelling lance,
And shame too long delayed and vain retreat!
For ne'er, O Liberty! with partial aim
I dimmed thy light or damped thy holy flame;
But blessed the paeans of delivered France,
And hung my head and wept at Britain's name.

Stanza III: "The blasphemies and horrors during the domination of the Terrorists regarded by the Poet as a transient storm, and as the natural consequences of former despotism and of the foul superstition of Popery. Reason, indeed, began to suggest many apprehensions; yet still the poet struggled to retain the hope that France would make conquests by no other means than by presenting to the observation of Europe a nation more happy and better instructed than under other forms of government."

"And what," said I, "though Blasphemy's loud scream
With that sweet music of deliverence strove!
Though all the fierce and drunken passions wove
A dance more wild than e'er was maniac's dream!
Ye storms, that round the dawning East assembled,
The Sun was rising, though ye hid his light!"

Stanza IV: "Switzerland, and the poet's recantation."

Forgive me, Freedom! O forgive those dreams!
I hear thy voice, I hear thy loud lament,
From bleak Helvetia's icy caverns sent —
I hear thy groans upon her blood-stained streams!
Heroes, that for your peaceful country perished,
And ye that, fleeing, spot your mountain-snows
With bleeding wounds; forgive me that I cherished
One thought that ever blessed your cruel foes!

Stanza V: "An address to Liberty, in which the Poet expresses his conviction that those feelings and that grand *ideal* of Freedom which the mind attains by the contemplation of its individual nature, and of the sublime surrounding objects, do not belong to men, as a society, nor can possibly be either gratified or realized, under any form of human government; but belong to the individual man, so far as he is pure, and inflamed with the love and adoration of God in Nature."

> The Sensual and the Dark rebel in vain,
> Slaves by their own compulsion! In mad game
> They burst their manacles and wear the name
> Of Freedom, graven on a heavier chain!
> O Liberty! with profitless endeavour
> Have I pursued thee, many a weary hour;
> But thou nor swell'st the victor's strain, nor ever
> Didst breathe thy soul in forms of human power.
> Alike from all, howe'er they praise thee,
> (Nor prayer, nor boastful name delays thee)
> Alike from Priestcraft's harpy minions,
> And factious Blasphemy's obscener slaves,
> Thou speedest on thy subtle pinions,
> The guide of homeless winds, and playmate of the waves!
> And there I felt thee! — on that sea-cliff's verge,
> Whose pines, scarce travelled by the breeze above,
> Had made one murmur with the distant surge!
> Yes, while I stood and gazed, my temples bare,
> And shot my being through earth, sea, and air,
> Possessing all things with intensest love,
> O Liberty! my spirit felt thee there.

Coleridge, then, finally comes to the conclusion that society cannot attain freedom through violent rebellion or even through peaceful reform. Liberty is something which the individual finds in his own noblest self; and he finds that noblest self through adoring *God's* noblest self

— that is, God's beautiful mountains and forests and streams.

Now that Southey and Coleridge are safe in the bosom of nature after the storm and stress of the Revolution, we may turn to Wordsworth in order to see how he responded to the same stimuli.

V

THE PRELUDE

Since *The Prelude* covers Wordsworth's imaginative and intellectual development from early childhood to 1798, by which time his characteristic view of nature had assumed definite form, it will provide the backbone of this lecture. For facts about the composition of the poem and its relation to the uncompleted *magnum opus* on "man, nature, and society," *The Recluse*, see De Selincourt's Variorum Edition.

Before we begin to analyze *The Prelude* we should remind ourselves of a fact which some students of Wordsworth forget — that memory tends to rearrange the past in such a way as to make it account for the present. We are here dealing, not with primary biographical sources, but with a highly imaginative man's account of those influences which he supposes to have made him the poet that he is. The poem is part of the abundant literature of romantic self-revelation, and inevitably has a large subjective element.

Book I deals with *Childhood and Schooltime*. Describing his boyhood in the Lake Country, Wordsworth relates that from his earliest days his senses were gradually attuned to the beauty of nature. The most intense and memorable of his early impressions, however, seem to have been those of solemn fear. Take for example the poaching incident, lines 317 ff., or better still the great "stolen boat" passage, lines 357 ff. Wordsworth is trying

to show that beauty enters our souls through fear even
before it appeals to us directly.

But nature soon began to impress the boy not merely
by scaring him, but by giving him sensuous joy. Such
moments are represented by the skating scene:

> Not seldom from the uproar I retired
> Into a silent bay, or sportively
> Glanced sideway, leaving the tumultuous throng,
> To cut across the reflex of a star
> That fled, and, flying still before me, gleamed
> Upon the glassy plain; and oftentimes,
> When we had given our bodies to the wind,
> And all the shadowy banks on either side
> Came sweeping through the darkness, spinning still
> The rapid line of motion, then at once
> Have I, reclining back upon my heels,
> Stopped short; yet still the solitary cliffs
> Wheeled by me — even as if the earth had rolled
> With visible motion her diurnal round!

Looking back on these impressions, Wordsworth feels
that they must have been for some purpose:

> Ye Presences of Nature in the sky
> And on the earth! Ye Visions of the hills!
> And Souls of lonely places! can I think
> A vulgar hope was yours when ye employed
> Such ministry, when ye through many a year
> Haunting me thus among my boyish sports,
> On caves and trees, upon the woods and hills,
> Impressed upon all forms the characters
> Of danger or desire; and thus did make
> The surface of the universal earth
> With triumph and delight, with hope and fear,
> Work like a sea?

The poet seems to remember that as early as the age
of ten he felt not merely the boyish thrill which he has
been describing, but a deeper and more spiritual delight.

> Even then I felt
> Gleams like the flashing of a shield; — the earth
> And common face of Nature spake to me
> Rememberable things.

Without his knowing it, these influences sank into his
mind to make him what at last he became — a great poet.
Here and elsewhere, as I have suggested, some allowance
needs to be made for the "autobiographical fallacy."
Not Wordsworth, but his sister, tells us that in these days
the future poet used to kill all the white butterflies he
could catch, "because they were Frenchmen." The white
cockade of the Bourbons is no doubt the associative link.
This little fact sheds light on *To a Butterfly*:

> Oh! pleasant, pleasant, were the days,
> The time, when in our childish plays,
> My sister Emmeline and I
> Together chased the butterfly!
> A very hunter did I rush
> Upon the prey; — with leaps and springs
> I followed on from brake to bush;
> But she, God love her! feared to brush
> The dust from off its wings.

That butterfly was a Frenchman.

Book II, *Schooltime* (*continued*), deals in a more intimate and informal way with Wordsworth's happy life at
Hawkshead Grammar School. In an interesting passage
he recalls his love of the sun:

Not as I since have loved him, as a pledge
And surety of our earthly life, a light
Which we behold and feel we are alive;
Nor for his bounty to so many worlds —
But for this cause, that I had seen him lay
His beauty on the morning hills, had seen
The western mountain touch his setting orb,
In many a thoughtless hour, when, from excess
Of happiness, my blood appeared to flow
For its own pleasure, and I breathed with joy.

The pleasure he derived from nature at this time, then, was purely esthetic, without any element of philosophy. But as Wordsworth writes of his past his matured sense of the philosophical significance of these joys is very keen. He now feels that something in him, something more than merely sensuous, must have reached out toward the beauty that he beheld. The following passage illustrates this belief in a way that casts light upon the *Immortality Ode*:

Blest the Babe,
Nursed in his Mother's arms, who sinks to sleep
Rocked on his Mother's breast; who with his soul
Drinks in the feeling of his Mother's eye!
For him, in one dear Presence, there exists
A virtue which irradiates and exalts
Objects through widest intercourse of sense.
No outcast he, bewildered and depressed;
Along his infant veins are interfused
The gravitation and the filial bond
Of nature that connect him with the world.
Is there a flower, to which he points with hand
Too weak to gather it, already love
Drawn from love's purest earthly fount for him

Hath beautified that flower; already shades
Of pity cast from inward tenderness
Do fall around him upon aught that bears
Unsightly marks of violence or harm.
Emphatically such a Being lives,
Frail creature as he is, helpless as frail,
An inmate of this active universe;
For feeling has to him imparted power
That through the growing faculties of sense
Doth like an agent of the one great Mind
Create, creator and receiver both,
Working but in alliance with the works
Which it beholds. — Such, verily, is the first
Poetic spirit of our human life,
By uniform control of after years,
In most, abated or suppressed; in some,
Through every change of growth and of decay,
Pre-eminent till death.

These lines are of great importance as showing how a
happy childhood holds the germ of the poetry of an adult
who has been faithful to the insight of childhood. The
mother's love for her babe, says Wordsworth, disposes
the child to feel love in nature, so that even his earliest
sense experiences are subconsciously associated in his mind
with an element of affectionate goodness in the external
world. The child's own instinctive love for his mother,
conversely, disposes him to take an attitude of filial love
toward the beautiful world in which he lives. This is the
"natural piety" of *My Heart Leaps Up*. And it is "the
first poetic spirit of our human life" because, like poetry,
it is partly a passive response to sense impressions and
partly a creative treatment of those impressions in terms
of inward feeling. This natural interplay of the objective

and the subjective is the privilege of childhood. The world suppresses it in most adults, but a few men, called poets, are able to preserve it. Wordsworth believes for a time that he has done so.

Book III, *Residence at Cambridge.* In 1787, at the age of seventeen, Wordsworth entered St. John's College, Cambridge. He roomed over the noisy college kitchens, but his window looked out upon the chapel of Trinity, where stood the statue of Newton,

> The marble index of a mind for ever
> Voyaging through strange seas of Thought, alone.

He did not try very hard for scholastic eminence, feeling that he had a special destiny with which Cambridge had little to do. His love of nature began to take on greater depth and maturity:

> To every natural form, rock, fruit or flower,
> Even the loose stones that cover the high-way,
> I gave a moral life: I saw them feel,
> Or linked them to some feeling: the great mass
> Lay bedded in a quickening soul, and all
> That I beheld respired with inward meaning.

This advance toward the final state of his poetic mind, however, was soon checked and smothered by the frivolities of college life.

> Easily I passed
> From the remembrances of better things,
> And slipped into the ordinary works
> Of careless youth, unburthened, unalarmed.
> *Caverns* there were within my mind which sun
> Could never penetrate, yet there did not
> Want store of leafy *arbours* where the light
> Might enter in at will. Companionships,

Friendships, acquaintances, were welcome all.
We sauntered, played, or rioted; we talked
Unprofitable talk at morning hours;
Drifted about along the streets and walks,
Read lazily in trivial books, went forth
To gallop through the country in blind zeal
Of senseless horsemanship, or on the breast
Of Cam sailed boisterously, and let the stars
Come forth, perhaps without one quiet thought.

The universities of this time were, as Southey was later
to express it, "haunts of intolerance, vice, and folly." In
Fleetwood (1805), Godwin makes his hero undergo at
Oxford experiences similar to those which Wordsworth
reports, except that the fictional character is much more
deplorably affected by his environment. Young Fleetwood
is brought up in the mountains of Wales as a child of
nature — free, innocent, instinctively benevolent. But Oxford has a corrupting influence on the youth. "Oh divinity
that presidest over the constellations, the meteors, and
the ocean, how was your pupil fallen! How the awestruck
and ardent worshipper changed into the shameless roarer
of a licentious catch!" Fleetwood goes to Switzerland
from the university, as Wordsworth is to do a little later.
We may note that Hugh Trevor, in Holcroft's novel of
that name, also finds Oxford a place where the natural
virtues are sophisticated. There is no reason to suppose
that Wordsworth was guilty of any serious misconduct
during his college days. De Quincey reports that for a
time he was something of a dandy, and Wordsworth
himself tells us that he once got slightly tipsy in John
Milton's room in Christ's College. A friend of Wordsworth occupied that historic chamber, and one night a

group of students gathered there and paid somewhat inappropriate tribute to "the lady of Christ's" by drinking too much. That incident is described in lines 286 ff.

We cannot suppose, however, that Wordsworth was ever very active as a shameless roarer of licentious catches. He simply wasted his time and got off the track of his true development. He is not greatly to be blamed for that. We may see from this great passage that he expected to find something which the university was not able to give him:

> Toil and pains
> In this recess, by thoughtful Fancy built,
> Should spread from heart to heart; and stately groves,
> Majestic edifices, should not want
> A corresponding dignity within.
> The congregating temper that pervades
> Our unripe years, not wasted, should be taught
> To minister to works of high attempt —
> Work which the enthusiast would perform with love.
> Youth should be awed, religiously possessed
> With a conviction of the power that waits
> On knowledge, when sincerely sought and prized
> For its own sake, on glory and on praise
> If but by labour won, and fit to endure
> The passing day; should learn to put aside
> Her trappings here, should strip them off abashed
> Before antiquity and stedfast truth
> And strong book-mindedness; and over all
> A healthy sound simplicity should reign,
> A seemly plainness, name it what you will,
> Republican or pious.

Missing that spirit at Cambridge, as we miss it at Harvard and Williams and Minnesota and Columbia, Wordsworth hardly took full advantage of such benefits as the academic environment actually provided.

Book V, *Summer Vacation*. In the Summer of 1788 he returned to Hawkshead for the long vacation. Even across the years, the zestful, almost gay, spirit of this book imparts to us his pleasure at getting back to the old scenes. But the intimacy of his contact with nature was interfered with by the frivolous, superficial, Cambridge attitude which clung to him:

> Yet in spite
> Of pleasure won, and knowledge not withheld,
> There was an inner falling off — I loved,
> Loved deeply all that had been loved before,
> More deeply even than ever: but a swarm
> Of heady schemes jostling each other, gawds,
> And feast and dance, and public revelry,
> And sports and games (too grateful in themselves,
> Yet in themselves less grateful, I believe,
> Than as they were a badge glossy and fresh
> Of manliness and freedom) all conspired
> To lure my mind from firm habitual quest
> Of feeding pleasures, to depress the zeal
> And damp those yearnings which had once been mine.

Book V, *Books*, is a sort of interlude dealing with the influence of literature on the poet's mind. He testifies that books have been second only to nature in forming his ideas. Lines 230 ff. advocate liberty in reading, and praise his mother for letting him browse at will. Wordsworth's education at Hawkshead Grammar School had been along lines of Rousseauistic freedom, though William Taylor could hardly have been aware of that fact. Wordsworth follows Rousseau in believing that education should be the

development, not the repression, of natural instinct.
Legouis and De Selincourt, however, are probably right
when they say that on this point Wordsworth is more
consistent than Rousseau. Émile's tutor is something of a
Foxy Grandpa, always spying on the child, presenting this
stimulus and withholding that. The boy is to suppose
himself free, but in reality he is about as free as a laboratory guinea pig. Wordsworth — at the time when he
wrote this passage — will have none of these mistrustful
restrictions and arbitrarily manufactured situations. We
may infer that Wordsworth thinks his mother a better
educator than Émile's ideal tutor. He insists that literary
instruction must not be forced or formalized, and must
not be allowed to usurp the place of nature in education.
He does not, however, share Rousseau's disapproval of
imaginative literature as mental food for the young child.
Tales of wonder and magic keep the boy's mind from
growing dry and stiff, and help him to see the marvelous
in nature. Conversely, the education of nature is the best
preparation for the maturer love of books, since a lad
reared as Wordsworth has been reared finds in literature
the nature which he already knows, now illumined by
genius.

Book VI, *Cambridge and the Alps.* When Wordsworth
returned to Cambridge in the autumn of 1788 the original
excitement of college life had subsided and, by being less
imitative of his environment, he derived more benefit from
it. He lived more to himself, read eagerly, though not
often in the books which his professors required, and responded to the quiet beauty of the university and its setting. The impressions of his childhood, too, returned to
him in meditations which led him to hope that he might

achieve greatness in literature. Nevertheless, he looks back on these pleasant days as a period of drifting.

When the "long vacation" of 1790 arrived, he took a walking-tour through France and the Swiss Alps with Robert Jones, a Welsh college friend. As we may see from the passage describing the Simplon Pass, lines 617 ff., he sometimes keenly felt the glories of the scenery. But such moods of almost mystical elevation are at this time rather rare. Wordsworth's imagination worked best in an atmosphere of peace and quiet — "emotion recollected in tranquility." His travels were too superficially and immediately exciting to afford the best material for his mind to work on. With twelve short weeks at their disposal, these young men hiked very rapidly, hurrying on to a new scene of beauty before they had had time to digest the previous one. Contemporary events in France, moreover, tended to obscure the deeper messages of the mountains. The Revolution had broken out, but the excesses of the Terror were still far away. In fact, during the summer of 1790 all France was celebrating a kind of love feast in which the sentimentally idealistic side of the movement was uppermost. Louis himself had taken the oath of allegiance to the new government, and everyone was everyone else's brother. In his *French Revolution*, Carlyle has painted a remarkable picture of these idyllic days. This carnival of universal brotherhood would be delightful to any young man of sensibility, and Wordsworth liked it extremely. But the carnival impressed him more than the meaning of the carnival. Everything conspired to make him feel gay and careless. His enjoyment of external nature kept him from sensing the true seriousness of the political situation, and the present temper of the French

kept him from opening the depths of his heart to the
beauty through which he passed.

Book VII, *Residence in London*. At the end of this
vacation Wordsworth returned to Cambridge. He took
his B.A. in January, 1791, and went to London. The city
pleased and excited him. The poet of nature gives us in
this book some charming glimpses of what a great city can
mean to a youth. And he never forgot that a city can be
beautiful — witness the sonnet *Composed upon West-
minster Bridge*. But looking back upon these days he feels
that the excitement of city life distracted him from his
true self. Even then he half unconsciously recognized that
the profound wells of his character were being covered up.
His thoughts kept turning to his boyhood in the Lake
Country. Perhaps some recollection of his own home-
sickness later entered into *The Reverie of Poor Susan*
(1797):

> At the corner of Wood Street, when daylight appears,
> Hangs a thrush that sings loud, it has sung for three years:
> Poor Susan has passed by the spot, and has heard
> In the silence of morning the song of the bird.
>
> 'Tis a note of enchantment; what ails her? She sees
> A mountain ascending, a vision of trees;
> Bright volumes of vapour through Lothbury glide,
> And a river flows on through the vale of Cheapside.
>
> . . . .
>
> She looks, and her heart is in heaven: but they fade,
> The mist and the river, the hill and the shade:
> The stream will not flow, and the hill will not rise,
> And the colours have all passed away from her eyes!

The memories of the Lake Country which come to
Wordsworth in London make up Book VIII, *Retrospect*.

The subtitle, *Love of Nature Leading to Love of Man*, indicates the significance of this part of the poem. Wordsworth begins by describing a rural fair held in the shadow of Mount Helvellyn. The "dalesmen" lead a life very different from that of the dwellers in the city:

> Immense
> Is the recess, the circumambient world
> Magnificent, by which they are embraced:
> They move about upon the soft green turf:
> How little they, they and their doings, seem,
> And all that they can further or obstruct!
> Through utter weakness pitiably dear,
> As tender infants are: and yet how great!
> For all things serve them: them the morning light
> Loves, as it glistens on the silent rocks;
> And them the silent rocks, which now from high
> Look down upon them; the reposing clouds;
> The wild brooks prattling from invisible haunts;
> And old Helvellyn, conscious of the stir
> Which animates this day their calm abode.
>   With deep devotion, Nature, did I feel
> In that enormous City's turbulent world
> Of men and things, what benefit I owed
> To thee, and those domains of rural peace,
> Where to the sense of beauty first my heart
> Was opened.

After giving an account of the peasants' virtues, which arise from their closeness to nature, Wordsworth tells of the growth of his feeling for these simple folk. As a boy, he had seen the dalesman against the background of his majestic surroundings. Hence in Wordsworth's youthful imagination the peasant took on something of the majesty of the hills.

                  A rambling school-boy, thus
I felt his presence in his own domain,
As of a lord and master, or a power,
Or genius, under Nature, under God,
Presiding; and severest solitude
Had more commanding looks when he was there.
When up the lonely brooks on rainy days
Angling I went, or trod the trackless hills
By mists bewildered, suddenly mine eyes
Have glanced upon him distant a few steps,
In size a giant, stalking through thick fog,
His sheep like Greenland bears; or, as he stepped
Beyond the boundary line of some hill-shadow,
His form hath flashed upon me, glorified
By the deep radiance of the setting sun:
Or him have I descried in distant sky,
A solitary object and sublime,
Above all height! like an aerial cross
Stationed alone upon a spiry rock
Of the Chartreuse, for worship. Thus was man
Ennobled outwardly before my sight,
And thus my heart was early introduced
To an unconscious love and reverence
Of human nature; hence the human form
To me became an index of delight,
Of grace and honour, power and worthiness.

If this ideal view of man was an illusion, says Wordsworth, it was at least a beneficent one. He scorns the
literal-minded rationalist who would wish to deprive him
of it, and thanks God that the good in man was magnified
by his boyish imagination before he became aware of the
evil:

                  Call ye these appearances —
Which I beheld of shepherds in my youth,

This sanctity of Nature given to man —
A shadow, a delusion, ye who pore
On the dead letter, miss the spirit of things,

                    .   .   .   .

                        But blessed be the God
Of Nature and of Man that this was so;
That men before my inexperienced eyes
Did first present themselves thus purified,
Removed, and to a distance that was fit;
And so we all of us in some degree
Are led to knowledge, wheresoever led,
And howsoever; were it otherwise,
And we found evil fast as we found good
In our first years, or think that it is found,
How could the innocent heart bear up and live!
But doubly fortunate my lot; not here
Alone, that something of a better life
Perhaps was round me than it is the privilege
Of most to move in, but that first I looked
At Man through objects that were great or fair;
First communed with him by their help.

It is, then, by making us look at humanity in relation to
objects which are great or fair that love of nature leads
to love of man.

Books IX and X, *Residence in France*, and Book XI,
France, are best considered as a unit. At the end of 1791
Wordsworth went to France, and stayed there through
1792. During this sojourn occurred an event not mentioned in the *Prelude*: he formed an irregular alliance
with a French girl named Annette Vallon, and had by her
a daughter — the "dear child" of *It is a beauteous evening*. The occurrence is not particularly astounding —
Wordsworth was not *born* poet laureate of England. Dur-

ing this period, too, he may well have had conscientiously radical ideas on the subject of marriage, as did a good many other young men. Though the importance of this affair should not be overstressed, it doubtless added a special element to the general disturbance of the time. It is reflected in the narrative poem *Vaudracour and Julia*, and in several dramatic lyrics in which a deserted mother laments her fate to her child — for example, the *Complaint of a Forsaken Indian Woman*. It would also be extremely interesting should the mysterious Lucy be Annette Vallon, transferred to the Lake Country and there imaginatively killed off for purposes of emotional relief.

In this part of *The Prelude*, Wordsworth tells us that when he came to France he was not greatly moved by the Revolution. For a person so familiar with the democracy of nature, the rights of man seemed too obvious to become excited about. The following lines will recall the first stage of Coleridge's feelings toward the Revolution:

> Add unto this, subservience from the first
> To presences of God's mysterious power
> Made manifest in Nature's sovereignty,
> And fellowship with venerable books,
> To sanction the proud workings of the soul,
> And mountain liberty. It could not be
> But that one tutored thus should look with awe
> Upon the faculties of man, receive
> Gladly the highest promises, and hail,
> As best, the government of equal rights
> And individual worth. And hence, O Friend!
> If at the first great outbreak I rejoiced
> Less than might well befit my youth, the cause
> In part lay here, that unto me the events
> Seemed nothing out of nature's certain course,
> A gift that was come rather late than soon.

It all seemed a part of the general return to nature:

> Youth maintains,
> In all conditions of society,
> Communion more direct and intimate
> With Nature, — hence, ofttimes, with reason too —
> Than age, or manhood, even. To Nature, then,
> Power had reverted: habit, custom, law,
> Had left an interregnum's open space
> For *her* to move about in, uncontrolled.

But the poet soon formed a friendship with a French army officer, Michel Beaupuy. This high-souled patriot made Wordsworth appreciate the causes of the Revolution, the loftiness of its aims, and the obstacles in its path, and filled him with such enthusiasm that he determined to cast in his lot with the Girondins, the moderate republican party opposed to the Jacobins. To what extent he actually engaged in French politics has been a disputed point, as has the exact reason for his return to England in December, 1792, or January, 1793. Harper favors the idea that his activity in the Girondist party made it unsafe for him to remain in France. But in lines 222 ff. of Book X Wordsworth seems to say that if "a chain of harsh necessity" had not dragged him back to England at this time he *would* have joined the ill-fated Girondins and *might* have perished with their leaders — a hypothetical escape for which, in the final text of the poem, he thanks Providence. And the corresponding passage of the 1805-1806 text explains what the "chain" was:

> In this frame of mind,
> Reluctantly to England I returned,
> Compelled by nothing less than absolute want
> Of funds for my support, else, well assured

That I both was and must be of small worth,
No better than an alien in the Land,
I doubtless should have made a common cause
With some who perished, haply perished too,
A poor mistaken and bewildered offering.

The semi-autobiographical *Vaudracour and Julia* contains a passage which may easily be interpreted to mean that he hoped to obtain in England money wherewith to support Annette Vallon. There may be some other explanation, but I know of no evidence for it. This, by the way, will suggest the usefulness of De Selincourt's Variorum Edition of *The Prelude*, which has received less attention than it deserves. The possibility that Wordsworth returned to France and Annette for a short time in 1793 is strengthened by important letters communicated to the *London Times Literary Supplement* of May 1 and June 12, 1930, by Professors J. M. Harper and J. R. MacGillivray.

In 1793, Wordsworth was greatly shocked when England declared war against France. It seemed as if his beloved country were fighting against all his ideals. The hostility of England and the other members of the Coalition made France desperate, and strengthened the violent Jacobin party. The consequent Reign of Terror appalled Wordsworth, but he continued to hope for the best; and when Robespierre was himself beheaded in July, 1794, he thought that the Golden Age had at last returned. Though separately published under the title *French Revolution as It Appeared to Enthusiasts At Its Commencement*, those beautiful lines beginning "O pleasant exercise of hope and joy!" really represent Wordsworth's feelings in the summer of 1794 after the death of Robes-

pierre. He discovered his mistake in the autumn of the
same year when France forsook revolutionary idealism
along with terroristic excesses, and began to wage aggres-
sive war in Spain, Italy, Germany, and Holland. An
equally crushing disillusionment came when England, as
we know, tried to stamp out liberal thought on her side
of the Channel. In the final version Wordsworth has
toned down the passage dealing with this subject; let us
take the harsher lines of the 1805-1806 version:

> Our Shepherds (this say merely) at that time
> Thirsted to make the guardian Crook of Law
> A tool of Murder; they who ruled the State,
> Though with such awful proof before their eyes
> That he who would sow death, reaps death, or worse,
> And can reap nothing better, child-like longed
> To imitate, not wise enough to avoid,
> Giants in their impiety alone,
> But, in their weapons and their warfare base
> As vermin working out of reach, they leagued
> Their strength perfidiously, to undermine
> Justice, and make an end of Liberty.

All this hastened an interesting development in the
mind of the poet. Both France and England had disappointed his hopes, and he was troubled about Annette
Vallon. Since his feelings were bruised and irritated, he
tried not to feel at all, but to cultivate pure, abstract
reason. This, remember, was the very time when Southey
was trying to counteract the influence of Rousseau by dieting upon Epictetus and Godwin. At Cambridge, where
mathematics has long occupied an honored place, Wordsworth had responded to the imaginative appeal of geometry:

> Mighty is the charm
> Of those abstractions to a mind beset
> With images, and haunted by herself,
> And specially delightful unto me
> Was that clear synthesis built up aloft
> So gracefully; even then when it appeared
> No more than a mere plaything, or a toy
> To sense embodied: not the thing it is
> In verity, an independent world,
> Created out of pure intelligence.
>
> (VI, 158 ff.)

As Edna St. Vincent Millay expresses it, "Euclid alone has looked on beauty bare." Wordsworth now wished to withdraw into a philosophy of cool geometrical reason, forgetting all the lessons of nature. Such a philosophy was waiting for him, as for many of his contemporaries, in Godwin's *Political Justice*:

> This was the time, when, all things tending fast
> To depravation, speculative schemes —
> That promised to abstract the hopes of Man
> Out of his feelings, to be fixed thenceforth
> For ever in a purer element —
> Found ready welcome. Tempting region *that*
> For Zeal to enter and refresh herself,
> Where passions had the privilege to work,
> And never hear the sound of their own names.
> But, speaking more in charity, the dream
> Flattered the young, pleased with extremes, nor least
> With that which makes our Reason's naked self
> The object of its fervour. What delight!
> How glorious! in self-knowledge and self-rule,
> To look through all the frailties of the world,
> And, with a resolute mastery shaking off

Infirmities of nature, time, and place,
Build social upon personal Liberty,
Which, to the blind restraints of general laws
Superior, magisterially adopts
One guide, the light of circumstances, flashed
Upon an independent intellect.

Authorities are unable to agree as to the dates of Wordsworth's "Godwinian period." The concluding books of *The Prelude* shift backward and forward in a baffling manner. Besides, since even Godwin himself is not a perfect Godwinian, we can hardly expect to find particular months or years during which Wordsworth's mind is enclosed in a trim little box to which a definite label can be affixed. Without troubling you with minute details, I shall offer the following summary of the matter. It agrees, I find, with the views of De Selincourt. So far as necessitarianism is concerned, the influence of Godwin begins to operate upon Wordsworth in 1793. It tends to make his thought somewhat colder and more mechanical, it begins to draw him away from nature, and it combines with the English declaration of war against France and with the Terror to diminish his revolutionary enthusiasm. But the death of Robespierre arouses his hopes, and we may suppose that Godwin's grip is relaxed for a time. The aggressions of the French armies in the autumn of 1794, however, discourage Wordsworth once more, and he more or less definitely espouses Godwin's rationalism and his purely abstract, theoretical, and individualistic radicalism. This phase is of very short duration. Godwin's influence begins to waver by the middle of 1795, and is definitely at an end before the close of 1796. This applies almost exactly to Coleridge and Southey, who, quite independently of Wordsworth, were going through the same experience at the same time. The collapse of Godwinism causes a doubt and distress which in later days Wordsworth seems inclined to associate with the Godwinian period itself. But in 1797, through the help of his sister and of Coleridge, Wordsworth is himself again, and the *Lyrical Ballads* are in preparation.

When Wordsworth was actually living through his Godwinian period, he seems not to have been particularly unhappy. It was a time of unrest, but rather interesting and exciting. The best means of observing his actual feelings during this phase of his development is not so much *The Prelude* as his letters, especially those written to his friend James Matthews. Here he figures as a fairly typical young Godwinian — "even to extravagance a necessitarian," Coleridge was to say of him — and does not seem at all anguished over that fact.

In a letter written to Matthews in June, 1794, he says:

I disapprove of monarchical and aristocratical governments, however modified. Hereditary distinctions, and privileged orders of every species, I think must necessarily counteract the progress of human improvement: hence it follows that I am not amongst the admirers of the British Constitution.

That has the true Frank Henley ring. He says that he does not want a revolution in England, but feels that one is imminent. The only way to avert it is to preach the advantages of "gradual and constant reform." But if he must choose between revolution and no reform at all, he will choose revolution.

In the same year, he proposes to Matthews that they found a reform magazine, to be called *The Philanthropist*:

Here at the very threshold I solemnly affirm that in no writings of mine will I ever admit of any sentiment which can have the least tendency to induce my readers to suppose that the doctrines which are now enforced by banishment, imprisonment, etc., etc., are other than pregnant with every species of misery. You know perhaps already that I am of that odious class of men called democrats, and of that class I shall ever continue.

That rash prophecy was not to be fulfilled.

The *Philanthropist* scheme fell through, as did an attempt to secure a post on the staff of a liberal newspaper. In 1795 he planned a volume of political satires and worked on it for a short time, but this venture also proved fruitless. Earlier, in 1793, he had written his *Letter to the Bishop of Llandaff*. This was never printed in Wordsworth's lifetime, and there is no evidence that it was ever sent to the person addressed. Richard Watson, Bishop of Llandaff, had been a strong Whig when Whiggism was fashionable, but he recanted all his liberal opinions in January, 1793, when he published a sermon on "The wisdom and goodness of God in having made both rich and poor." That theme alone would give him ample opportunity to be unctuously conservative, but he added an appendix attacking the Revolution along Burkian lines. Wordsworth's letter, written soon after the publication of Watson's sermon, is really an attack on Burke through Watson. It contains the usual pro-revolutionary ideas, expressed in Wordsworth's excellent prose. Not being able to foresee "Just for a handful of silver he left us," Wordsworth charges Watson with apostasy.

As for the poetry of this period, you probably know that in 1793 Wordsworth published two longish poems, *An Evening Walk* and *Descriptive Sketches*. These were brought out by Joseph Johnson, a close friend of Godwin and the publisher for the radical group. They have little real connection, however, with Wordsworth's feelings at this time.

An Evening Walk was written between 1787 and 1789, before the outbreak of the Revolution. It is an immature but mildly pleasing poem in heroic couplets, and, except for hints of Wordsworth's future ability to write with his eye on the subject, completely in the tradition of the early romantic descriptive poetry of the eighteenth century. The time of day encourages a little superficial melancholy, and there is a touch of sentimental humanitarianism in the description of a beggar-woman. *Descriptive Sketches*, also in heroic couplets, was written in 1791 and 1792, but it arises directly from the walking tour of the summer of 1790. Although more mature than *An Evening Walk*, it is still the familiar eighteenth century mixture of description and reflection. Wordsworth praises the simple Swiss peasants, says the proper things about William Tell, and ends with a rather perfunctory-sounding complimentary address to revolutionary France.

The most important poem actually composed during the Godwinian period is the strong, gloomy, *Guilt and Sorrow*. It was begun as early as 1791, but the first draft was not finished until 1794 and the whole poem was rewritten in the following year. Its theme is the misery caused by war, and the helplessness of the poor in an unjustly organized society.

The poetic drama, *The Borderers*, written in 1795 and 1796, occupies an ambiguous position in Wordsworth scholarship. Some students regard it as an exposition of Godwinism, and some as an exposure of that philosophy.

Probably it represents that transitional stage to which I
have already referred: Wordsworth quite evidently distrusts his old master's guidance, but he has not yet found
a decisive refutation of his syllogisms. He can only show,
in a spirit which combines despairing acquiescence with
flashes of indignant protest against the chain of necessity
which binds him, the fearful consequences of individual
reason that has lost its sense of moral responsibility to
mankind. The villain Oswald, who corrupts and deceives
Marmaduke, seems intended to be the complete Godwinian. In him Godwin's individualism, which, like that of
the nineteenth century utilitarians, is intended to serve
altruistic ends, has been perverted by the cruelty of man
into a monstrous selfishness. He behaves like Edmund in
King Lear, and has much the same cold, cynical, materialistic, intellectualistic, Machiavellian attitude toward life.
His name, incidentally, is that of one of the lesser villains
of Shakespeare's tragedy. I see no force in Garrod's
assertion that Oswald and Marmaduke fail because they
are imperfect Godwinians and hence do not trust their
intellects enough. Their villainous plans, to be sure, fail
partly for that reason; unconquerable nature creeps in to
betray them. But from the viewpoint of the author the
real tragedy, the failure of their lives as human beings,
is that they did not sufficiently listen to the demands of
feelings which, to their cold Godwinian minds, seemed
irrational.

Read *The Borderers* and form your own opinion of it.
Perhaps you will be aided in doing so if we glance for a
moment at Book III of *The Excursion*, where the character called Solitary tells his life story up to the time
when, a disillusioned recluse, he appears in the poem.

Solitary is based partly upon Joseph Fawcett, a brilliant young Unitarian minister some of whose radical sermons Wordsworth heard in his Godwinian days. He is also, however, to some extent a picture of what Wordsworth thinks he himself had been while under the influence of *Political Justice*.

Solitary relates that he was happily married to a lovely girl who bore him two children. Relinquishing a successful career as a dissenting preacher, he retired to a Devonshire cottage and there lived quietly and innocently for seven years. But the children fell ill and died; the mother succumbed to melancholia and died also. This shock inhibited Solitary's emotional faculties, but left his intellectual faculties in a state of dangerous freedom and activity. (May we conjecture that this part of the story, though its actual events bear no resemblance to Wordsworth's relations with Annette Vallon, provides the psychological equivalent of that episode in the poet's life?) Then the Revolution broke out, and Solitary's pent-up emotions were released in a burst of enthusiasm. He returned to the city, wrote revolutionary poetry, and took up his old work of preaching.

Then, in response to the events which are now familiar to us, Solitary goes through the same process of disillusionment as Wordsworth, Coleridge, and Southey. He becomes a Godwinian rationalist, and reliance upon reason makes him cold, hard, and cynical. At last, profoundly unhappy, he makes a desperate effort of idealism. Though he indulges in no pantisocratic scheme, he goes to America, hoping to find in the Indian that favorite eighteenth century abstraction, natural man:

                                    Let us, then, I said,
                   Leave this unknit Republic to the scourge
                   Of her own passions; and to regions haste,
                   Whose shades have never felt the encroaching axe,
                   Or soil endured a transfer in the mart
                   Of dire rapacity. There, Man abides,
                   Primeval Nature's child. . . .
                                            .   .   .   .
                   So, westward, toward the unviolated woods,
                   I bent my way; and roaming far and wide,
                   Failed not to greet the merry Mocking-bird;
                   And, while the melancholy Muccawis
                   (The sportive bird's companion in the grove)
                   Repeated o'er and o'er his plaintive cry,
                   I sympathised at leisure with the sound;
                   But that pure archetype of human greatness,
                   I found him not. There, in his stead, appeared
                   A creature, squalid, vengeful, and impure;
                   Remorseless, and submissive to no law
                   But superstitious fear, and abject sloth.

Thus thwarted, he returns to England and goes to the
Lake Country. But he has cut himself off from nature;
his heart is dry and cold. And so he is found reading
Candide among the mountains and waterfalls.

   Though I do not wish to press the parallel too closely,
it seems to me that when Wordsworth was finishing *The
Borderers* at Racedown in 1796, he was in a mental state
not unlike that of Solitary. He had made a physical
return to nature, but the complete spiritual return to
nature still lay a short distance in the future. He could no
longer call himself a Godwinian, but he could not confidently call himself anything else. Figuratively speaking,
The Borderers is the work of a man who reads *Candide*

in the hills of Dorset, but who can find no pleasure in doing so.

But we must return to Book XI of *The Prelude*. Wordsworth tells us that throughout the bad Godwinian days his sister Dorothy prevented him from believing that all the inspirations of his boyhood had been sentimental delusions. She represented the almost forgotten voice of nature, and kept reminding him of his destiny as a poet. She was the Beatrice through whose ministry he escaped from the *selva selvaggia* of rationalism. Wordsworth's poems contain many loving tributes to his sister. *To a Butterfly*, with its delicate suggestion of her gentleness, has already been quoted; and we shall later find in *Tintern Abbey* an important passage concerning her. But perhaps these lines from *The Sparrow's Nest* are most successful in showing her influence on her brother:

> The Blessing of my later years
> Was with me when a boy:
> She gave me eyes, she gave me ears;
> And humble cares, and delicate fears;
> A heart, the fountain of sweet tears;
> And love, and thought, and joy.

Books XII and XIII have as their subject *Imagination and Taste, How Impaired and Restored*. In Wordsworth's boyhood, love of nature had led to love of man. Cold Godwinian individualism had destroyed this feeling of brotherhood with the physical and the human world. But through his sister's help and Raisley Calvert's legacy, he throws off Godwinism and at last regains contact with nature.

Wordsworth's experiences have given him a new

thoughtfulness. He returns to nature with weighty questions in his mind. Why does not mankind as a whole
attain the virtue and happiness which are sometimes attained by individuals?

> What one is,
> Why may not millions be? What bars are thrown
> By Nature in the way of such a hope?

It is no longer possible for him to say, with Godwin, that
the millions will reach the level of the one when they
become as rational as the one. Oswald in *The Borderers*
is the embodiment of logic, and the embodiment of vil-
lainy. Wordsworth now begins to believe, with Rousseau,
that purely rational intelligence divorced from the intui-
tions of the heart is misleading and destructive. No bars
are thrown by *nature* in the way of human hopes. The
bars consist of "what man has made of man." The human
heart, as Rousseau taught, contains a seed of pure goodness, and if we live in the light of nature that seed will
bear fruit. It is in shutting ourselves off from the influences of nature that we go astray and fail to fulfill our
destiny.

Not long after his establishment at Racedown, then,
Wordsworth is turning from Godwin to Rousseau. To
say that he became a disciple of Rousseau, however, would
be misleading. Probably the resemblances between the
two writers are caused quite as much by common dependence upon prevalent eighteenth century ideas as by the
direct influence of one upon the other. And Wordsworth
differs from the great continental romanticist in several
respects, of which four deserve to be pointed out as essential. His general philosophy is based more firmly upon
eighteenth century psychology; he makes a closer con-

nection between nature as an ideal abstraction and nature
as scenery; he leans more toward transcendentalism; and
he has a stronger desire for discipline and control. Nevertheless, if, despite our earlier reservations on this point,
we allow Godwin and Rousseau to stand for two rather
markedly different tendencies in the thought of the period,
Wordsworth's movement from the former to the latter
between 1796 and 1798 is quite evident.

Wordsworth believes that the Lake Country shepherds
are on the whole the happiest and best of men. Although
by no means perfect, they are the least corrupted people
he knows, and their virtues show what nature intended
man to be. Hence he dedicates himself to the task of
studying these simple folk, and of writing about them and
the environment that has made them what they are:

> Of these, said I, shall be my song; of these,
> If future years mature me for the task,
> Will I record the praises, making verse
> Deal boldly with substantial things; in truth
> And sanctity of passion, speak of these,
> That justice may be done, obeisance paid
> Where it is due: thus haply shall I teach,
> Inspire, through unadulterated ears
> Pour rapture, tenderness, and hope, — my theme
> No other than the very heart of man,
> As found among the best of those who live,
> Not unexalted by religious faith,
> Nor uninformed by books, good books, though few,
> In Nature's presence: thence may I select
> Sorrow, that is not sorrow, but delight;
> And miserable love, that is not pain
> To hear of, for the glory that redounds
> Therefrom to human kind, and what we are.

This promise is fulfilled in the *Lyrical Ballads*, in *Michael*, and in other poems. With the exception of *Michael*, however, most of Wordsworth's really great poems deal with himself in relation to nature rather than with the dalesman in relation to nature.

Book XIV of *The Prelude, Conclusion*, looks back to survey the road that Wordsworth's spirit has traversed. The following passage provides a good summary. I give it as it stands in the 1805-1806 text because the final version contains an element of Christian orthodoxy which was not characteristic of Wordsworth at the time when his philosophy of nature took form.

> I never, in the quest of right and wrong,
> Did tamper with myself from private aims;
> Nor was in any of my hopes the dupe
> Of selfish passions; nor did wilfully
> Yield ever to mean cares and low pursuits;
> But rather did with jealousy shrink back
> From every combination that might aid
> The tendency, too potent in itself,
> Of habit to enslave the mind, I mean
> Oppress it by the laws of vulgar sense,
> And substitute a universe of death,
> The falsest of all worlds, in place of that
> Which is divine and true. To fear and love,
> To love as first and chief, for there fear ends,
> Be this ascribed; to early intercourse,
> In presence of sublime and lovely forms,
> With the adverse principles of pain and joy,
> Evil as one is rashly named by those
> Who know not what they say. By love, for here
> Do we begin and end, all grandeur comes,
> All truth and beauty, from pervading love;

That gone, we are as dust. Behold the fields
In balmy spring-time, full of rising flowers
And happy creatures; see that pair, the Lamb
And the Lamb's Mother, and their tender ways
Shall touch thee to the heart; in some green bower
Rest, and be not alone, but have thou there
The One who is thy choice of all the world;
There linger, lulled and lost, and rapt away,
Be happy to thy fill; thou call'st this love
And so it is, but there is higher love
Than this, a love that comes into the heart
With awe and a diffusive sentiment;
Thy love is human merely; this proceeds
More from the brooding Soul, and is divine.

This love more intellectual cannot be
Without Imagination, which, in truth,
Is but another name for absolute strength
And clearest insight, amplitude of mind,
And reason in her most exalted mood.
That faculty hath been the moving soul
Of our long labour: we have traced the stream
From darkness, and the very place of birth
In its blind cavern, whence is faintly heard
The sound of waters; followed it to light
And open day, accompanied its course
Among the ways of Nature, afterwards
Lost sight of it bewildered and engulphed,
Then given it greeting as it rose once more
With strength, reflecting in its solemn breast
The works of man and face of human life,
And lastly, from its progress have we drawn
The feeling of life endless, the great thought
By which we live, Infinity and God.

(De Selincourt, pp. 480-482)

Wordsworth has given us a poet's account of the growth of a poet's mind. It is now our task to analyze what he has told us. What are the component elements of the "philosophy of nature" which has become associated with his name? Whence does it come, and whither does it go? To what extent is it shared by his contemporaries? Such questions as these will engage us for the next few days.

VI

ROMANTIC ANTI-INTELLECTUALISM

The Wordsworthian philosophy of nature, unscientific as it may seem, is grounded in the psychology of the eighteenth century. Wordsworth owes much to the theory of sensationalism. This theory finds its source in Locke, who had tried to show that all mental growth results from the action of sense impressions upon the blank surface of the child's mind. Locke's necessarily complete environmentalism, highly influential throughout the eighteenth century, supports the belief of men like Godwin in perfectibility. Create the right environment for man, and there is no limit to his development. The same idea is implicit in pantisocracy. In 1749, David Hartley's *Observations on Man* had elaborated Locke's theory by tracing the "laws of association," which seek to explain how sense impressions combine into larger and more highly organized units.

The Prelude is full of sensationalism and associationism. It traces all mental development back to primary sense impressions, which have been bound together and made to grow in fullness and intensity by the laws of association. The same theory explains this famous passage from *Expostulation and Reply*:

> The eye — it cannot choose but see;
> We cannot bid the ear be still;
> Our bodies feel, where'er they be,
> Against or with our will.

> Nor less I deem that there are Powers
> Which of themselves our minds impress;
> That we can feed this mind of ours
> In a wise passiveness.

If the mind of a human being is the sum of the sensory stimuli which have reached it, one need only catch him young enough and place him amidst the goodness and majesty of nature in order to have him develop like Lucy in *Three Years She Grew*. For the sake of the experiment, let us suppose that these familiar lines are spoken, not by Nature, but by a personification of the term, "sense impressions":

> Myself will to my darling be
> Both law and impulse: and with me
> The Girl, in rock and plain,
> In earth and heaven, in glade and bower,
> Shall feel an overseeing power
> To kindle or restrain.
>
> She shall be sportive as the fawn
> That wild with glee across the lawn
> Or up the mountain springs;
> And hers shall be the breathing balm,
> And hers the silence and the calm
> Of mute insensate things.
>
> The floating clouds their state shall lend
> To her; for her the willow bend;
> Nor shall she fail to see
> Even in the motions of the Storm
> Grace that shall mould the Maiden's form
> By silent sympathy.
>
> The stars of midnight shall be dear
> To her; and she shall lean her ear

In many a secret place
Where rivulets dance their wayward round,
And beauty born of murmuring sound
Shall pass into her face.

And vital feelings of delight
Shall rear her form to stately height,
Her virgin bosom swell;
Such thoughts to Lucy I will give
While she and I together live
Here in this happy dell.

That lovely poem is no less indebted to the teachings of
Locke and Hartley than the lines from *Tintern Abbey*:

These beauteous forms,
Through a long absence, have not been to me
As is a landscape to a blind man's eye:
But oft, in lonely rooms, and 'mid the din
Of towns and cities, I have owed to them
In hours of weariness, sensations sweet,
Felt in the blood, and felt along the heart;
And passing even into my purer mind,
With tranquil restoration.

In interpreting such passages it is important to remember
that Wordsworth means what he is saying. Here he uses
the word "sensations" as a scientific term, for he thinks
it a literal fact that these sensations pass from the blood
to the feelings, and from the feelings to the mind.

It was Professor Arthur Beatty, in *William Wordsworth: His Doctrine and Art in Their Historical Relations*, who first showed the full extent of Wordsworth's
debt to eighteenth century psychology. But like so many
students of sources and influences, Professor Beatty over-
emphasizes the similarities between the poet and his

scientific sources, and underestimates the differences, which are after all more important than the similarities. Over this scientific skeleton Wordsworth throws a garment of strong religious feeling. In his philosophy, the sense impressions which come to the child are not cold, mechanical stimuli. They are almost spirits; certainly they are emanations of the one great Spirit that "rolls through all things."

Pure eighteenth century sensationalism is entirely passive. Closely associated with the theory of necessity, it implies that we are the helpless totals of our experience. To Wordsworth, on the other hand, the influence of nature depends upon us as well as upon nature. True, if our minds are attuned to nature, "wise passiveness" is often the most desirable attitude; but unless we go to her prepared to find what she has to give us, we shall not find it. Remember the effect of American scenery upon the wild young man in *Ruth*:

> Whatever in those climes he found
> Irregular in sight or sound
> Did to his mind impart
> A kindred impulse, seemed allied
> To his own powers, and justified
> The workings of his heart.

There is love for us in nature, but unless we have love for her in us the process is not complete. Satisfying contact with God in nature demands an exercise of the creative or poetic imagination: "From thyself it comes. . . . Thou must give." Thus in *Tintern Abbey* Wordsworth says:

> Therefore am I still
> A lover of the meadows and the woods,

> And mountains; and of all that we behold
> From this green earth; of all the mighty world
> Of eye, and ear, — *both what they half create,*
> *And what perceive.*

Right seeing, then, is a creative as well as a passively receptive process, recalling Blake's advice that we should see through, not with, the eye. This of course is the philosophical attitude known as transcendentalism. It gives a wholly new color to the determined and mechanistic sensationalism which Wordsworth inherited from the eighteenth century. Whether Wordsworth was ever able to work out a really satisfactory adjustment between his transcendentalism and his desire to believe in the controlling power of external nature is a question which must be discussed later.

Underlying all the specific differences between this eighteenth century heritage and the use which Wordsworth made of it is the fact that Wordsworth's view of nature is essentially non-rationalistic. We may recall that the most popular, though by no means the only conception of nature in the age of Pope, included a rationalistic view of the universe as a neat and comprehensible mechanism based upon broad, general principles like those of geometry. It included a pseudoclassic conception of literature giving allegiance to rules derived from Aristotle and his interpreters. It included the idea that truth and common sense are more or less identical, and excluded mysticism and genuine religious fervor. Being rationalistic, it generally implied a great deal of reliance upon logic and analytical intellect, and very little reliance upon instinct, emotion, and intuition.

It should have become apparent that the romantic conception of nature is in most respects the reverse of the rationalistic and pseudoclassic conception of nature. This reversal, however, occurred very slowly and irregularly, and the roots of the change run far back into the eighteenth century. Nor must we exaggerate the duration and force of the dominance of rationalism and pseudoclassicism. The normally romantic quality of English thought and hence of English literature was for a time interfered with, but it was never stamped out. It is wholesome to remember that, to the French critics of his own day, Pope was an extremely romantic person. Some of his early poems, such as *Eloisa to Abelard*, have plenty of romantic feeling. His close friend Thomas Parnell is always mentioned in discussions of early romanticism because of his *Night-Piece on Death*. Towards James Thomson, fountainhead of romantic nature poetry, the great Augustan was well disposed, and he even added a few touches to *The Seasons*. Facts like these should preserve us from thinking in water-tight compartments. As I stated at the outset of this course, the rationalistic and pseudoclassical conception of nature never by any means obliterated a more primitivistic, Arcadian, sentimental, religious, and romantic conception of nature, bearing implications of innocence, freedom, spontaneity, and the validity of untutored feeling as a guide to truth. From the very beginning of the eighteenth century, moreover, this conception of nature was related in a vague way to the blessings of rustic life and the beauties of scenery. All one can say, then, is that at the close of the seventeenth and the opening of the eighteenth century England came nearer than at any other time to being dominated by standards which were alien to her native ways of thinking and writing.

But these standards were never all-powerful, and they had hardly taken definite form when they began to slough down into the transitional mid-eighteenth century flux from which arose what we call the romantic movement.

We have already seen that the political and social ferment of the revolutionary period cannot as a whole be classified as romantic. It is often based upon a rationalism which is repugnant to the romantic spirit, and is often attacked by conservatives who use romantic arguments. But when the temper of reform is tinged with a utopianism which draws encouragement from illusions about the state of nature, or when it stresses the natural goodness of common humanity, the influence of the romantic conception of nature is manifest.

We are now turning to aspects of romantic naturalism which are less confusingly mingled with non-romantic features. It is difficult to decide which element to take up next. When we try to get one olive out of the bottle, all the other olives come tumbling out with it. Let us begin, however, with the romantic opposition to rationalism, logic, analytical intellect, and scientific method.

One cannot say that the romanticist is an enemy of reason unless one is a very hot antiromanticist and has a very restricted conception of reason. The great romanticists were men of the highest intelligence; they loved, praised, and practised reason of a special kind which has been extremely influential ever since. At its worst, eighteenth century reason implies finespun, impractical, deductive syllogizing. At its next worst, it implies unillumined common sense. At its best, it implies a genuinely scientific method of thought, sceptical in spirit, and concerned more with analysis than with synthesis. But on the whole eighteenth century reason, at least in intention, is cool, exact, and logical. That is the ideal standard or norm to which it aspires. Romantic reason, on the other hand, is warm, fervent, shot through with emotion. It emphasizes the value of instinct, intuition, and imagination in thinking. It aspires to free man from enslavement to mere observation and inference, and gives him a kind of creative dominance over his own senses and the messages which they bring him.

Now the romanticists, in order to support their conception of reason and in order to win freedom to apply it, kept up a persistent sniping at the cool, logical, analytical, eighteenth century kind of reason — "that false secondary power by which we multiply distinctions," as Wordsworth called it. In Wordsworth, indeed, this anti-intellectualism is very strong, and it is closely associated with his philosophy of nature. In *The Poet's Epitaph* (1799), for example, he addresses various small-souled persons who are imagined as approaching his grave:

> Physician art thou? — one, all eyes,
> Philosopher! — a fingering slave,
> One that would peep and botanize
> Upon his mother's grave?
>
> . . . .
>
> A moralist perchance appears;
> Led, Heaven knows how! to this poor sod:
> And he has neither eyes nor ears;
> Himself his world, and his own God;
>
> One to whose smooth-rubbed soul can cling
> Nor form, nor feeling, great or small;
> A reasoning, self-sufficing thing,
> An intellectual All-in-all!

Remembering that Wordsworth had had personal experience of this frigid intellectualism, we may hazard the
guess that, with the zeal of a convert, he is kicking his
old master, William Godwin.

Everyone knows the lines in *The Tables Turned*:

> One impulse from a vernal wood
> May teach you more of man,
> Of moral evil and of good,
> Than all the sages can.
>
> Sweet is the lore which Nature brings;
> Our meddling intellect
> Misshapes the beauteous forms of things: —
> We murder to dissect.

That suspicion of analysis, of dissection, is typical of the
tendency under discussion. Logic is chiefly analytic. Romantic thought is chiefly synthetic. It wants large inspiring wholes, and it is very impatient of any factual obstacle
that may lie in the way of obtaining them. Thus in *The
Excursion* the Wanderer, in exhorting Solitary, tells him
to

> Enquire of ancient Wisdom; go, demand
> Of mighty Nature, if 'twas ever meant
> That we should pry far off yet be unraised;
> That we should pore, and dwindle as we pore,
> Viewing all objects unremittingly
> In disconnection dead and spiritless;
> And still dividing and dividing still,
> Break down all grandeur.
>
> (IV, 957 ff.)

The same feeling passes into several poems of Wordsworth's later years, when he finds himself living in

> a chilled age, most pitiably shut out
> From that which *is* and actuates, by forms,
> Abstractions, and by lifeless fact to fact
> Minutely linked with diligence uninspired,
> Unrectified, unguided, unsustained
> By godlike insight.
>
> (*Musings Near Aquapendente*, 1837)

The anti-intellectualism which we have observed in Wordsworth runs far back into the eighteenth century. One thinks immediately of Rousseau, for it was part of his attack upon the Enlightenment. In his *Discourse on the Moral Effect of the Sciences and Arts*, he regards the evils of the age as the result of our deserting "that happy state of ignorance in which the wisdom of providence has placed us":

Let men learn for once that nature would have preserved them from science, as a mother snatches a dangerous weapon from the hands of her child. Let them know that all the secrets she hides are so many evils from which she protects them, and that the very difficulty they find in acquiring knowledge is not the least of her bounty towards them. Men are perverse; but they would have been far worse, if they had had the misfortune to be born learned. . . . Virtue! sublime science of simple minds, are such industry and preparation needed if we are to know you? Are not your principles graven on every heart? Need we do more, to learn your laws, than examine ourselves, and listen to the voice of conscience, when the passions are silent?

Here is that idea of reason as the highest common denominator of human hearts which, as we have seen, is itself the incongruous offspring of rationalism.

Such disciples of Rousseau as Bernardin de Saint-Pierre carry on this cult of the blessings of ignorance after Rousseau himself has forsaken or greatly modified

his paradoxes. In a prose tale, *Le Café du Surate*, Saint-
Pierre employs two characters to show the evil consequences of thinking. One is a Persian savant "who had
written all his life on theology, and who no longer believed
in God." The other is a Confucian who had tried to
understand the cause of the sun's radiance, and who of
course went blind and thereupon denied the existence of
the sun. In *Paul and Virginia*, the hero embraces and
kisses a tree which Virginia had planted, exclaiming, "Oh,
she who planted this tree made the inhabitants of this
forest a more useful and lovely present than if she had
given them a library!" Here is "one impulse from a
vernal wood," not to speak of

> Poems are made by fools like me,
> But only God can make a tree.

It is a very old story.

But although Rousseau had a considerable influence
upon Wordsworth and other English romanticists in this
matter, anti-intellectualism is too generally pervasive in
English literature from about the middle of the eighteenth
century to justify us in ascribing the whole tradition to
Rousseau. That writer himself probably owed much of
his anti-intellectualism to English sources.

Analytical intellect is severely handled by several of the
eighteenth century writers whom we associate with the
early stirrings of the romantic movement. The prevalent
shrinking away from the vices of the town toward rural
innocence has as a corollary the notion that some causal
relation exists between virtue and ignorance on the one
hand, and between vice and learning on the other. Heart
and head are persistently opposed. In *Night Thoughts*,
for example, Edward Young addresses a scholarly sceptic:

> Would you be still more learned than the learn'd?
> Learn well to know how much need not be known,
> And what that knowledge, which impairs your sense.
> Our needful knowledge, like our needful food,
> Unhedg'd, lies open in life's common field:
> And bids all welcome to the vital feast.
> You scorn what lies before you in the page
> Of nature, and experience, moral truth;
> Of indispensible, eternal truth;
> Fruit on which mortals, feeding, turn to gods:
> And dive in science for distinguisht names,
> Dishonest fomentation of your pride;
> Sinking in virtue as you rise in fame.
> Your learning, like the lunar beam, affords
> Light, but not heat; it leaves you undevout,
> Frozen at heart, while speculation shines.

A great deal more heat, even at the expense of light, is Young's ideal.

William Collins, in his ode, *The Manners*, displays ideas on education such as Rousseau would have approved. He speaks of book-science as the bride of doubt, and commends instead a direct and loving contemplation of nature:

> O thou who lov'st that ampler range
> Where life's wide prospects round thee change,
> And with her mingling sons allied,
> Throw'st the prattling page aside,
> To me, in converse sweet, impart
> To read in man the native heart;
> To learn, where science sure is found,
> From nature as she lives around.

A strong anti-intellectualism helps to buttress the evangelical piety of William Cowper. The following passage

from Book III of *The Task* is an irritating example of
that uneasy jocularity which a certain type of obscurantist
regards as the most crushing attitude to adopt toward
science:

> Some drill and bore
> The solid earth, and from the strata there
> Extract a register, by which we learn
> That he who made it, and revealed its date
> To Moses, was mistaken in its age.
> Some, more acute, and more industrious still,
> Contrive creation; travel nature up
> To the sharp peak of her sublimest height,
> And tell us whence the stars; why some are fix'd,
> And planetary some; what gave them first
> Rotation, from what fountain flowed their light.
> Great contest follows, and much learned dust
> Involves the combatants; each claiming truth,
> And truth disclaiming both. And thus they spend
> The little wick of life's poor shallow lamp,
> In playing tricks with nature, giving laws
> To distant worlds, and trifling in their own.

This is almost unworthy of a modern fundamentalist.

It is hardly necessary to say that Blake's whole philosophy is based upon the most intense hostility to the
analytical spirit. For him, logic is the very soul of evil, the
mocking Spectre that rose over Albion,

Saying: "I am God, O Sons of Men! I am your Rational Power!
Am I not Bacon and Newton and Locke, who teach Humility to
      Man,
Who teach Doubt and Experiment? and my two wings, Voltaire,
      Rousseau?
Where is that Friend of Sinners, that Rebel against my Laws,

Who teaches Belief to the Nations and an unknown Eternal Life?
Come hither into the desert and turn these stones to bread!
Vain, foolish Man! wilt thou believe without Experiment,
And build a World of Phantasy upon my great Abyss,
A World of Shapes in craving lust and devouring appetite?

(Jerusalem, f. 54, 15-24)

His mission in life is to banish this Spectre from the human mind:

The Negation is the Spectre, the Reasoning Power in Man:
This is a false Body, an Incrustation over my Immortal
Spirit, a Selfhood which must be put off and annihilated alway.
To cleanse the Face of my Spirit by self-examination,
To bathe in the waters of Life, to wash off the Not Human,
I come in Self-annihilation and the grandeur of Inspiration;
To cast off Rational Demonstration by Faith in the Saviour,
To cast off the rotten rags of Memory by Inspiration,
To cast off Bacon, Locke, and Newton from Albion's covering,
To take off his filthy garments and clothe him with Imagination.

(Milton, ff. 42 and 43)

Blake is so extreme in all his ideas that it is perhaps unfair to call him to the witness-stand. But exaggeration, if we make due allowance for its distorting effect, at least has the virtue of making us see the thing exaggerated. Sometimes one feels that Blake *says* what other romanticists *mean* to say.

In many of Wordsworth's contemporaries appears the same anti-intellectualism — less as a result of Wordsworth's influence than as a common heritage from the eighteenth century. It helps to support the transcendentalism of Coleridge. His letter of October 9, 1797, to Thomas Poole is full of the romantic longing for synthesis:

From my early reading of fairy tales and genii, etc., etc., my mind has been habituated *to the Vast*, and I never regarded *my senses* as in any way the criteria of my belief. I regulated all my creeds by my conceptions, not by my *sight*, even at that age. Should children be permitted to read romances, and relations of giants and magicians and genii? I know all that has been said against it; but I have formed my faith in the affirmative. I know no other way of giving the mind a love of the Great and the Whole. Those who have been led to the same truths step by step, through the constant testimony of their senses, seem to me to want a sense which I possess. They contemplate nothing but *parts*, and all parts are necessarily little. And the universe to them is but a mass of *little things*. It is true, that the mind *may* become credulous and prone to superstition by the former method; but are not the ex-perimentalists credulous even to madness in believing any absurdity, rather than the grandest truths, if they have not the testimony of their own senses in their favor? I have known some who have been *rationally* educated, as it is styled. They were marked by a microscopic acuteness, but when they looked at great things, all became a blank and they saw nothing, and denied (very illogi-cally) that anything could be seen, and uniformly put the negation of a power for the possession of a power, and called the want of imagination, judgment, and the never being moved to rapture, philosophy.

Shelley seems to feel that rationalism is among the traditions which oppress man and keep him from asserting the love in his heart. It is associated with age, impotence, and hate; while his own emotional, Platonic, and tran-scendental kind of reason is associated with youth, love, and hope. Thus in *The Revolt of Islam* he says of the revolutionary gospel preached by Cythna:

> New lore was this — old age, with its gray hair,
> And wrinkled legends of unworthy things,

And icy sneers, is nought: it cannot dare
  To burst the chain which life for ever flings
  On the entangled soul's aspiring wings,
So it is cold and cruel, and is made
  The careless slave of that dark power which brings
Evil, like blight, on man, who, still betrayed,
Laughs o'er the grave in which his living hopes are laid.

And if the spirit of analysis is the enemy of Shelley's gospel of love, it is equally the enemy of Keats's gospel of beauty. We may recall his comment upon Apollonius' betrayal of Lamia:

Do not all charms fly
At the mere touch of cold philosophy?
There was an awful rainbow once in heaven:
We know her woof, her texture; she is given
In the dull catalogue of common things.
Philosophy will clip an Angel's wings,
Conquer all mysteries by rule and line,
Empty the haunted air, and gnomed mine —
Unweave a rainbow, as it erstwhile made
The tender-personed Lamia melt into a shade.

Opposition to peeping and botanizing is very prevalent among minor romantic writers. Thus Charles Lloyd sings that in the humble cottage

Peace affords a purer joy
  Than Luxury could e'er dispense;
There courtly vices ne'er annoy
  The ignorance of innocence.

There, if the systematic school
  No sophist laws for me enact
To chain the free-born mind to rule —
  The native feelings teach to act.
              (*Address to a Cottage*)

The association of antirationalism with the back-to-nature theme is characteristic. If Lloyd celebrates "the ignorance of innocence," John Clare celebrates *The Happiness of Ignorance*:

> Ere I had known the world, and understood
> How many follies Wisdom names its own,
> Distinguishing things evil from things good,
> The dread of sin and death — ere I had known
> Knowledge the root of evil — had I been
> Left in some lone place where the world is wild,
> And trace of troubling man was never seen,
> Brought up by Nature as her favourite child,
> As born for nought but joy where all rejoice,
> Emparadised in ignorance of sin,
> Where Nature tries with never-chiding voice,
> Like tender nurse, nought but our smiles to win —
> The future, dreamless, beautiful would be;
> The present, foretaste of eternity.

There is plainly a difference between the shrinking retreatism of Lloyd or Clare and the boldly mystical affirmations of Blake. But the difference is such as might be expected to exist between two stages of a single process. First, withdrawing from "knowledge of good and evil," one finds the merely negative "happiness of ignorance." But this happiness leads in turn to a superrational kind of knowledge which the earlier retreat has made possible — a knowledge which is not the root of evil, but the root of beneficent illusion. This is perhaps the psychological relation between two attitudes which are found side by side in romantic literature. I do not mean that the process occurs systematically in the history of the romantic movement. Weaklings like Lloyd and Clare hardly rise above the level of retreat; Blake rises from that level very rapidly, and seldom if ever relapses to it. Most romantic writers stand somewhere between these extremes, mingling in their work both negative and positive anti-intellectualism.

It may be said that some of the examples which have been presented are wholesome protests against abstract, bookish theorizing in favor of direct observation of nature or against pedantic fact-grubbing in favor of constructive thought, and that they are therefore not hostile to the spirit of genuine science. Of course I am not attempting to impose an identity of attitude upon all the authors quoted. They differed greatly in their likes and dislikes: Collins' *The Manners* is not Blake's *Jerusalem.* I wish merely to suggest that these protests, and many others that might be cited, arise from a basically anti-intellectualistic attitude.

Even this statement needs to be qualified. We must try to understand how it is that such romanticists as Wordsworth, Coleridge, and Shelley have a strong and intelligent interest in science but are nevertheless anti-scientific. Though eighteenth century thought as a whole may be called rationalistic in the broader sense of that term, there is a cleavage between abstract, theoretical, rationalism and the empirical or scientific rationalism which gradually gained strength during the century. The latter is at bottom more hostile to romanticism than the former, but there is a circumstance which sometimes obscures that fact. Orthodox rationalism of the older type tended to neglect the concrete. Scientific empiricism, on the contrary, paid close attention to the concrete, and so of course did romanticism. Consequently, during the

eighteenth and early nineteenth century there was a most
complex and delicate interplay between the spirit of scientific investigation and the spirit of romanticism. Their
very different motives for cultivating the real did not
always prevent them from putting out feelers toward
each other. Throughout its course, romanticism has indulged in a series of unhappy love affairs with science.
Its devotion to the real impels the attempt to unite; its
desire to find within the real something "more" than real
causes the subsequent disillusionment and divorce. Hence
the decay of abstract geometic rationalism, so far as its
indifference to the concrete is concerned, is attended by an
uneasy and intermittent *rapprochement* between empiricism and romanticism. Both at least say, "Look at nature
with your own eyes," and to say this is to have much in
common. But their ways of looking, and the results which
they hope to derive from looking, are essentially so different that they soon begin to quarrel. The extent of the
rapprochement and the bitterness of the quarrel depend
upon the temperament of the individual writer. Yet
though Wordsworth bases his philosophy of nature upon
Locke's psychology, while Blake regards Locke as first
cousin to the devil, they are both in the long run antago-
nistic to the scientific view of life.

The remarks which I have just made, and the evidence
which I presented earlier in this lecture, may receive
additional support as we pass on to related topics. Meanwhile, please refrain from setting down in your notebooks
that the romanticists were not thinkers. They were often
very acute and powerful thinkers, and with all their suspicion of learning they were often more learned than
many a devoted logic chopper. They had a grievance,

however, against a kind of reason which was hostile to
their conception of nature and which threatened to rob
them of the illusion they desired. Against that reason they
reasoned with all their might. They doggedly resisted the
invasion by analytical thought of realms which they
desired to preserve for the free play of the imagination.
Not content with defensive tactics, they sometimes con-
ducted bold raids into the realms of logic and science,
seeking to recapture territory which had been lost during
the seventeenth and eighteenth centuries. We shall observe
the results of their campaign when we consider the
transcendental aspect of romanticism. At present it is
enough to know that romantic naturalism usually implies
a hostile attitude toward analytic reason.

VII

EXTERNAL NATURE

The love of external nature — birds, flowers, trees, streams, mountains, scenery in general — is obviously an important element in romantic naturalism. To Wordsworth and many of his contemporaries all of the visible universe which remained untouched, or only slightly touched, by the hand of man, symbolized the fundamental beauty and goodness of nature. For them, indeed, "nature" and "scenery" were almost synonymous, as they often are for us. This trend of romanticism runs much further back into the eighteenth century than time will permit us to follow. The story is told in a number of works, notably in Myra Reynolds' *The Treatment of Nature in English Poetry between Pope and Wordsworth.*

The familiar statement that the Augustan age cared nothing for external nature is true only in a very general and comparative sense. It certainly was an urban age, and not inclined to go into ecstasies about sparrows — or, for that matter, about anything else. But it would be hard to name a time when actual hatred of the country was universal. Some expressions of dislike for rural scenes which students have drawn from the literature of this period are merely reactions against the pastoral fad. In *Windsor Forest,* Pope himself is trying to write nature poetry. He is handicapped by the glossy, artificial diction of his time, and by the pseudoclassic notion that he should paint a generalized scenery piece instead of looking directly at real objects with his own eyes. But parts of the poem — the description of the pheasant, for example — are highly successful even when measured by the standards which we have inherited from Wordsworth. Lady Winchilsea, Ambrose Philips, Parnell, Thomson, Dyer, Somerville, Thomas and Joseph Warton, Shenstone, Goldsmith, Collins, Gray, and other eighteenth century poets, show a gradual movement of imagination from the park to the mountain, an increasingly genuine interest in natural scenes, an increasing tendency to relate them to subjective emotion, and an increasing ability to represent nature in images derived from the qualities of the object itself rather than from some abstract standard of verbal propriety. In the 1780's the movement culminates in Cowper, Blake, and Burns. Wordsworth is the direct heir of all this eighteenth century nature poetry. He knows it thoroughly, and is strongly influenced by it.

As for Wordsworth's contemporaries, to name those who loved external nature would merely be to call the roll of the romanticists. Think of Hazlitt's *On Going a Journey* (for the tendency is hardly less marked in prose than in poetry), Byron's *Childe Harold*, Shelley's *Skylark*, Keats's *Nightingale*. The only notable dissenter is Charles Lamb, who had a peculiar city-of-London romanticism, made up of old streets, old houses, old books, and old memories. In answer to Wordsworth's invitation to Cumberland he writes:

Separate from the pleasure of your company, I don't much care if I never see a mountain in my life. I have passed all my days in London, until I have formed as many and intense local attachments, as any of you mountaineers can have done with dead nature.

When at last he does visit the Lakes, he confesses, "I have satisfied myself that there is such a thing as that which tourists call *romantic*, which I very much suspected before." Yet "after all, Fleet Street and the Strand are better places to live in for good than amidst Skiddaw." But Lamb, as I have said, is an exception.

The romantic revival of enthusiasm for external nature had very important results. It not only widened and freshened the stock of literary themes, but contributed to the renascence of lyric poetry. That renascence also originated in the movement toward a simplicity of which folk song and ballad were attractive models. Since these kinds of poetry were rich in natural imagery, there was a union at this point between literary primitivism and the love of external nature. But I am speaking not so much of the pure song-poem as of those more elaborate and serious lyrics in which the singing element, apart from the music of the verse, becomes what Brunetière calls the *chant intérieur*.

This sort of poetry demands an interweaving of extreme objectivity with extreme subjectivity: that is, it demands either the expression or suggestion of vivid images drawn from the direct perception of external objects, and it demands either the expression or suggestion of a bond between those objects and the deepest emotions of the poet as a unique individual. Such a lyric, then, uses external nature to clarify and give body to inward feeling, and uses inward feeling to give significance to external things.

Now let us turn to the average poet of the Augustan age, remembering that no such person ever existed. Although he was by no means incapable of enjoying natural things and scenes, his enjoyment seldom stirred him deeply. He would grant that both he and the nightingale were "parts of one tremendous whole"; but since he was infinitely further advanced in the neatly graduated scale of being, the idea of any close spiritual communion between himself and the bird would have seemed nonsensical.

The nightingale, if he dealt with it in a poem, must be regarded as an example of a general type. The details of physical surroundings, habit, shape, color, sound, which distinguished this particular nightingale from other nightingales were no business of his. He should even beware of distinguishing the type-nightingale *too* sharply from other species of bird. It might be safer to speak merely of "the feathered songster of the grove." Since he was a classicist, his material was not the incommensurable factor, but the highest common denominator. If a discreet particularization seemed desirable, there were certain proper things to say about nightingales. The mythological background should at least be hinted at, and the bird should be called Philomela. This generalized bird should sing in a generalized grove, and its mood should be one of tenderly mournful enjoyment of unrequited love. Its passion, however, must be held within the bounds of good sense. The subject demanded a quiet elegance of manner, and the verse should be mellifluously smooth. It would be best to keep "Waller's sweetness" in mind; "Denham's strength" would be out of place. There were also certain things which should *not* be said on such a subject. Any attempt at sublimity would be incongruous, but at the other extreme, "low" words must be avoided. Our contemporary, T. S. Eliot, in his *Sweeney Among the Night-*

ingales, mentions the "liquid droppings" which stained the shroud of Agamemnon. Such a phrase in a serious poem would make an Augustan apoplectic; associated with so lofty a personage as Agamemnon, it would kill the critic. With his dying breath he would remark that the entire basis of the poem is defective, for no person named Sweeney should ever be found among nightingales.

Lady Mary Wortley Montagu knew how to handle these matters. In one of her letters written to Pope from Constantinople she quotes a Turkish love song beginning, in literal translation, "The nightingale now wanders in the vines. Her passion is to seek roses." This she improves into:

> Now Philomel renews the tender strain,
> Indulging all the night her pleasing pain.

Even supposing that the song of the nightingale did arouse the deeper feelings of our average Augustan poet, those feelings would probably not appear in his poem. The fine shades of emotion which differentiated his response from all other responses to a similar situation were no more fitting as poetic material than the objective bird's peculiarities — those "streaks of the tulip" which, as Johnson's Imlac says, are not the proper concern of the poet. The desideratum was a normal intellectual response given a neat little turn of ingenuity and colored by a moderate amount of such emotion as any man of sense might feel — "what oft was thought, but ne'er so well expressed." Hence our poet would probably not write an entire poem about a nightingale: there would not be sufficient material. The bird would be worth a couplet or two — perhaps a decorative simile — in some

longer sequence of versified ideas. If by chance the poet
should decide to use the bird as the basis of an entire
poem, the resultant three or four octosyllabic quatrains
might be entitled *To Arabella, on Hearing a Nightingale*; and the theme would be that while Arabella sings
much better than Philomela, she is unfortunately less susceptible to the tender passion. The poet might go on to
say that the nightingale's inferiority in song was owing
to the sincerity of his love, and that this was also true of
Arabella's most obedient humble servant. Or the twist
might be satirical: would that certain poets — *we* know
who — resembled the nightingale in| the modest self-
effacement of its devotion to song! Or the bird might
provide the text of a sensible little discourse on any idea
that it might suggest. But in all these cases the bird
would be merely the occasion for saying sentimental or
witty or improving things. The stimulus would glance off
the surface of the poet's heart and bury itself in a mass of
stock phrases, stock thoughts, and stock emotions.

The standards which governed the poetry of the Augustan age, then, gave small scope for the writing of
serious lyric poetry, since they were hostile to concreteness in treatment of the subject, hostile to subjectivity in
treatment of personal emotion, and hostile to the needful
interweaving of objective and subjective. In his *Essay
Supplementary to the Preface to the Lyrical Ballads*,
Wordsworth declares:

It is remarkable that, excepting the *Nocturnal Reverie* of Lady
Winchilsea, and a passage or two in the *Windsor Forest* of Pope,
the poetry of the period intervening between the publication of
the *Paradise Lost* [1667] and the *Seasons* [1726-1730] does not
contain a single new image of external nature; and hardly pre-

sents a familiar one from which it can be inferred that the eye of
the poet had been steadily fixed upon his object, much less that his
feelings had urged him to work upon it in the spirit of genuine
imagination.

This, though an exaggeration, is an exaggeration of
the truth. But even within the period mentioned by Wordsworth the exceptions are more numerous than he
indicates, and they increase geometrically as the eighteenth century goes on. Wordsworth feels that falsely
"poetic" diction and lack of steady observation of nature
go hand in hand. Some of the worst eighteenth century
diction, however, occurs when poets are beginning to look
at nature with their own eyes but have not yet ceased to
draw their phrases from the stock of professional lingo
— as when Thomson says,

> But let not on your hook the tortured worm,
> Convulsive, twist in agonizing folds.

But this is a disease of transition. On the whole we cannot doubt that if the poet opens his senses to life his diction will be true to his impressions.

Although lack of time prevents us from tracing these
developments, we can observe their final outcome by reading romantic nature poetry. Obviously a great change
has taken place. Love of external nature has sharpened
the poet's vision, deepened his capacity to feel, and impelled him to sing as few have sung since the seventeenth
century. Poetry once more is "simple, sensuous, and passionate." There is a negative side to all this, but so much
in my treatment of romanticism is negative that here I
am eager to emphasize the very real benefits which this
trend of romanticism has conferred upon poetry. And
through poetry it has benefitted human life, for it has

added to man's happiness by relating his emotions to the most beautiful and enduring elements in his environment.

As students of literature, we should learn to recognize each poet's special manner of dealing with nature. We should know Byron's eloquent, effective, but somewhat rhetorical way of painting a big picture in broad strokes. We should know Shelley's light, bright, ethereal atmosphere, his unearthly interpretation of earth, his fondness for projecting himself into nature and sharing the life of the west wind, the skylark, and the cloud. And we should know the luxurious richness of Keats, a richness that in his mature work never blurs the fresh vividness of his imagery.

Keats is almost purely esthetic in his feeling for external nature. To him she is a great repository of those sights and sounds and smells which constitute the truth that is beauty. Her aid to man's spirit is great, but it is exerted through nobly sensuous delight. The same can hardly be said of the Lakists. Their sensuous love of nature, strong as it is, is heavily mingled with ethical and instrumental considerations. As they gaze upon the beauties of nature, esthetic joy becomes moral and spiritual medicine. This fact need not be illustrated from Wordsworth, for it is implicit and explicit throughout his work. The same feeling is very strong in Coleridge. In a letter of April, 1798, he declares:

I love fields and woods and mountains with an almost visionary fondness. And because I have found benevolence and quietness growing within me as that fondness increased, therefore I should wish to be the means of implanting it in others.

Several of Coleridge's poems between 1797 and 1799 attempt to carry out this wish. Thus the passage from

Osorio printed in *Lyrical Ballads* as *The Dungeon* reads:

> With other ministrations thou, O Nature!
> Healest thy wandering and distempered child;
> Thou pourest on him thy soft influences,
> Thy sunny hues, fair forms, and breathing sweets,
> Thy melodies of woods, and winds, and waters,
> Till he relent, and can no more endure
> To be a jarring and a dissonant thing,
> Amid this general dance and minstrelsy;
> But, bursting into tears, wins back his way,
> His angry spirit healed and harmonized
> By the benignant touch of love and beauty.

And the message of *This Lime-Tree Bower My Prison* is that

> Henceforth I shall know
> That Nature ne'er deserts the wise and pure;
> No plot so narrow, be but Nature there,
> No waste so vacant, but may well employ
> Each faculty of sense, and keep the heart
> Awake to Love and Beauty!

Coleridge's work shows that nature, which begins by inspiring his love of liberty, later comes to be a stimulus to patriotism and thus indirectly helps to induce his later conservatism. In *Fears in Solitude* (1798), for example, we find:

> But, O dear Britain! O my Mother Isle!
> How shouldst thou prove aught else but dear and holy
> To me, who from thy lakes and mountain-hills,
> Thy clouds, thy quiet dales, thy rocks and seas,
> Have drunk in all my intellectual life,
> All sweet sensations, all ennobling thoughts,
> All adorations of the God in nature,

There lives nor form nor feeling in my soul
Unborrowed from my country!

A similarly patriotic attitude toward English scenes was aroused in Wordsworth by his trip to Germany. But the results of this transition from love of nature to love of *English* nature are not fully apparent in the period of most devout nature worship, just before the turn of the century. Nature is then primarily a healing and inspiring force rather than an incitement to one-hundred-per-cent patriotism.

The minor poets who cluster about Wordsworth and Coleridge share the feeling of their masters. Charles Lloyd writes:

Methinks he acts the purposes of life
And fills the measures of his destiny
With best approved wisdom, who retires
To some majestic solitude; his mind
Raised by those visions of eternal love,
The rock, the vale, the forest, and the lake,
The sky, the sea, and everlasting hills.

Passages of the same tenor in other writers are almost innumerable.

The later group of romantic poets, of which Byron, Shelley, and Keats are the chief members, depart rather far from the Wordsworthian philosophy of nature, and are much less inclined to discover sermons in stones. Each makes his own adjustment between his love of nature and his personal view of life. At Keats we have already glanced. Shelley imposes on external nature his vision of an ideal world of which the essence is the love of freedom and the freedom of love. The west wind is a great radical propagandist, scattering, one might say, not merely leaves but leaflets "to quicken a new birth."

And all through nature as seen by Shelley runs the spirit of love, a highly idealized sexuality, often Platonic in thought and expression, but with much too large a fleshly element to be labeled as Platonic without qualification. His own rapidly shifting loves for this, that, and the other woman are a reflection of the way in which his "nature" behaves. It is *Love's Philosophy* that

> The fountains mingle with the river
>   And the rivers with the Ocean,
> The winds of Heaven mix for ever
>   With a sweet emotion;
> Nothing in the world is single;
>   All things by a law divine
> In one spirit meet and mingle.
>   Why not I with thine?

This is the spirit which in springtime animates the garden of *The Sensitive Plant*:

> And the Spring arose on the garden fair,
> Like the Spirit of Love felt everywhere;
> And each flower and herb on Earth's dark breast
> Rose from the dreams of its wintry rest.
>
> .   .   .   .
>
> Then the pied wind-flowers and the tulip tall,
> And narcissi, the fairest among them all,
> Who gaze on their eyes in the stream's recess,
> Till they die of their own dear loveliness;
>
> And the Naiad-like lily of the vale,
> Whom youth makes so fair and passion so pale
> That the light of its tremulous bells is seen
> Through their pavilions of tender green;

And the rose like a nymph to the bath addressed,
Which unveiled the depth of her glowing breast,
Till, fold after fold, to the fainting air
The soul of her beauty and love lay bare:

    . . . .

For each one was interpenetrated
With the light and the odour its neighbour shed,
Like young lovers whom youth and love make dear
Wrapped and filled by their mutual atmosphere.

A comparison between this poem and Erasmus Darwin's *Loves of the Plants* will help you to understand what the early nineteenth century did to the eighteenth.

One more example of this, to me, extremely interesting point. In Act IV of *Prometheus Unbound*, when Prometheus' abstract love of man and his specific love of Asia combine to cause the overthrow of Jupiter, the hate that has ruled the world, then the love in the physical universe is liberated, and at last the moon can sing her love song to the earth. The moon cries:

The snow upon my lifeless mountains
Is loosened into living fountains,
My solid oceans flow, and sing, and shine:
   A spirit from my heart bursts forth,
   It clothes with unexpected birth
My cold bare bosom: Oh! it must be thine
     On mine, on mine!

Gazing on thee I feel, I know
Green stalks burst forth, and bright flowers grow,
And living shapes upon my bosom move:
   Music is in the sea and air,
   Winged clouds soar here and there,
Dark with the rain new buds are dreaming of:
     'Tis love, all love!

Byron's attitude toward nature is equally distinctive. In the spring of 1816, when the circumstances of his life have turned him into the proud and stricken creature which he has earlier taken a sentimental pleasure in pretending to be, he seeks refuge in nature, going up the Rhine, spending the summer in Switzerland, and then coming down into Italy. These travels form the basis of Cantos III and IV of *Childe Harold*. At the beginning of Canto III the hero "wanders forth again,"

> Proud though in desolation; which could find
> A life within itself, to breathe without mankind.
>
> Where rose the mountains, there to him were friends;
> Where rolled the ocean, thereon was his home;
> Where a blue sky, and glowing clime, extends,
> He had the passion and the power to roam;
> The desert, forest, cavern, breaker's foam,
> Were unto him companionship; they spake
> A mutual language, clearer than the tome
> Of his land's tongue, which he would oft forsake
> For Nature's pages glassed by sunbeams on the lake.
>
> (*Childe Harold*, III, 22, 23)

This retreat to nature is not unlike the earlier and more negative stage of the process displayed by Wordsworth and Coleridge. Sometimes, too, Byron reminds us strongly of the more affirmative stage of the Wordsworthian nature philosophy:

> Are not the mountains, waves, and skies, a part
> Of me and of my soul, as I of them?
> Is not the love of these deep in my heart
> With a pure passion?
>
> (*Childe Harold*, III, 75)

A major difference between the two poets, however, prevents our regarding Byron as anything like a disciple of Wordsworth. In Wordsworth's most characteristic poems, nature is given a voice that speaks to all humanity. Only a few maladjusted souls are unfitted to receive her message. Moreover, as we know, love of nature leads to love of man. But Byron prizes nature for her glorious *in*humanity. She, with him her son, stands apart in majestic scorn of the human herd.

> Is it not better, then, to be alone,
> And love Earth only for its earthly sake?
> By the blue rushing of the arrowy Rhone,
> Or the pure bosom of its nursing lake,
>
> . . . .
>
> Is it not better thus our lives to wear,
> Than join the crushing crowd, doomed to inflict or bear?
>
> I live not in myself, but I become
> Portion of that around me; and to me
> High mountains are a feeling, but the hum
> Of human cities torture: I can see
> Nothing to loathe in nature, save to be
> A link reluctant in a fleshly chain,
> Classed among creatures, when the soul can flee,
> And with the sky, the peak, the heaving plain
> Of ocean, or the stars, mingle, and not in vain.
>
> (*Childe Harold*, III, 51, 52)

Much in Byron's relations with nature recalls the bad young man in *Ruth* whose irregularity is encouraged by the irregularities of nature. Mother Nature and her son Byron share the same proud, moody, turbulent emotion. For Wordsworth, nature is "the guide of all his moral being;" for Byron, she is the mirror of his melancholy.

And so at the end of Canto IV Childe Harold turns to the ocean as that aspect of nature least controlled by man:

> Roll on, thou deep and dark blue Ocean — roll!
> Ten thousand fleets sweep over thee in vain;
> Man marks the earth with ruin — his control
> Stops with the shore; — upon the watery plain
> The wrecks are all thy deed, nor doth remain
> A shadow of man's ravage, save his own,
> When, for a moment, like a drop of rain,
> He sinks into thy depths with bubbling groan,
> Without a grave, unknelled, uncoffined, and unknown.

In English literature, Byron's mood is not very common. It is more frequently found in continental literature, for it is associated with the melancholy state of mind known in Germany as *Weltschmerz* and in France as *mal du siècle*. That it sometimes crops up in English literature, however, is shown by Godwin's *Fleetwood* (1805). I have already told how the hero of this novel is corrupted at the university. He later goes to Paris and becomes extremely dissipated. Then he discovers that his mistress is inconstant, and of course heads straight for the Swiss Alps.

> I loathed existence and the sight of day. I fled from Paris and sought the craggy and inhospitable Alps; the most frightful scenes alone had power to please, and produced in me a kind of malicious and desperate sentiment of satisfaction.

Thanks to the influence of the scenery, however, Fleetwood's feelings become softened and elevated. He has a remarkable moment of reverie when he sees the chapel dedicated to William Tell. The passage is valuable as running through the gamut of romanticism from the primitivistic to the mystical levels:

I thought of William Tell; I thought of the simple manners which still prevail in the primitive cantons; I felt as if I were in the wildest and most luxuriant of the uninhabited islands of the South Sea. I was lost in visions of paradise, of habitations and bowers among the celestial orbs, of the pure rewards and enjoyments of a happier state.

So Fleetwood, healed by the mountains, ends by loving man and nature and everything else. Byron's "malicious and desperate sentiment of satisfaction" does not, like that of Godwin's hero, pass on to the Wordsworthian level. In fact it passes on to the cynicism of *Don Juan*, where he makes merciless and delightful fun of the cult of nature. I hope I am right in thinking that the following wicked lines will be a relief to you:

> Young Juan wandered by the glassy brooks
>   Thinking unutterable things; he threw
> Himself at length within the leafy nooks
>   Where the wild branch of the cork forest grew;
> There poets find material for their books,
>   And every now and then we read them through,
> So that their plan and prosody are eligible,
> Unless, like Wordsworth, they prove unintelligible.
>
> He (Juan, and not Wordsworth) so pursued
>   His self-communion with his own high soul,
> Until his mighty heart, in its great mood,
>   Had mitigated part, though not the whole
> Of its disease; he did the best he could
>   With things not very subject to control,
> And turned, without perceiving his condition,
> Like Coleridge, into a metaphysician.
>
> He thought about himself, and the whole earth,
>   Of man the wonderful, and of the stars,

And how the deuce they ever could have birth;
  And then he thought of earthquakes, and of wars,
How many miles the moon might have in girth,
  Of air-balloons, and of the many bars
To perfect knowledge of the boundless skies; —
And then he thought of Donna Julia's eyes.

In thoughts like these true wisdom may discern
  Longings sublime, and aspirations high,
Which some are born with, but the most part learn
  To plague themselves withal, they know not why:
'Twas strange that one so young should thus concern
  His brain about the action of the sky;
If *you* think 'twas philosophy that this did,
I can't help thinking puberty assisted.

(Don Juan, I, 90-93)

That one of the great romantic poets should thus mock what we have come to regard as a major romantic tendency raises a puzzling question which we are not yet ready to answer except by saying that a pendulum which swings far to the right will swing far to the left. But there is another question which must be considered at once.

Although I have entitled this lecture "External Nature," much of what I have said has been more concerned with subjective attitudes toward the external than with the external itself, with what the romanticists put into nature than with what they actually saw there. No one will deny that the main theme of *Tintern Abbey* is the deep spiritual joy which the loving contemplation of nature can give to man. Yet the state described in the most famous lines of the poem is one which rises above enjoyment, however spiritual, of the fruits of direct perception. For a moment the objective "dwelling" is forgotten, and there is a more or less mystical contact between the soul of Wordsworth and the Spirit that "rolls through all things." We get another hint of mystical aspiration earlier in the poem when Wordsworth speaks of

that blessed mood,
In which the burthen of the mystery,
In which the heavy and the weary weight
Of all this unintelligible world
Is lightened: — that serene and blessed mood,
In which the affections gently lead us on, —
Until, the breath of this corporeal frame
And even the motion of our human blood
Almost suspended, we are laid asleep
In body, and become a living soul;
While with an eye made quiet by the power
Of harmony, and the deep power of joy,
We see into the life of things.

Are we to say, then, that the goal of this loving attention to natural objects is the disappearance of those objects in a flash of mystical immediacy? Are we here confronted with an inconsistency which runs through the fabric of romanticism? Without much hope of being able to answer this question, I shall begin to deal with it in the next lecture.

VIII

DESCENDENTALISM AND TRANSCENDENTALISM

In your own reading it must often have struck you that although romanticism loves to burrow deeply into the soil of the actual, it also loves to soar above the actual into the intangible and mysterious. It has a realistic side, and it has a transcendental side. Transcendentalism may be defined as belief in the dominance of the intuitive and spiritual elements of mentality over sense experience. At present, however, I am thinking of transcendentalism less as a definite philosophical position than as the general upward-looking and supersensuous spirit which accompanies the downward-looking and realistic element in romanticism. The concluding section of the course will be devoted to transcendentalism in the more technical sense, but I cannot explain the romantic conception of nature without touching upon its transcendental element.

The seeming divergence between the realistic and transcendental sides of romanticism has led some scholars to protest that no single explanation of the term can cover them both. In a valuable paper "On the Discrimination of Romanticisms" (*Publications of the Modern Language Association of America*, Vol. XXXIX, pp. 229-253), Professor A. O. Lovejoy urges us to speak, not of romanticism, but of romanticisms. Yet without attempting to bring under a single head everything to which this perplexing tag has at one time or another been affixed, I would point out that there is much in common

between what might be called "naturalistic" and "super-
naturalistic" romanticism. Where would Professor Lovejoy undertake to divide that stream of associations which
passes through Fleetwood's mind as he stands before
Tell's chapel? The interpreter of romanticism, to be sure,
is in a sad predicament. If he regards it as a unity, he is
haunted by a sense of its plurality; if he regards it as a
plurality, he is haunted by a sense of its unity. Though
fully realizing this dilemma, I wish to say something in
support of a unitarian view of romanticism so far as its
naturalistic aspect is concerned.

In *Sartor Resartus,* Carlyle says of that very romantic
figure, Professor Diogenes Teufelsdröckh, that his character has both a descendental and a transcendental element. He is intensely earthly, and intensely spiritual. He
enjoys taking us into the barnyard and making us look at
real things; but, like Martin Luther, he wishes us to
remember that the egg which we lift from the straw is a
miracle. His philosophy of clothes includes the descendental idea that it would be amusing to see a naked House
of Lords, but it also includes the transcendental idea that
all matter is merely a garment for the spiritual reality of
the universe. The character of Teufelsdröckh, which of
course is the character of Carlyle, does not fall apart.
He does not oscillate between burrowing down into the
soil of the actual and soaring up into the intangible and
mysterious: he burrows into the soil of the actual for the
sake of something intangible and mysterious in its depths.
Sometimes, to be sure, one element is emphasized at the
expense of the other; but the elements are not inconsistent.
They are two aspects of one view of life — a view which
might be expressed by saying that the real is wonderful
and that the wonderful is real.

This formula perhaps approaches the core of romanticism. Novalis, one of Carlyle's deep Teutons, writes:

The world must be romanticized. If we do this, we shall discover in it the meaning it had from the beginning. The lower self becomes, through this process, identified with its higher self. . . . By giving the common a nobler meaning, the ordinary a mysterious aspect, the known the dignity of the unknown, the finite the appearance of the infinite — I romanticize.

Although England never went far toward formulating an explicit philosophy of romanticism, this fusion of the descendental and the transcendental is apparent in a great deal of English romantic literature. At a particular time or in a particular personality either the descendental or the transcendental aspect may predominate, but not to the total exclusion of the other. The romanticist so persistently tries to find in trees the thrill of the unknown, and so persistently tries to give the unknown the tangibility of trees, that when we study this period it seems not only easier but more fruitful to let descendentalism and transcendentalism run together in our minds than severely to keep them separate. In the historiography of ideas, a distinction which was not apparent to the writers under consideration may be misleading in direct proportion to its neatness and clarity.

Coleridge's account in *Biographia Literaria* of the plan underlying *Lyrical Ballads* is very much to the point:

It was agreed that my endeavors should be directed to persons and characters supernatural, or at least romantic; yet so as to transfer from our inward nature a human interest and a semblance of truth sufficient to procure for those shadows of imagination that willing suspension of disbelief for the moment, which constitutes poetic faith. Mr. Wordsworth, on the other hand, was to propose to himself as his object, to give the charm of novelty to things of every day, and to excite a feeling analogous to the supernatural, by awakening the mind's attention to the lethargy of custom, and directing it to the loveliness of the world before us.

Here in a single volume of poetry we have the two different but harmonious elements of the romantic program. Were we to sum up that program in a single phrase, we could hardly find a better than the one which Carlyle uses to describe Teufelsdröckh's philosophy, "natural supernaturalism" — though "supernatural naturalism" would serve equally well.

The history of the romantic fusion of descendentalism and transcendentalism is difficult to trace. One may say, however, that the most characteristic thought of the late seventeenth and early eighteenth centuries gave little satisfaction either to man's interest in the natural or to his yearning for the supernatural. In order to connect this topic with what was said in the preceding lecture about the average Augustan poet and his nightingale, an illustration will be drawn from eighteenth century esthetics. As an expression of pseudoclassic ideals, Isaac Hawkins Browne's *On Design and Beauty* is far more philosophical than Pope's *Essay on Criticism*. I cannot date the poem, but Browne was born in 1705 and it was a work of his youth. The author declares that the simplicity desirable in art must not become so abstract as to melt into vastness:

> Yet here, unless due boundaries be placed,
> Oft will the Simple spread into the Vast;
> Vast, where the symmetry of parts akin
> Lies too remote, and is but dimly seen.
> In Nature's wondrous frame if aught appear
> Vast, or misshapen, or irregular,

> 'Tis that the mighty structure was designed
> A whole proportioned to the all-seeing Mind.
> But art is bounded by perception still,
> And aims not to oppress the mind, but fill.

In avoiding the Scylla of the vast, however, the artist must steer clear of the Charybdis of the minutely circumstantial:

> Nor less their fault, who shunning this extreme
> Grow circumstantial, and but crowd the scheme.
> Beauty, when best discerned, is most complete,
> But all is Gothic which is intricate.

Browne's ideas may be extended from the plastic art to the poetry, and from the poetry to the general thought, of his age. That thought was sufficiently detached from reality to be abstract, and yet not sufficiently detached from reality to provide the illusion of living in a thrillingly mysterious universe. It thwarted both the desire to roam the infinite and the desire to look upon and touch real objects. Hence in the gradual reaction against this kind of thought, there would be a tendency for the two neglected planes, the natural and the supernatural, to combine in an alliance against the rationalistic enemy. In romanticism, the two extremes which Browne is anxious to avoid — vastness and the intricacy of Gothic detail — are combined and often reconciled.

The alliance between the descendental and the transcendental does not come all at once, and the proportions of the two elements are far from even — either in chronological divisions of the movement, or in individual authors, or throughout particular works. On the whole, the early manifestations of the romantic spirit in the age of Pope and throughout the age of Johnson are descendental. The primary impulse is toward the simple and the real — a movement of feeling from the corrupted city to the innocent country; from hard pavements to grassy paths; from the disillusionments of worldly ambition to the simple satisfactions of rustic contentment; from the complex and over-sophisticated present to the naïve and spontaneous past; from the bewilderment of learning to the sure guidance of untutored instinct. But all this, while no doubt chiefly descendental, is full of hints which point forward to the other trend of romanticism. The sentimentality of this early phase of the movement, its desire for thrills and mystery and glamour and illusion, its opposition of feeling to thinking — these have transcendental implications; they predict the transcendental attitude, and actively prepare for it.

Early romanticism, in which descendentalism dominates over an obscure but never wholly negligible transcendentalism, gradually gives place to a stage in which descendentalism and transcendentalism are more evenly balanced. James Thomson may perhaps stand for the first stage, and the Wordsworth of 1798-1805 for the second.

The equilibrium of the second stage is difficult to maintain. Descendentalism tips the scales toward realism in literary technique and toward the scientific attitude in philosophy; transcendentalism tips the scales toward impressionism in literary technique and toward mysticism in philosophy. Wordsworth at his greatest is remarkably successful in keeping the balance, but even in his best period one sometimes feels the unsteadiness which raises the question that we asked concerning *Tintern Abbey*. He loves external and tangible nature too genuinely to be a mystic, but when anything pulls him toward the extreme of realism he makes a compensatory move toward the opposite extreme of mysticism.

But I have begun to touch upon matters which I prefer to reserve for later discussion. At present it is enough to say that the second stage is of short duration. It gives place to one in which the balance shifts the other way, so that transcendentalism dominates over descendentalism. The attempt to find the vast within the circumstantial becomes less and less satisfactory; going up in the air, after all, gives more inspiring results than delving into the earth. Yet the true romanticist carries his love of earth up into the air with him, and his mistiest transcendentalism is tinged with descendentalism. Shelley will stand as an example of this third stage.

We may suspect that this little graph is too neat to be true. But it is pretty, and perhaps it has a limited kind of validity. Thus much, at all events, by way of a theoretical attempt to keep romanticism from falling apart into romanticisms at this point.

In a less abstract way, the savage, the peasant, and the child do something to justify a unitarian conception of romantic naturalism. The romanticists aspired to something "higher" than analytical reason, and yet they were greatly interested in beings who have not yet attained even the merely analytical stage. In the light of what has been said about the fusion of descendentalism and transcendentalism, this fact is not difficult to understand. The naïve and primitive souls admired by the romanticist are above logic precisely because they are below it. In being close to nature they are close to the supernatural, and partake of that "sense sublime of something far more deeply interfused" which can never be attained through "that false secondary power by which we multiply distinctions." In fact, this mingling of the subrational with the supposedly superrational is a cardinal trait of romanticism. Whether there is such a thing as the superrational, and whether any conscious attempt to rise above logic is not inevitably to fall below it, no matter how gracefully the collapse is sublimated by mystical terminology, are questions to be asked, but hardly to be answered. In any case the romanticists believed in the superrational and in their efforts to describe it to mankind often drew their examples from the subrational.

Our next step, therefore, will be to examine these three very popular figures of romantic literature. For a fuller discussion of them, especially of the first, I must refer you to my own *Noble Savage*. Practically all of my material, indeed, will be drawn from that book; but even at the expense of some repetition I wish to relate the savage, the peasant, and the child to the view of romanticism which I am trying to develop in this course.

IX

SAVAGE, PEASANT, AND CHILD

It would be uncritical to exaggerate the importance of the noble savage. He is more popular in the earlier than in the later manifestations of romanticism, and more popular with minor writers than with the really great men. Of these, none are at any time willing to adore him unreservedly, though several show admiration for one or more aspects of his character.

But the noble savage is interesting in that he does, at various times and in the hands of various writers, provide a vehicle for many romantic ideas. He can illustrate what a blessing it is to be ignorant of bewildering books; to what a low level man has deteriorated; to what a high level, since his native equipment is so promising, man may develop; the benign influence of scenery; the natural goodness of man and the badness of the civilization which, despite his natural goodness, he has somehow managed to create; the stupidity of building cities when the woods are so much better; the stupidity of making money when contentment depends upon not having any; the superiority of feeling to thinking; the possibility of finding God in nature; the benefits and pleasures of free and unsophisticated love; the fact that natural man is a natural poet — and other things of the same general kind.

Although the virtues of the noble savage are more or less the same wherever he is found, those virtues are differently displayed by different races. The American

Indian is the aristocrat of the group. His scorn of civilization, lively sense of gratitude, natural mysticism, dignity,
oratorical ability, hospitality, and courage are all very
impressive. His bloodthirstiness provides agreeable thrills,
and it can always be explained in terms of resistance to
European oppression or by glances at the vices of "more
refined nations." We might think him too stolid for romantic tastes, but he is supposed to be a true Man of
Feeling beneath his stoical exterior.

The South Sea Islander is a slighter, less imposing,
more amiable figure. Tahiti and other such islands provide
a number of female noble savages. In fact, from the
abundant eighteenth century voyage-literature down to
present-day books like O'Brien's *Mystic Isles of the South
Seas*, the noble Polynesian tradition has been suffused
with a hankering for a freer and more spontaneous kind
of love than our own corrupt civilization provides. For a
perfect example see Byron's last poem, *The Island* — an
ideal motion picture story of mutiny, marooning and the
love of a Scotch sailor and a native woman on a Pacific
isle. The ever-watchful *Anti-Jacobin* had earlier satirized
the South Seas fad by making Mr. Higgins dilate upon
the joys of pastoral life in Tahiti, "where the office of
shepherd is a perfect sinecure, there being no sheep on the
island," and by inserting this amusing passage in the
burlesque *Progress of Man*:

> There laughs the sky, there Zephyr's frolic train,
> And light-winged loves, and blameless pleasures reign:
> There, when two souls congenial ties unite,
> No hireling Bonzes chant the mystic rite:
> Free every thought, each action unconfined,
> And light those fetters which no rivets bind.

· · · ·

Each shepherd clasped, with undisguised delight,
His yielding fair one — in the captain's sight;
Each yielding fair, as chance or fancy led,
Preferred new lovers to her sylvan bed.
Learn hence, each nymph, whose free aspiring mind
Europe's cold laws, and colder customs bind —
O! learn, what Nature's genial laws decree —
What Otaheité is, let Britain be!

The African Negro joins the noble savage club rather late, and is never so prominent a member as the Indian or the South Sea Islander. Probably owing to the influence of Aphra Behn's *Oroonoko*, whose hero was an African king before his enslavement, the Negro is sometimes depicted as a fallen monarch of nature. William Roscoe's *The Wrongs of Africa* will provide an example. *The West Indies*, a long poem written by James Montgomery of Sheffield to celebrate the abolition of the slave trade in 1807, undertakes to prove that the Negro is quite as noble a noble savage as the Indian. But a more typical treatment of the Negro is William Blake's *The Little Black Boy*, which I have shown to be the best of a number of poems in which the Negro speaks for himself, pleading for sympathy and understanding, not as a noble savage, but as a human being. In short, the literary Negro of the period is more closely associated with humanitarianism than with primitivism.

Some authors regard in the light of the noble savage tradition other more or less primitive peoples who happen to be known to them. Walter Scott's Highlanders have a touch of the noble savage. He once compares Rob Roy to an Arab chief, and at another time to an American Indian. The natives of Albania who figure so importantly in

Canto II of *Childe Harold* are noble savages of a rather fierce and lawless kind, as might be expected of the children of Byronic nature.

Whether the Lake Country shepherd admired by Wordsworth can be spoken of as a noble savage even in a loose and figurative sense is doubtful. Wordsworth was never a lover of actual wildness in men or institutions. In fact, he has been claimed as an enemy of the savage on the basis of the *Excursion* passage describing Solitary's vain attempt to find natural man in the American forest. We must not forget, however, that Solitary's speech is dramatic. His ideas are by no means those which Wordsworth wishes to enforce, for he exists to be lectured into a more wholesome view of life. And few seem to have noticed that at the very end of the Wanderer's long exhortation in answer to Solitary occur the lines:

> Here closed the Sage that eloquent harangue,
> Poured forth with fervour in continuous stream,
> Such as, remote, 'mid savage wilderness,
> An Indian Chief discharges from his breast
> Into the hearing of assembled tribes,
> In open circle seated round, and hushed
> As the unbreathing air, when not a leaf
> Stirs in the mighty woods.
>
> (IV, 1275 ff.)

Although I have found a number of Wordsworth passages which suggest a more or less approving interest in the Indian, the fact remains that this poet was never really enthusiastic about savages. Nevertheless, it is tempting to compare the noble savage and the noble peasant. Michael at least reminds one of the dignified and stoical old sachem of tradition. In Wordsworth, too, the Indian can respond to nature much as the peasant does:

Think, how the everlasting streams and woods,
Stretched and still stretching far and wide, exalt
The roving Indian, on his desert sands.

(Prelude, VII, 745 ff.)

One may at least say that the noble savage and the noble
peasant are similarly motivated. Both reflect a revulsion
against "what man has made of man." Both preach
the gospel of nature worship, innocent simplicity, and
anti-intellectualism. They are related also in that Wordsworth's conception of the shepherd is influenced by Rousseau's conception of natural man, which in turn owes
something to the noble savage tradition.

Wordsworth's contemporaries often speak of indige-
nous rustics in the same terms that they apply to the
savage. You will remember that Pope had written in the
Essay on Man:

Lo, the poor Indian! whose untutored mind
Sees God in clouds, or hears him in the wind.
His soul proud science never taught to stray
Far as the solar walk or milky way;
Yet simple nature to his hope has given,
Behind the cloud-topped hill, an humbler heaven.

And so Henry Kirke White, a young contemporary of
Wordsworth who died in 1806, writes:

Lo! the unlettered hind who never knew
To raise his mind excursive, to the heights
Of abstract contemplation.

The simple peasant, he goes on, has a deep religious sense
because his gratitude has been aroused by the generosity
of nature. Since the sophisticated philosopher does not
experience this mood,

What is the pomp of learning? The parade
Of letters and of tongues? E'en as the mists
That pass away and perish.

Both the poor Indian and the poor peasant, then, may be
used to exemplify the benefits of the "natural" religion
which will be taken up in the next lecture.

My point is not that the idealized peasant is an outgrowth of the noble savage, but that the two figures are
harmoniously related in romantic thought. Of course the
idealized peasant has an independent line of development
which reaches back even further than the ancestry of the
noble savage. At the opening of the eighteenth century
the pastoral was still a highly sophisticated, artificial,
and traditional type, treating in a veneered and affected
way the elegant loves and elegant poetic talents of completely unreal shepherds and shepherdesses. It was simply
a special variety of pseudoclassic poetry, with definite
rules of its own. No one thought that it implied writing
about real rustics in a real country setting. But as the
eighteenth century goes on, the conventional pastoral
gives place more and more to seriously sympathetic portrayals of English country folk. Of course the peasant is
idealized as well as realized: the development shows the
usual descendental-transcendental mixture. The simple
shepherd is made the vehicle for the increasingly popular
notions about the wickedness of cities and the desirability
of innocent contentment in the lap of nature. As a matter
of fact these ideas were commonplaces of the old conventional pastoral, but when they are rather solemnly applied
to actual English peasants instead of to "the gay Corin
of the groves" they begin to mean something —

> Not in Utopia, subterranean fields,
> Or some secreted island, heaven knows where!
> But in the very world.

The clash between early romantic pastoral sentiment and the industrial revolution is particularly emphatic in Goldsmith's *Deserted Village*. This poem represents perhaps the highest point in favorable depiction of rustic character up to Wordsworth himself, though we must not forget "the rude forefathers of the hamlet" in Gray's *Elegy*. The tendency to view country life through rose-colored glasses had gone so far by the 1780's that George Crabbe, one of the few genuinely realistic minds in English literature, tried to deflate it in *The Village* (1783). Thinking of his own unhappy boyhood in the desolate fen country of Norfolk, he gives a gloomy picture of the ugliness, ignorance, and toilsome poverty of the rustic's existence.

> I paint the cot,
> As truth will paint it, and as bards will not.

Glancing at Goldsmith's "Sweet Auburn, loveliest village of the plain," he declares that

> Since vice the world subdued and waters drowned,
> Auburn and Eden can no more be found.

But the tide of nature worship swept over his head and on to Wordsworth, who, we see, had plenty of traditional background for his idealization of the Lake Country dalesman.

You will find in romantic writers, especially in those of Wordsworth's generation, a strong sympathy for all sorts of simple rural folk, and you will often justly infer that these lowly ones are lofty because of their very lowliness — because they are close to that light of nature from

which the learned and sophisticated have turned away.
But we must pass on to the child as seen by the romantic
imagination.

To Wordsworth, childhood is a sublime and sacred
thing. Despite his attempts to congratulate himself upon
the philosophical insight of maturity, he constantly yearns
back to the warm, fresh perceptions of boyhood, and
associates that warmth and freshness with the heaven
from which, "trailing clouds of glory," the child has newly
come. Probably his greatest tribute to the child is the
eighth stanza of the *Immortality Ode*, beginning:

> Thou, whose exterior semblance doth belie
> Thy soul's immensity;
> Thou best philosopher, who yet dost keep
> Thy heritage, thou eye among the blind,
> That, deaf and silent, read'st the eternal mind —
> Mighty prophet! Seer blest!

Many of Wordsworth's contacts with nature are valued
not so much in themselves as because they bring back
more intense and delightful childhood experiences of the
same sort. The butterfly and the sparrow's nest remind
him of early days with his sister. An apt instance of this
retrospective response to natural stimuli is *To the Cuckoo*
(the one beginning "O blithe newcomer"):

> Though babbling only to the vale,
> Of sunshine and of flowers,
> Thou bringest unto me a tale
> Of visionary hours.
>
> Thrice welcome, darling of the Spring!
> Even yet thou art to me
> No bird, but an invisible thing,
> A voice, a mystery;

The same whom in my schoolboy days
I listened to; that Cry
Which made me look a thousand ways
In bush, and tree, and sky.

.   .   .   .

And I can listen to thee yet;
Can lie upon the plain
And listen, till I do beget
That golden time again.

In his most characteristic period, Wordsworth dwells much upon the intuitive wisdom which children derive from nature. Several of the *Lyrical Ballads* deal with this theme. *Anecdote for Fathers* is a very funny poem, and it is hard not to smile at parts of *We Are Seven*; but in the latter, one cannot fail to be impressed by the vain hammering of the literal-minded adult's sense of fact against the child's intuitive sense of truth.

For the background of this topic I refer you to a dissertation by the late Professor A. C. Babenroth: *English Childhood. Wordsworth's Treatment of Childhood in the Light of English Poetry from Prior to Crabbe*. Professor Babenroth was able to show that this element, like other elements of Wordsworth's philosophy of nature, has deep roots in the past. During the eighteenth century there was a gradual growth of sympathy for childhood, a gradual fusion of this sympathy with the cult of nature, and a gradually mounting belief that the child's innocence and intuitiveness are precious as showing what a rich heritage we bring into the world, and how sinfully we squander it.

But all this I must pass by in order to concentrate upon

a single variety of the romantic child — one which might be called the child of nature, or the Lucy type, in whom romantic interest in childhood unites with the romantic love of external nature.

The child of nature — sometimes a boy, but more often a girl — grows up in some rustic or sylvan region more or less uncorrupted by civilization. From a spirit of goodness immanent in the scenery she draws beauty, innocence, an instinctive moral sense, and often an intuitive insight into the heart of things. In the work of Wordsworth, Lucy herself is by no means the only example. We need only glance at Ruth, who

> Had built a bower upon the green
> As if she from her birth had been
> An infant of the woods.

When nature says of Lucy that

> a lovelier flower
> On earth was never sown,

she is using a conventional metaphor in a more than conventional sense. The flower, quietly absorbing sunlight and moisture and transforming them into fragrance and beauty, is just what a child should be. Lucies are often associated with flowers in the romantic mind. Thus Southey compares Emma, a Somersetshire lass, to

> a plant whose leaf
> And bud and blossom all are beautiful.

Southey, in fact, is very fond of Lucies. In *A Tale of Paraguay* he has a pair of them, brother and sister:

> The boy in sun and shower
> Rejoicing in his strength to youthhead grew;
> And Mooma, that beloved girl, a dower
> Of gentleness from bounteous nature drew,
> With all that should the heart of womankind imbue.

Here the influence of Wordsworth's *Three Years She Grew* is unmistakable.

In the work of other writers of the age these flower-maidens are almost as numerous as those in *Parsifal*, though their character is quite different. Of Haidee, the pirate's wild and beautiful daughter in *Don Juan*, Byron says that "like a lovely tree, she grew to womanhood." Mary Mitford's father, John Mitford, dedicated a group of poems to a dead girl who bore the initials A. B. I have never attempted to identify her, but she was certainly reared as a Lucy, and she is explicitly called a "child of nature,"

> The mildest and the maidenliest creature born,
> So gentle, and so gracious — in serene
> And tender hope, the opening blossom grew.

The influence of scenery upon these children of nature is especially clear in the heroine of Thomas Campbell's *Gertrude of Wyoming*:

> It seemed as if those scenes sweet influence had
> On Gertrude's soul, and kindness like their own
> Inspired those eyes affectionate and glad,
> That seemed to love whate'er they looked upon.

And though this strain of romantic thought is not prominent in Shelley, one recognizes its presence in the *Revolt of Islam*, where the mysterious woman who interprets

the vision of the first canto represents herself as having
been a child of nature:

> Woe could not be mine own, since far from men
>   I dwelt, a free and happy orphan child,
> By the sea-shore, in a deep mountain-glen;
>   And near the waves, and through the forests wild,
>   I roamed, to storm and darkness reconciled:
> For I was calm while tempest shook the sky:
>   But when the breathless heavens in beauty smiled,
> I wept, sweet tears, yet too tumultuously
> For peace, and clasped my hands aloft in ecstasy.

The Lucy ideal enters not only into the poems but into
the lives of several romantic writers. The influence of
nature upon little Hartley Coleridge begins in the cradle.
In *The Nightingale* his father writes:

>   And I deem it wise
> To make him Nature's playmate. He knows well
> The evening-star; and once, when he awoke
> In most distressful mood (some inward pain
> Had made up that strange thing, an infant's dream)
> I hurried with him to our orchard-plot,
> And he beheld the moon, and hushed at once,
> Suspends his sobs, and laughs most silently,
> While his fair eyes, that swam with undropped tears,
> Did glitter in the yellow moon-beam!

In one of her letters, Dorothy Wordsworth describes
her brother's daughter Dora as a free, wild creature.
She reports that Coleridge jokingly says of the child,
"The wild-cat of the wilderness was not so wild as she"
— a garbling of the lines in Wordsworth's own *Ruth*,
"The panther in the wilderness Was not so fair as he."
Dorothy Wordsworth herself is plainly a child of nature,

and is so regarded by her brother and by Coleridge. She was always a little too close to nature to be a romantic naturalist. She felt it very intensely, but — or, perhaps, and therefore — was seldom able to discourse solemnly *about* it. Her closest approach to philosophizing lies in such beautiful simple statements as "Grasmere calls the heart home to quiet." And what we generally find in her journals is a direct response to the loveliness of lovely things — often surprisingly in the manner of a modern imagist poet. De Quincey compares Dorothy's life to that of Ruth in the earlier part of her brother's poem. She was, he adds, like a gipsy. "Her time fleeted away like some golden age, or like the life of primeval man." From *Tintern Abbey* we learn that she preserved Wordsworth's own youthful feeling for nature. As he grew older, she must have seemed to him almost savage, almost pagan, in the immediacy of her response to the beauty of the visible world. In his heart he would probably envy her a little for her fresh sensuousness, but his explanation would be that which accounts for the seeming indifference of the child in the sonnet beginning *It is a beauteous evening*:

> Dear child! dear girl! that walkest with me here,
> If thou appear untouched by solemn thought,
> Thy nature is not therefore less divine:
> Thou liest in Abraham's bosom all the year;
> And worshipp'st at the Temple's inner shrine,
> God being with thee when we know it not.

Much the same explanation, by the way, accounts for the influence of nature upon the peasant Michael:

> And grossly that man errs, who should suppose
> That the green valleys, and the streams and rocks,
> Were things indifferent to the Shepherd's thoughts.

> Those fields, those hills — what could they less? had laid
> Strong hold on his affections, were to him
> A pleasurable feeling of blind love,
> The pleasure which there is in life itself.

These simple hearts, then, enjoy the privilege of an unconscious communion with the supernatural in the natural.

The Prelude and *France: an Ode*, respectively, show that Wordsworth and Coleridge thought of *themselves* as having been children of nature. We have already glanced at the similarity in this respect between the actual Wordsworth and the fictional Fleetwood, Godwin's hero. The parallel is really very close. Godwin makes Fleetwood declare:

> My earliest days were spent among mountains and precipices, amidst the roaring of the ocean and the dashing of waterfalls. A constant familiarity with these objects gave a wildness to my ideas, and an uncommon seriousness to my temper.

He adds that he had been "a wild roe among the mountains of Wales," while Wordsworth speaks in *Tintern Abbey* of the days

> when like a roe
> I bounded o'er the mountains.

Fleetwood says, "In Merionethshire I had been a solitary savage," and Wordsworth says that his own boyhood was

> as if I had been born
> On Indian plains, and from my mother's hut
> Had run abroad in wantonness, to sport,
> A naked savage, in the thunder shower.
> (*Prelude* I, 297 ff)

Byron also thought that he had been a child of nature.

See *I would I were a careless child*, and *When I roved a young Highlander*, in which he longs for the days when he was

> Untutored by science, a stranger to fear,
> And rude as the rocks where my infancy grew.

These lines were written when he was a student at Cambridge, towards which he felt very much as did Wordsworth, Coleridge, Southey, Shelley, Godwin's Fleetwood, and Holcroft's Hugh Trevor in their college days. One cause of the melancholy of the Byronic hero is the fact that beneath all his sin and cynicism he is a thwarted male Lucy.

> His early dreams of good outstripped the truth,
> And troubled manhood followed baffled youth.

Earlier in this lecture we noted several points of contact between the savage and the peasant. It may be added that a good many children of nature are also the children either of savages or of rustic folk. In a late poem, *Presentiments*, Wordsworth addresses the spirit of prophetic intuition:

> The naked Indian of the wild,
> And haply too the cradled child,
> Are pupils of your school.

Another associative link is found in Felicia Hemans' poem, *I Dream of All Things Free*. She dreams of a ship, a stag, an eagle, mountain brooks, and, in the last stanza,

> Of a happy forest child,
>   With the nymphs and fauns at play;
> Of an Indian midst the wild,
>   With the stars to guide his way:

My heart in chains is bleeding,
And I dream of all things free!

Lucy, in short, is harmoniously related to the other popular figures of illusioned primitivism. It is quite evident, moreover, that she cannot be dismissed as a mere literary fad. If we wish to understand her we cannot do better than look back to the eighteenth century and consider how Lord Chesterfield desired to rear Philip Stanhope — a natural child, to be sure, but hardly a child of nature. The contrast will suggest that a reaction was needed, though like most reactions it went to extreme lengths.

The savage, the peasant, and the child were introduced primarily as examples of the fusion of descendentalism and transcendentalism in romantic nature. They seem to imply a desire to descend from sophistication and intellectualism towards the primitive simplicity of sense experience. On the other hand, they seem to imply a desire to rise above the trammels of the man-made world into a purer realm of spiritual intuition. But these desires are united in that the "something higher" is best reached by lying close to the heart of nature in the wigwam, the sheepfold, or the cradle — so close that the happy savage or dalesman or child feels the divine impulse which sets the heart of nature throbbing with love and beauty.

And so these figures, which we might expect to be almost entirely descendental in their significance, are strongly tinged with transcendentalism. We are about to see, conversely, that the religion of nature, which we might expect to be almost entirely transcendental, includes a large descendental element. I shall not, however, continue to labor a point which will be apparent to you now if it is ever to be apparent at all. You will perhaps agree that the cult of the naïve and primitive is not so completely foreign to the high fervor of *Tintern Abbey* as to demand a pluralistic view of romantic naturalism. Beneath all the diversity lies a unifying network of roots too stubbornly interlaced to be hacked apart.

X

THE RELIGION OF NATURE

Toward the close of the seventeenth century, rationalistic philosophy exerted a powerful influence upon theology. It was desirable that religion should become a part of the systematic and reasonable universe in which men supposed themselves to be living. At this time, therefore, a group of theologians attempted to show that religion is after all just a matter of common sense. The outcome of this well-meant endeavor to provide a rational basis for faith was that by the beginning of the eighteenth century religion had lost most of the poetry and fervor which constitute its value. It would be more accurate to say that this endeavor was itself largely a symptom of the temporary decay of the religious spirit, for the theologians would have had little effect if people had not been prepared to receive their message.

The movement known as deism is the extreme but logical consequence of the attempt to achieve a reasonable kind of religion by believing in God without believing in supernatural revelation. To the deist, God does not reveal himself through scripture, through the traditions of the church, or even through personal religious experience. He reveals himself solely through his creation — a universe operating according to natural laws with which, once having enunciated them, he is sensible enough not to interfere. This God is neither a stern lawgiver nor a loving father, but a colorless abstraction inferred to satisfy

the demands of logic. Having been inferred, he is relegated as far as possible to the background, and is seldom
invoked except when rhetorical elevation is demanded.
Deism is supposed to embody the universal moral principles of common sense. It is not Christianity or Judaism
or Mohammedanism, but "the religion of nature." This is
a fair statement of the general theory of deism. In practice, however, deistic thought shaded all the way from a
vaguely optimistic "broadmindedness," often astonishing-
ly like that of present-day modernism, to a bitterly destructive scepticism which is not easy to distinguish from flat
atheism.

Meanwhile Christian orthodoxy, having made a tamer
compromise with rationalism, jogged contentedly along
a wide, level road. The average Anglican divine simply
went through the forms of worship and pulled wires to
get a fatter living. His chief aversion was what he termed
"enthusiasm" — belief that one has had a private and
special revelation of God's goodness. A personal religious
illumination was the worst possible form. Churchmen of
a higher type might engage in theological exposition or
controversy, but they usually did so in a cold-blooded,
hairsplitting, technical spirit. Many of the best minds in
the church, too, were in private hardly less sceptical than
the avowed deists against whom they fulminated. Religion
was all very well for the common people, but persons of
quality knew better. You may remember Addison's *Spec-
tator* paper, Number 50, giving selections from an Indian
chief's private journal of his visit to London. He admires
St. Paul's, but cannot imagine what it is for:

It is probable that when this great work was begun . . . there
was some religion among this people; for they give it the name of

a temple, and have a tradition that it was designed for men to pay their devotion in. And indeed there are several reasons which make us think that the natives of this country had formerly among them some sort of worship; for they set apart every seventh day as sacred: but upon my going into one of these holy houses on that day, I could not observe any circumstance of devotion in their behavior.

The inevitable reaction against this sham religion follows two channels: an attack in the name of genuinely critical rationalism upon more or less the whole structure of Christian faith; and an attack in the name of true religion upon the intellectualism which had deprived Christianity of its emotional and imaginative elements. The two movements may seem to be inconsistent, but we have here the same kind of necessary confusion as beset us in connection with the naturalism of the French Revolution. We are no more confused about the matter than the eighteenth century was. Religion had fallen into such a state that it could be assailed either because it was not reasonable enough or because it was too reasonable.

The former current of reaction concerns us little. The sceptically rationalistic attack upon religion is largely a continuation of the destructive side of deism. At the outbreak of the French Revolution it joins hands with political radicalism, and hence, as notably in the case of Tom Paine, is represented by several of the English Jacobins. Through Godwin, but even more through the French sceptic Volney, it influences the young Shelley, who was expelled from Oxford for his pamphlet on *The Necessity of Atheism*. In a thin but steady stream of "free thought" it comes down through Victorian England, until today we find it represented at its worst by the "village atheist" type, and at its best by men like Bertrand Russell.

It is rather the second current of reaction, the attempt to restore fervor, mystery, and poetry to religion, which pertains to romanticism. An honest attempt to trace this reaction forces the admission that in this as in other respects scholars have often exaggerated the spiritual deadness of the eighteenth century in order to achieve a neat contrast between the eighteenth and the nineteenth. Genuine religious emotion no more completely perished in the eighteenth century than genuine love for external nature. The various dissenting sects never quite lost the fervor of their ancestors, the Puritans. A thin but steady trickle of mysticism, moreover, ran from the seventeenth century into the eighteenth. There were those who read Jacob Boehme, and those who read Emmanuel Sweden-borg. Professor Saurat, in *Blake and Modern Thought*, shows that Blake's strange mythology used many frag-ments of a tradition of occultism which survived through-out the century. And though the center of the Church of England was smug and stuffy, the Low Church wing was never wholly without evangelical ardor, and the High Church wing never wholly without ritualistic poetry. In the 1720's and '30's we have the famous divine William Law, who moved from an earnestly evangelical to an earnestly mystical viewpoint. Some of his ideas were carried into non-theological literature by Henry Brooke, author of *The Fool of Quality*, and by the minor poet John Byrom, author of *Universal Beauty*. We have the great Methodist movement, the essence of which was just that "enthusiasm," that sense of personal salvation through personal relationship with Christ, which was so distasteful to the orthodox. William Cowper, though never technically a Methodist, was greatly influenced by Wesleyan thought. Bishop Joseph Butler's famous *Analogy* (1736) has a transcendental aspect which later inspired Newman. It is interesting to remember Newman's assertion, that, far from having been a Catholic spy in the Anglican camp, he had drawn from eighteenth century works of Protestant theology all the essential doctrines which finally made him leave the Church of England.

The importance of all this should not be exaggerated. It would still be true to say that even at the beginning of the nineteenth century organized religion on the whole was cold and sleepy. England had to wait almost until the middle of the nineteenth century for the full results of the earlier ferment. Nevertheless, the stirrings of a religious revival are perfectly apparent in the eighteenth century; and Wordsworth's religion of nature, while it has a large element of originality, also has a historical background.

Of the transcendental element in Wordsworth's religion of nature more will be said in a subsequent lecture. He plainly desires to rise above the rational plane into a realm where religious emotion will not be chilled by the sneer of logic. To this aim his anti-intellectualism, of which the eighteenth century origins were recently glanced at, is subservient. The descendental element in Wordsworth's religion is of course an extreme development of the eighteenth century renascence of interest in external nature. In trying to understand the combination of these two elements you will recall my earlier explanation of how romantic thought fuses descendentalism and transcendentalism. I shall try, however, to account more specifically for this fusion as it occurs in Wordsworth's creed.

Long before the psalmist sang "I will lift up mine eyes unto the hills," external nature and religious emotion were interwoven in men's hearts. The anthropologist who seeks to explain this association will find a bewildering wealth of material. He can point to the animism which assumes the existence of a spirit in every natural object, and which quite literally "sees God in clouds, or hears him in the wind"; to sympathetic magic as represented by springtide festivities and rain-making ceremonies, remote ancestors of Shelley's *The Cloud*; to sacrificial or otherwise holy localities — "high places of Israel," druidic groves, sin-absolving rivers, oracular caves. More or less sublimated reminiscences of these primitive and beautiful things exist in all of us. They existed strongly in Wordsworth. The boy who saw the mountain striding to punish him for a stolen boat ride never quite grew up — until he ceased to be a great poet. When at the end of *Nutting* he says that "there is a spirit in the woods," he means something at least as much like a pagan tree spirit as like the spirit that "rolls through all things" in *Tintern Abbey*. Professor De Selincourt writes:

It is interesting to notice that when Wordsworth began to write *The Prelude* he still delighted to conceive of Nature not merely as the expression of one divine spirit, but as in its several parts animated by individual spirits who had, like human beings, an independent life and power of action. This was obviously his firm belief in the primitive paganism of his boyhood, and long after he had given up definite belief in it he cherished it as more than mere poetic fancy.

For De Selincourt's evidence on this point, as well as the citation itself, see page 506 of his edition of *The Prelude*.

But the anthropologist whom we invited to probe the

nexus between nature and religious feeling must consider other groups of facts. Ethics have always been closely related to religion, and popular ethics constantly appeal to the testimony of external nature. There must have been sermons in stones from almost the earliest days of man. Sacred literature frequently commands us to consider the lilies of the field, or, for a quite different purpose, to go to the ant; and we perhaps transfer to the lily and the ant something of the reverence which we feel for the source of these directions.

If our anthropologist has the breadth of view which his subject demands somewhat more often than it receives, he will also recognize the indissoluble kinship between esthetic and religious feeling. Beauty and holiness; the beauty of holiness; the holiness of beauty — whatever phrase is used, this age-old psychological bond cannot be broken. The hills to which the psalmist lifted up his eyes were perhaps the abode of magic. They were certainly the abode of beauty, and help was to come from their loveliness as well as from the Lord.

It is not at all surprising, then, that Wordsworth's desire for an emotional and non-theological sort of religion should have found expression through his unusually strong sense of natural beauty. The fusion is all the easier to understand when we remember that the age of Pope had been comparatively neglectful of both elements of Wordsworth's religion, and that throughout the second half of the eighteenth century a reaction against that neglect had been leading up to the climactic outburst of descendental-transcendental nature worship which appears in *Tintern Abbey*.

But no aspect of romanticism can be explained solely in

terms of reaction from the age of Pope. Ideas do collide and bounce apart, but they also flow into each other and undergo subtle evolutionary changes. In the historiography of ideas, a simple "bouncing" explanation often means that our knowledge is not great enough to provide a more complex but more accurate "flowing" explanation. What I have been saying about the religion of Wordsworth is true enough as far as it goes, but its simplicity needs to be ruffled by the statement that Wordsworth's creed is historically related to the more optimistic and affirmative kind of eighteenth century deism. The relation is similar to that which exists between his naturalism viewed as a psychology and the associationism of Locke. In both cases certain ideas are accepted as a working basis and then transfigured by being regarded in a light quite different from that in which they were originally conceived.

The link between deism and Wordsworth is suggested by the phrase, "religion of nature." Deism called itself a religion of nature, and the same term may surely be applied to Wordsworth's creed. Any religion of nature infers the Creator from his creation. That is equally true of the deist and of Wordsworth. The difference lies in the viewpoint from which the creation is regarded. Speaking very broadly, the deistic conception of nature was the physico-mathematical one characteristic of official eighteenth century rationalism. It regarded the concrete objects of the physical universe chiefly as convenient illustrations of general laws. The divine was not immanent in these objects. God made them, devised the laws which govern them, and then left them severely alone. The creation therefore aroused only the sort of awe which a

mathematician might feel when confronted by an extremely neat theorem. This theorem could have been worked
out only by a super-mathematician, and there was no
objection to calling him God; but, except in theological
controversy, the game of reason could be played without
him. The Creator, in short, was kept out of his creation.

Now, remembering my first lecture, consider what
happens as the eighteenth century goes on. The rationalistic conception of nature merges with and becomes largely
subordinate to the primitivistic and sentimental conception of nature. The primitivistic and sentimental conception of nature merges with and expresses itself through
the growing enthusiasm for rural scenes and simple folk.
Terms like "reason" and "common sense" begin to acquire
transcendental connotations. Along with all this, the sub-
merged desire for emotional and imaginative religion
comes to the surface. The creation, which now consists
not of geometrical axioms but of mountains and trees and
birds, cries out for its Creator. And the Creator returns.
He does not, in the special development which we are
tracing, come back as a personal ruler or father of mankind. Such conceptions are too closely associated with the
intellectualist theology and the oppressive conservatism
which have become repugnant to the young romantic
naturalists. It is still necessary that religion should be a
religion of *nature*, that the Creator should be conceived
only in terms of his creation. And so God returns to
nature as an abstract and impersonal but loving and intimate something that breathes in every flower of the
beautiful world. Deism, warmed and romanticized, has
turned into Wordsworth's pantheism. The remote super-
mathematician has become

A presence that disturbs me with the joy
Of elevated thoughts; a sense sublime
Of something far more deeply interfused,
Whose dwelling is the light of setting suns,
And the round ocean and the living air,
And the blue sky, and in the mind of man.
A motion and a spirit, that impels
All thinking things, all objects of all thought,
And rolls through all things.

(*Tintern Abbey*)

Not merely lack of time, but lack of knowledge, forbids my giving a completely specific account of how this transformation took place. That it did take place seems evident enough, but the details of the process are buried more deeply in eighteenth century thought than I have yet been able to delve. Of course we may turn to the always useful Rousseau, who quite possibly influenced Wordsworth in this matter. Rousseau's religion was a highly emotionalized variety of deism, and he was a great interpreter of the beauties of nature. In his *Confession of Faith of a Savoyard Vicar* the two elements are combined, for the *Credo* is delivered at sunrise on a mountain-top. Most students will agree, however, that in Wordsworth's representative works religious emotion and the love of external nature are even more inextricably blended than they are in Rousseau. In fact no one either before, contemporary with, or after Wordsworth fuses quite so closely as he the God of the emotionally and antitheologically religious person and the nature of the lover of streams and mountains.

Here we may recall that "spy nosey" whom the government agent heard Wordsworth and Coleridge discussing

in 1797. Though Spinoza's total philosophy would have
been repugnant to Wordsworth, certain features of it, as
refracted and passed on to him by Coleridge, may have
helped him to bring God into a close relationship with
nature. To a man who was trying to spiritualize eighteenth century science, Spinoza's religious devotion to
natural law would be inspiring. The philosopher's insistence upon unity might be interpreted in such a way as to
encourage the romantic fusion of the descendental and
the transcendental. Spinoza's identification of God and
the universe, however, is less Wordsworthian than it appears to be at first glance. In the philosophy of Spinoza God is by no means identified with *natura naturata*
— nature in its passive aspect, the material things, or
"modes," which present themselves to our senses. God
is identified with *natura naturans* — nature in its active
and shaping aspect, the creative processes which make
up the underlying reality, or "substance," of the universe. Hence Wordsworth, in order to extract real
nourishment from Spinoza, would need to assume a
closer relationship between *natura naturata* and *natura
naturans* than is possible under the philosopher's system.
One solution might be to say — as Spinoza never said —
that comprehension of spiritual and active nature descends
to us *through* material and passive nature; and this
indeed closely approaches Wordsworth's own position.
We may guess that Coleridge's interpretation of Spinoza's
philosophy would heighten its transcendental implications
and neglect its rationalistic implications. But having no
certain evidence on this point we can only recognize the
rather strong possibility that Wordsworth indirectly drew
something from Spinoza. In a paper entitled "Words-

worth and Philosophy" (*Publications of the Modern Language Association of America*, Vol. XLIV, pp. 1116 ff.), N. P. Stallknecht suggests that Spinoza may have influenced Wordsworth in other respects than those just mentioned. It seems to me that Mr. Stallknecht over-emphasizes the mysticism of both Spinoza and Words-worth, but the argument deserves your attention.

In considering the religion of Wordsworth, we should recognize a distinction between a man's beliefs and the expression of those beliefs in the excited language of poetry. In cold blood, Wordsworth would never have equated scenery and nature, or nature and God. But to many romanticists, of whom Wordsworth is the great example, scenery provided the best evidence of what the universe fundamentally is and ought to be. Flowers and birds, grassy fields, streams, mountains, were felt to possess the untrammelled beauty, simplicity, spontaneity and unreflective goodness which find an echo in the heart of man whenever he casts off the perverting influences of civilization. The nature who takes Lucy unto herself is more, far more, than the "sun and shower" in which the child grew, but it is *through* the sun and shower that nature's educative force can best be exerted. Thus wild and semi-wild scenery became a body of symbols repre-senting the romantic ideal of nature. And since the symbol often looms as large as what it symbolizes, "nature" was often taken as synonymous with "scenery"; although just as great abstractions loom up behind sacred images, so behind natural objects hovered the universal spirit which gave those objects their value. With Wordsworth, love of external nature sometimes causes the symbol to absorb the thing symbolized, so that trees and mountains seem to have an efficacy of their own such as might be ascribed by a Catholic to a religious image. But in both cases the uninitiated may be deceived by a verbal code which the adept is using with full understanding. Just as the Catholic knows that the efficacy of a relic is derived from God, so Wordsworth knows that natural objects derive their "power to kindle or restrain" from the "wisdom and spirit of the universe." When Wordsworth tries to say all this in poetry, however, these distinctions run together like pieces of hot metal. At the height of his naturalistic enthusiasm, nature as God, nature as the universe and its laws, and nature as visible beauty, are almost inextricably mingled. When the dove descends to the Sangrael, what theology can distinguish the gift from the giver? Indeed, this sublime confusion of the physical and the metaphysical, of the descendental and the transcendental, is perhaps the essence of romanticism. In prose, Wordsworth would probably never have declared "I am a pantheist," but the poetry of his best period is intensely pantheistic; and those who refuse to grant that fact are moved chiefly by a desire to redeem him from heresy. He redeemed himself only too soon, but that is another story.

A man's religion, when unregulated by the doctrines of any organized sect, is a very personal thing, and it would be vain to expect to find in other writers an exact duplicate of Wordsworth's faith. We do find, however, a close approximation of that faith in several of his contemporaries. Indeed, the fundamental desire to find the supernatural within the natural is widespread.

In *Biographia Literaria*, Coleridge rather pathetically says:

And if in after time I have sought a refuge from bodily pain

and mismanaged sensibility in abstruse researches, which exercised
the strength and subtilty of the understanding without awakening
the feelings of the heart; yet still there was a long and blessed
interval, during which my natural faculties were allowed to expand and my original tendencies to develope themselves; — my
fancy, and the love of nature, and the sense of beauty in forms and
sounds.

Coleridge is thinking of his lost youth, but what he says
applies especially to the great nature-worshipping years
at the turn of the century, during which he had somewhat
the same creed as Wordsworth. In June, 1796, he writes
to the more or less atheistic John Thelwall: "We have a
hundred lovely scenes about Bristol which would make
you exclaim, 'O admirable *Nature*!' and *me*, 'O gracious
God!'" The implication is that they would be saying the
same thing in different terminology. This, we may remember, is the sort of religion to which Coleridge converted
Godwin in 1800.

In *Frost at Midnight* (1798) Coleridge expresses the
hope that his son will "wander like a breeze" among the
lakes and mountains, so that he may

> see and hear
> The lovely shapes and sounds intelligible
> Of that eternal language which thy God
> Utters, who from eternity doth teach
> Himself in all, and all things in himself.

Here God and nature are intimately related, but Coleridge recognizes more fully than Wordsworth frequently
does a distinction between God and the symbolic language
which he uses to instruct and inspire mankind. We shall
see later, moreover, that even when Coleridge approaches

Wordsworth most closely he differs from Wordsworth in having a more transcendental view of nature.

Many of the best illustrations of the religion of nature are found in portrayals of savages, peasants, and children. Here are some Indians in Southey's *Madoc* who tell the Christian voyagers:

> And we too . . . we know
> And worship the Great Spirit, who in clouds
> And storms, in mountain-caves and by the fall
> Of waters in the woodland solitudes,
> And in the night and silence of the sky,
> Doth make his being felt.

These savages have somewhat more than a glimmer of the spiritual light shed through nature upon a Swiss peasant in Wordsworth's *Descriptive Sketches*:

> He holds with God himself communion high,
> There where the peal of swelling torrents fills
> The 'sky-roofed temple of the eternal hills,
>
> . . . .
>
> Awe in his breast with holiest love unites,
> And the near heavens impart their own delights.

As for the child, we need only remember the *Immortality Ode*, where the evidence of the fact that "heaven lies about us in our infancy" is the freshness and vividness of the child's joy in nature.

A Catholic student once asked me why the romantic naturalists did not go to a priest and have done with it. She was thinking primarily of St. Francis and his descendental-transcendental attitude toward nature. Although I reminded her that there was some difference between preaching to birds and letting birds preach to us, I felt that her question was a fruitful one. In Germany and France, the romantic movement stimulated a revival of Catholicism. Certain French critics, in fact, have defined romanticism as the literary expression of the Catholic spirit. Novalis, who declared that the world must be romanticized through a union of its highest and lowest elements, was an ardent Catholic. In a way very significant for us, Chateaubriand shifts from nature worship to the traditional faith, both stages of his development being equally romantic. Historical circumstances delayed a similar movement in England, but at last Tractarianism established a tardy parallel in this respect between English and continental romanticism. And Tractarianism was to some extent prepared for by the medieval revival of the romantic period proper, which did much to soften the bitterness that Englishmen felt toward Catholicism. Moreover, when Wordsworth and Coleridge grew conservative, they turned to a religious orthodoxy which, though far from Catholic, was at least ready to emphasize essential points of contact between Anglicanism and Catholicism. The Tractarians' reverence for church tradition was to find support in Wordsworth's *Ecclesiastical Sonnets*; their other-worldliness and antiliberalism were to find support in Coleridge's transcendental Toryism.

My student's answer to her own question was that the romantic naturalists desired the Catholic thrill but shrank from the Catholic discipline. Without quarreling with that suggestive remark, I would resort to somewhat different terms. It seems to me that the religion of nature is associated with the side of romanticism which has a large descendental element and which is liberal in spirit, while romantic Catholicism and its fainter adumbrations in England are associated with the side of romanticism which has a large transcendental element and which is conservative in spirit. These two very different religions are related to the extent that either may be used by romanticism as a weapon in combating forces hostile to the illusioned view of life. To point out this relationship is not to indulge in a mere quibble. Psychology is teaching us that men's minds are to be compared and contrasted less according to what they say than according to the desires which underlie their words.

But at the turn of the century anyone who invited a young English romanticist to go to a priest would have been drowned in a flood of noble remarks about priestcraft and kingcraft, chains of monkish superstition, pedantic theology, the light of natural reason, the dictates of the heart, and the spirit of universal nature. The romantic naturalist had come to associate organized religion with the soul-blighting spirit of rationalism in theology and with conservatism in politics. Hence he disliked formal worship, and could pray anywhere but in a church. Joseph Hucks, a minor member of the Bristol group, says that true religion shuns "the grandeur of the Gothic pile" in order to roam through the woods and listen to the birds.

> Where'er she goes, where'er her eye surveys,
> In Nature's works she reads her Maker's praise.

Similarly, Robert Southey, in *Stanzas Written at Alentajo*, addresses the orthodox worshipper:

> Go, thou, and seek the House of Prayer!
> I to the woodlands bend my way,
>   And meet Religion there!
> She needs not haunt the high-arched dome to pray,

> Where storied windows dim the doubtful day:
>   At liberty she loves to rove,
> Wide o'er the heathy hill or cowslipt dale.

In *Joan of Arc*, the same poet provides us with a figure who will not only answer my Catholic student's question but will sum up the religion of nature. The Maid of Orleans — simple peasant girl who saw so much more than apples in the orchard, intuitive mystic, champion of the oppressed, victim of kingcraft and priestcraft — was a tempting subject for a romantic naturalist. In the first edition, Southey, in deference to the received legend and to the epic formula, lets his heroine be controlled and guided by the Christian Olympus; but in the second edition, which was published in the great naturalistic year of 1798, all this machinery is discarded, and Joan appears as a true child of nature, a Lucy-saint. Her faith arises from the benign influence of the forests in which she was reared; she owes her spiritual power to her ignorance of those rationalistic subtleties which have corrupted religion.

For us the most important scene of the poem is that in which Joan is examined by the ecclesistical court summoned by the Dauphin to determine the authenticity of her mission. The champion of the heart confronts the forces of the head.

When the learned bigots, who have gone blind from staring at the sun, ask Joan whether she has been faithful to the observances of Mother Church, she astounds them by replying that churches have always roused in her a feeling of repugnance:

> The forms of worship in mine earlier years
> Waked my young mind to artificial awe,

And made me fear my God. Warm with the glow
Of health and exercise, whene'er I passed
The threshold of the house of prayer I felt
A cold damp chill me.

In childhood, then, she worshipped "a God of terrors,"
but gradually she cast off her "artificial awe," and in true
descendental-transcendental fashion associated " the glow
of health and exercise" with the effulgence of the divine
spirit.

I saw the eternal energy pervade
The boundless range of nature;
. . . Then I felt
That he who formed this goodly frame of things
Must needs be good . . .
Methinks it is not strange, then, that I fled
The house of prayer, and made the lonely grove
My temple.

Feeling herself a part of "this goodly frame of things,"
Joan has no conviction of sin. "Was it strange," she asks,

that when I felt
How God had made my spirit quick to feel
And love whate'er was beautiful and good,
And from aught evil and deformed to shrink
Even as with instinct — father! was it strange
That in my heart I had no thought of sin,
And did not need forgiveness?

The ecclesiastics are far from satisfied. The whole
queer business smacks of witchcraft. Was it true that she
had taken part in certain ungodly assemblies at a place
called the Fountain of the Fairies, near Domprein?
"There is," Joan readily admits,

> a fountain in the forest called
> The Fountain of the Fairies.

The spot, folk say, is visited at midnight by elves who
leave their circles on the sward. As a child Joan heard
these tales "with a delightful wonder." When she grew
older "the strange and fearful pleasure" which she took
in visiting the fountain did not disappear, but gave place
to

> Deeper delight and more mysterious awe.
> A blessed spot! Oh, how my soul enjoyed
> Its holy quietness! with what delight,
> Escaping from mankind, I hastened there
> To solitude and freedom!

The fountain is more than a refuge from the trammels of
civilization and the terrors of the Church. It provides
mystical contact with the God of nature:

> On a rock I sat;
> The glory of the tempest filled my soul,
> And when the thunders pealed, and the long flash
> Hung durable in heaven, and on my sight
> Spread the gray forest, memory, thought were gone;
> All sense of self annihilate, I seemed
> Diffused into the scene.

It is interesting to observe that, although at the time
when he wrote this poem Southey could not have been
influenced by Wordsworth, Joan's religion is not only
Wordsworthian but develops in a rather Wordsworthian
manner. Wholesome exercise in beautiful surroundings;
pleasantly scarey thrills; a bit of pagan superstition; a
sense of escape to quietness; "deeper delight and more
mysterious awe;" mystic communion with the supernatural in nature — the parallel is suggestive.

As I said a moment ago, the more or less pantheistic
religion of the Lake poets gradually loses its intensity
and settles down into an edifying but not very interesting
orthodoxy. Coleridge then looks askance at the theological implications of his old friend's poetry:

The word Nature, from its extreme familiarity, and in some
instances, fitness, as well as from the want of a term, or *other*
name, for God, has caused very much confusion in the thought and
language of men. Hence a Nature-God, or God-Nature, not God
in Nature.

But Wordsworth himself was soon free from any suspicion of heresy. In *The Excursion* one can plainly observe the transition from the old nature cult to a state of
mind in which natural objects are merely incitements to
piety. Eventually be becomes a bulwark of the Church
of England.

Coleridge and Wordsworth, in their orthodox and
conservative days, regard nature chiefly as a temple in
which God may be worshiped when no regular service of
the Established Church is in progress. They sometimes,
as in two examples which are to be given, describe nature in ecclesiastical terms, as if they felt an impulse to
sprinkle holy water on the scenes of their earlier pantheism. The following lines from Coleridge's *To Nature*,
written probably in 1820, suggest that the poet regards
such worship as a beneficent exercise of the imagination:

> It may indeed be phantasy, when I
> Essay to draw from all created things
> Deep, heartfelt, inward joy that closely clings;
>
> . . . .
>
> So let it be; and if the wide world rings
> In mock of this belief, it brings

No fear, nor grief, nor vain perplexity.
So will I build my altar in the fields,
And the blue sky my fretted dome shall be,
And the sweet fragrance that the wild flower yields
Shall be the incense I will yield to Thee,
Thee only God! and thou shalt not despise
Even me, the priest of this poor sacrifice.

A similar conception of the worship of God through,
rather than in, nature appears in Wordsworth's *Devotional Incitements* (1832). He combines the theme with
a soothingly conservative message. This sort of religion
is wholesome for the poor man. It places his labor among
nature's offerings to God, and encourages industry, regularity, and obedience:

Kind Nature keeps a heavenly door
Wide open for the scattered poor.
Where flower-breathed incense to the skies
Is wafted in mute harmonies;
And ground fresh cloven for the plough
Is fragrant with an humbler vow;
Where birds and brooks from leafy dells
Chime forth unwearied canticles,
And vapours magnify and spread
The glory of the sun's bright head —
Still constant in her worship, still
Conforming to the eternal Will.

We have, then, first deistic separation of God from nature; then romantic interfusion of God and nature; then
a more orthodox distinction between a God and a nature
which are nevertheless on close and friendly terms.

Our attitude toward the religion of nature will depend
upon our personal religious ideas. Many will regard it

as an unalloyed blessing to mankind. Without attacking this viewpoint I shall merely remind you that the spiritual distress aroused by evolutionary science in the Victorian era and in our own day is partly the result of this religion. Though only a few romanticists, and these only for a short time, approached actual pantheism, the general effect of romantic naturalism was to inculcate a vaguely religious attitude in which "Nature" and "God" were more or less interchangeable terms. Hence nineteenth century science, by making it difficult to believe in the romantic conception of nature, made it difficult for many persons to believe in God, and plunged them either into the depths of despair or into the still lower depths of intellectual dishonesty. In this sense, *Tintern Abbey* predicts Tennyson's agonized question, "Are God and Nature then at strife?"

XI

AT LENGTH THE MAN PERCEIVES IT DIE AWAY

The Lake poets gradually cease to find in nature the guide of all their moral being. This change, sympathetically regarded, is rather tragic. Somewhere in his letters Coleridge tells how he and his children went out one day and shouted "Dr. Dodd!" in order to enjoy the echo. At first I failed to understand why the name of a famous forger of Dr. Johnson's time should have been chosen for this purpose; but remembering the childish custom of shouting "Board of Health" in order that the echo may say something that sounds like "Go to Hell," I decided that Coleridge shouted "Dr. Dodd" in order that the echo might say something that sounded like "God." This may stand as a symbol of romantic naturalism. It was not long before the Lakists perceived that the tones of the echo had originated in their own vocal chords; and this discovery, while it could be interpreted in a way flattering to their imaginative powers, diminished their sense of the objective significance of nature.

Here is perhaps the best place to offer the unorthodox thesis that Wordsworth began to lose his spontaneous enjoyment of nature almost as soon as he knew its value, and that his philosophy is in part a subconscious attempt to find a compensation for that loss. This idea does not conflict with what has been said heretofore. Wordsworth's philosophy of nature was sincere, and it gave him deep spiritual satisfaction. I would merely suggest that this philosophy is tinged with an anxious and defensive element, as if he hoped by means of it to preserve something even more precious that was slipping from his grasp. He so frequently says that he is glad that he does not feel toward nature as he did in his youth; then almost in the same breath says wistfully that he *does* feel *almost* as he did in his youth; then in the next breath, or the next poem, says that he hopes he will die if he ever *stops* feeling as he did in his youth.

In *Tintern Abbey*, for example, Wordsworth distinguishes the stages in his attitude toward nature up to 1798, when the poem was written. Brushing aside "the coarser pleasures of my boyish days, and their glad animal movements," he tells how he felt when, a youth of twenty-three, he visited this spot five years before:

> I cannot paint
> What then I was. The sounding cataract
> Haunted me like a passion: the tall rock,
> The mountain, and the deep and gloomy wood,
> Their colours and their forms, were then to me
> An appetite; a feeling and a love,
> That had no need of a remoter charm,
> By thought supplied, nor any interest
> Unborrowed from the eye. — That time is past,
> And all its aching joys are now no more,
> And all its dizzy raptures. Not for this
> Faint I, nor mourn nor murmur; other gifts
> Have followed; for such loss, I would believe,
> Abundant recompense.

Then comes the great passage which was quoted in the preceding lecture, expressing the poet's mature attitude toward nature — one of more or less mystical pantheism.

But if Wordsworth were completely resigned to the loss of the old aching joys and dizzy raptures, would he now turn to his sister and ask her to keep alive before him his own earlier feelings?

> Oh! yet a little while
> May I behold in thee what I was once,
> My dear, dear Sister! and this prayer I make,
> Knowing that Nature never did betray
> The heart that loved her . . .
> Therefore let the moon
> Shine on thee in thy solitary walk;
> And let the misty mountain-winds be free
> To blow against thee: and, in after years,
> When these wild ecstasies shall be matured
> Into a sober pleasure; . . .
> Oh! then,
> If solitude, or fear, or pain, or grief,
> Should be thy portion, with what healing thoughts
> Of tender joy wilt thou remember me,
> And these my exhortations!

The time will come, says Wordsworth, when Dorothy will have the complete philosophy of nature; but he hopes that the substitution of sober pleasure for wild ecstasies will not be unduly hastened. "She gave me eyes, she gave me ears." He knows that she has the sensuousness indispensible to poetry, and he trusts that she may keep it "yet a little while" as a living reminder of what he "was once." We recall the almost desperate "or let me die" of *My heart leaps up*.

The *Ode on Intimations of Immortality*, which uses the last three lines of *My heart leaps up* as a heading or motto, definitely expresses Wordsworth's tragedy:

There was a time when meadow, grove and stream,
The earth, and every common sight,
        To me did seem
        Apparelled in celestial light,
The glory and the freshness of a dream.
It is not now as it hath been of yore; —
        Turn wheresoe'er I may,
        By night or day,
The things which I have seen I now can see no more.

        The Rainbow comes and goes,
        And lovely is the Rose,
        The Moon doth with delight
Look round her when the heavens are bare,
        Waters on a starry night
        Are beautiful and fair;
The sunshine is a glorious birth;
        But yet I know, where'er I go,
That there hath passed away a glory from the earth.
            .   .   .   .
Whither is fled the visionary gleam?
Where is it now, the glory and the dream?

This is not merely Wordsworth's tragedy, but mankind's:

Heaven lies about us in our infancy!
Shades of the prison-house begin to close
        Upon the growing Boy,
But He beholds the light, and whence it flows,
        He sees it in his joy;
The Youth, who daily farther from the east
        Must travel, still is Nature's Priest,
        And by the vision splendid
        Is on his way attended;
At length the Man perceives it die away,
And fade into the light of common day.

In the three stanzas which were added when the ode was taken up and finished in 1806, he asserts that the richness of human experience makes up for what has been lost; that nature, if no longer so exciting, has become more deeply significant. Yet his real consolation, after all, is that there are times when wisdom is unnecessary, times when the youthful mood comes back in all its freshness.

Wordsworth was always to catch an occasional flicker of the visionary gleam. The last stanza of a poem of 1818, *Composed upon an Evening of Extraordinary Splendour and Beauty*, is pathetically reminiscent of the *Immortality Ode*. The poet recognizes that the light is fading, and no longer tries to find a philosophical consolation for what he has lost:

> Such hues from their celestial Urn
> Were wont to stream before mine eye,
> Whene'er it wandered in the morn
> Of blissful infancy.
> This glimpse of glory, why renewed?
> Nay, rather speak with gratitude;
> For if a vestige of those gleams
> Survived, 'twas only in my dreams.
> Dread Power! whom peace and calmness serve
> No less than Nature's threatening voice,
> If aught unworthy be my choice,
> From THEE if I would swerve;
> Oh, let thy grace remind me of the light
> Full early lost, and fruitlessly deplored;
> Which at this moment, on my waking sight
> Appears to shine, by miracle restored;
> My soul, though yet confined to earth,
> Rejoices in a second birth!

— 'Tis past, the visionary splendour fades,
And night approaches with her shades.

We have Crabb Robinson's authority for the statement that although Wordsworth was not buried until 1850, he died in 1814, the year of *The Excursion*. By 1806, indeed, he had written most of his really great poems. If we removed from Wordsworth's collected works the hundreds of poems composed after about 1806, his reputation as one of the four or five greatest English poets would be undiminished; while if we removed every poem written between 1797 and 1806, we should have a versifier of ethical platitudes who sometimes surprises us with a fine poem.

Wordsworth rapidly lost that sensuousness which is the basis of all poetry; he lost the capacity to rejoice in sensations of sight and sound and smell and touch and taste for their own sake. His mind always had a strong hortatory tendency; and an almost Miltonian sense of the loftiness of his poetic mission gave him a bardic self-consciousness, an impulse to take the reader by the buttonhole and impart a message. In the poems of the great 1797-1806 period, his sensuousness and his didacticism are harmonized in that union of feeling and thinking which constitutes the best poetry. But the equilibrium is of short duration: didacticism soon gets the upper hand. The images in his later poems are seldom derived from genuine sense impressions. The objects of nature which he now writes *about* are not enjoyed as real things, but are merely symbols consciously chosen to sugar-coat some ethical pill.

They fade,
The mist and the river, the hill and the shade:

> The stream will not flow, and the hill will not rise,
> And the colours have all passed away from her eyes!

This means the death of poetry. In 1798, Wordsworth
had reproached Peter Bell because

> A primrose by a river's brim
> A yellow primrose was to him,
> And it was nothing more.

Up to about 1806, Wordsworth wrote about real primroses that were also something more. After that his
primroses continued to be something more, but they gradually ceased to be primroses.

Wordsworth knew what was happening to him better
than anyone else. He wrote *To a Skylark* in 1805, when
he was fully aware of the coming change. Up he soars
with the lark; but soon, conscious of a different destiny,
drops back to earth:

> Up with me! up with me into the clouds!
>   For thy song, lark, is strong!
> Up with me, up with me, into the clouds!
>   Singing, singing,
> With clouds and sky about thee ringing,
>   Lift me, guide me, till I find
> The spot which seems so to thy mind!
>
>   .   .   .   .
>
> Happy, happy liver,
> With a heart as strong as a mountain river
> Pouring out praise to the almighty Giver,
> Joy and jollity be with us both!

Then observe how the metre changes with the mood:

Alas! my journey, rugged and uneven,
Through prickly moors or dusty ways must wind;
But hearing thee, or others of thy kind,
As full of gladness and as free of heaven,
I, with my fate contented, will plod on,
And hope for higher raptures, when life's day is done.

This recalls some verses by our own child poet, Hilda Conkling. One day she met a butterfly.

It said a small word, "Follow."
"I cannot follow," I told him;
"I have to go the opposite way."

Wordsworth knew that he had to go the opposite way from the skylark, as Hilda from the butterfly. His philosophy of nature is in part a compensation mechanism, a yearning bridge thrown out between what he has been and what he is to become. Surely he says this plainly enough in *The Prelude*:

Oh! mystery of man, from what a depth
Proceed thy honours. I am lost, but see
In simple childhood something of the base
On which thy greatness stands; but this I feel,
That from thyself it comes, that thou must give,
Else never canst receive. The days gone by
Return upon me almost from the dawn
Of life: the hiding-places of man's power
Open; I would approach them, but they close.
I see by glimpses now; when age comes on,
May scarcely see at all; and I would give,
While yet we may, as far as words can give,
Substance and life to what I see, enshrining,
Such is my hope, the spirit of the Past
For future restoration.

(XII, 272 ff.)

As "the hiding-places of man's power" recede further and further into the past, Wordsworth sometimes desperately feels that superstition would be preferable to insensibility. This familiar sonnet is a case in point:

> The world is too much with us; late and soon,
> Getting and spending, we lay waste our powers:
> Little we see in Nature that is ours;
> We have given our lives away, a sordid boon!
> This Sea that bares her bosom to the moon;
> The winds that will be howling at all ours,
> And are up-gathered now like sleeping flowers;
> For this, for everything, we are out of tune;
> It moves us not. — Great God! I'd rather be
> A pagan suckled in a creed outworn;
> So might I, standing on this pleasant lea,
> Have glimpses that would make me less forlorn;
> Have sight of Proteus rising from the sea;
> Or hear old Triton blow his wreathed horn.

And in *The Excursion* the Wanderer exclaims:

> Life's autumn past, I stand on winter's verge;
> And daily lose what I desire to keep;
> Yet rather would I instantly decline
> To the traditionary sympathies
> Of a most rustic ignorance, and take
> A fearful apprehension from the owl
> Or death-watch: and as readily rejoice,
> If two auspicious magpies crossed my way; —
> To this would rather bend than see and hear
> The repetitions wearisome of sense,
> Where soul is dead, and feeling hath no place.
>
> (IV, 611 ff.)

But of course no real remedy lies in this direction. Though romanticism may sometimes feel a lurking sympathy with superstition, it cannot recognize the full strength of the bond without surrendering the loftiness of its illusions.

The exact reasons for the decay of Wordsworth's poetic sensuousness are hidden from us. We can point, however, to factors which doubtless contributed to it. Marriage to an estimable but not very exciting woman who bore him five children between 1803 and 1810 had a quieting effect, and blunted the old keen stimulus of association with his sister. For him who had spoken of poetry as "emotion recollected in tranquility," there was less and less emotion, and more and more tranquility — not the deep tranquility that lets us "see into the heart of life," but the insensitive tranquility of the world that "is too much with us." The disturbances which ruffled this uninspiring peace and quiet were not of the sort that would draw him closer to nature. In 1806, an estrangement arose between him and Coleridge, his partner in the creation of the naturalistic illusion. A personal tragedy played a still more important part: in 1804 his beloved brother John was drowned, and the blow crushed something within him.

Wordsworth's loss of the visionary gleam was accompanied by a growing conservatism. Though neither of these related developments was wholly the cause or the effect of the other, Wordsworth's illusioned view of nature was so closely bound up with an illusioned view of man that a cooling of his attitude toward man probably contributed to a cooling of his attitude toward nature. The growth of Wordsworth's conservatism also interfered with his spontaneous enjoyment of nature by encouraging his inherent didactic tendency. In a manner familiar to students of Victorian literature, he felt more and more the obligation to impart wholesome lessons to the public, forgetting that poetry instructs, if at all, through the contagion of beauty.

The change that came over Coleridge was somewhat different. He had always been more transcendental than Wordsworth. Actual things meant less to him: in his thought the creative imagination which gave significance to what it beheld was always more important than the objective world. As he becomes more and more deeply immersed in German philosophy, he recedes further and further from the concrete. By 1809, when he begins to publish *The Friend*, he is primarily a philosopher rather than a poet, and a philosopher to whom physical nature is not in itself particularly significant. Moreover, as we have seen, the religious conservatism which grows along with his transcendentalism makes him disapprove of nature worship. In a letter of August, 1820, he attacks Wordsworth's old idea of the benign influence of mountains upon mountaineers:

Whether mountains have any particular effect on the native inhabitants by virtue of being mountains exclusively, and what that effect is, would be a difficult problem. At least the influence acts indirectly only, as far as the mountains are the *causa causae*, or occasion of a pastoral life instead of an agricultural. . . . I will not conceal from you that this inferred dependence of the human soul on accidents of birthplace and abode, together with the vague, misty, rather than Mystic, confusion of God with the world, and the accompanying nature-worship of which the asserted dependence forms a part is the trait in Wordsworth's poetic works which I most dislike as unhealthy and denounce as contagious.

This is the man who had written *Frost at Midnight* and *This Lime-Tree Bower My Prison*. More will be said later about Coleridge's transcendentalism. At present it is enough to understand that his final philosophy implies the dominance of man's creative will over the material world. Since it now seems to him that the philosophy of nature subordinates mind to matter, he objects to any "inferred dependence of the human soul on accidents of birthplace and abode," even though the abode may be the Lake Country.

Unfortunately, by the time Coleridge came fully to believe in the dominance of man's creative will over the material world, his own creative will had temporarily lost its power to dominate anything, even the conduct of his own life. He had begun taking opium in the form of laudanum as early as 1797, and the habit grew on him until he was soon a slave of the drug. At first opium stimulated Coleridge's imagination, and some of the magical strangeness of *The Ancient Mariner*, *Kubla Khan*, and *Christabel* is traceable to it. Its ultimate effect, however, was to paralyze the creative faculty, and to leave the mind active but disorganized and sundered from the normal sources of its happiness in the external world.

The Pains of Sleep is a striking portrayal of the seamy side of opium taking, but the poem which shows most clearly how Coleridge becomes cut off from the inspiration of nature is *Dejection: an Ode*. The date of this poem, April 4, 1802, marks a definite stage in his career. What we now call the *reproductive* imagination — the ability to absorb sense impressions, retain them in the mind, and recall them to consciousness — was never displayed by Coleridge more strikingly than in this poem. Indeed, his perceptiveness, which can see the "peculiar tint of yellow green" in the sunset, is agonized and almost

pathological in its intensity. But he feels himself losing
that *inward* and *creative* imagination which alone can
give meaning to his perceptions. In 1798 he had ended
France: an Ode with the lines:

> Yes, while I stood and gazed, my temples bare,
> And shot my being through earth, sea, and air,
> Possessing all things with intensest love,
> O Liberty! my spirit felt thee there.

That power to shoot his being into nature and fill it with
liberty and love has now decayed. Tragically, it has decayed just at the time when his philosophical studies have
convinced him that this transcendental power is the most
important thing in the world, for objective nature has no
spiritual significance unless this power is brought to bear
upon it:

> A grief without a pang, void, dark, and drear,
> A stifled, drowsy, unimpassioned grief,
> Which finds no natural outlet, no relief,
> In word, or sigh, or tear —
> O Lady! in this wan and heartless mood,
> To other thoughts by yonder throstle wooed,
> All this long eve, so balmy and serene,
> Have I been gazing on the western sky,
> And its peculiar tint of yellow green:
> And still I gaze — and with how blank an eye!
> And those thin clouds above, in flakes and bars,
> That give away their motion to the stars;
> Those stars, that glide behind them or between,
> Now sparkling, now bedimmed, but always seen;
> Yon crescent Moon, as fixed as if it grew
> In its own cloudless, starless lake of blue;
> I see them all, so excellently fair,
> I see, not feel, how beautiful they are!

I may not hope from outward forms to win
The passion and the life, whose fountains are within.

O Lady! we receive but what we give,
And in our life alone does Nature live:
Ours is her wedding-garment, ours her shroud!
  And would we aught behold, of higher worth,
Than that inanimate cold world allowed
To the poor loveless ever-anxious crowd,
    Ah! from the soul itself must issue forth
A light, a glory, a fair luminous cloud
      Enveloping the Earth —
And from the soul itself must there be sent
    A sweet and potent voice, of its own birth,
Of all sweet sounds the life and element!

Nothing so interesting happened in the case of Robert Southey. He was a true-hearted, estimable gentleman and scholar, an accomplished writer of history and biography, a dependable editor and critic. Like many other bookish persons, he had creative hankerings and some creative ability as a youth. He grew up in stirring times, and he responded in poetry. But his excitement soon died down. All through his life he wrote reams of verse, much of it preserving an afterglow of the emotions that had moved him in earlier days. He was quite intelligent enough to know how poetry should sound, and quite skillful enough to manufacture a very fair imitation of the real thing. No one, however, would assert that after 1805 or thereabouts nature was to Southey more than a body of attractive material about which to make the proper romantic remarks. We need to remember that the romantic attitude can become quite as stereotyped and conventional as the pseudoclassic attitude. Indeed, one might make out a good case for saying that the "new poetry" of our own times is partly a rebellion against conventionalized romanticism, just as romantic poetry was partly a rebellion against conventionalized classicism.

Along with the decay of naturalistic enthusiasm in the Lake poets appears a growing conservatism in political, social, and religious matters. You will remember that these poets return to nature after passing through two disillusioning stages of radicalism: the first, one of revolutionary ardor; the second, one combining eighteenth century sensibility with the abstract and theoretical rationalism of Godwin. During their period of nature worship, or at least until toward the end of that period, they have more temperately liberal opinions without being active reformers. They believe that reform as the world understands the term is impracticable, and that it is better for men to bring their souls into contact with nature than to clamor for their rights. This attitude, though not in itself conservative, easily slips into conservatism. Meanwhile our poets are rather glad to be sheltered from the turmoil of actual affairs. In 1797, John Thelwall, the old Jacobin, came down from Wales to visit Coleridge at Nether Stowey. "Citizen John," teased Coleridge, "this is a fine place to talk treason in." "Nay, Citizen Samuel," answered Thelwall, "it is rather a place to make a man forget that there is any necessity for treason." The poems of this group sometimes sound a note of almost selfish satisfaction at being withdrawn from the hubbub of the world. From his retreat in the Lake Country, Wordsworth looks out at all the strife and confusion, saying:

But list! a voice is near;
Great Pan himself, low-whispering through the reeds,
"Be thankful, thou; for if unholy deeds
Ravage the world, tranquillity is here!"
(*Composed by the Side of Grasmere Lake*)

But this Lucretian detachment gives place to a renewed interest in events — an interest which becomes distinctly conservative. As I said in commenting on Coleridge's *Fears in Solitude*, that very love of nature which Wordsworth and Coleridge had once associated with love of liberty now becomes associated with nationalism of a more or less fundamentalist sort.

The reversal of the opinions of the Lakists can be explained in various ways. First of all, they grew up. In 1805, to take a date by which their turn toward conservatism is clearly marked, Wordsworth is thirty-five, Coleridge is thirty-three, and Southey is thirty-one. Though far from being graybeards, they are a little too old for us to expect them to retain all the ardors of youth. Then, too, as men of their time, they shared in the general conservative reaction which followed the French Revolution. You have already been reminded of how England was scared into a distrust of all forms of liberalism — a panic like that in our own country after the Bolshevist revolution. From 1793 to the collapse of Napoleon in 1814, moreover, England was almost continuously at war with France, and we know what a strong conservative influence can be exerted by a really good war. Napoleon was responsible for the transformation of many a young English Jacobin into a stout Tory. After he became First Consul of the French Republic in 1799, and more especially after he was crowned Emperor of the French in 1804, there was no longer a revolutionary France for a liberal Englishman to sympathize with. Under the Corsican, France was a constant menace to England, and Pitt's rôle changed from that of Judas to that of the noble defender of his country.

In 1803, Dorothy Wordsworth writes of William to her friend Mrs. Clarkson:

Surely there never was a more determined hater of the French, nor one more willing to do his utmost to destroy them if they really do come. . . . He wants all the people of England instructed in the use of arms.

In corroboration of this is a letter written to Sir George Beaumont in October of the same year by Wordsworth himself:

They are sadly remiss at Keswick in putting themselves to trouble in defence of the country. . . . At Grasmere, we have turned out almost to a man. We are to go to Ambleside on Sunday, to be mustered, and to put on, for the first time, our military apparel.

Thanks to Napoleon, the old days of killing white butterflies have returned. How well one knows that pride in the filling of the local quota, that scornful glance at a less patriotic community, that thrill of putting on, "for the first time," the uniform of one's country! "O pleasant exercise of hope and joy!"

Beginning at about this time, Wordsworth writes a large number of poems which might cause a hasty reader to suppose that he is a devoted advocate of freedom. See especially the section in the collected works entitled *Poems Dedicated to National Independence and Liberty.* But upon more careful inspection it becomes evident that Wordsworth is merely championing the freedom of small nations which, if aroused, might make trouble for Napo-

leon. Once Napoleon falls, Wordsworth becomes a supporter of the Holy Alliance, in which the love of liberty
is anything but a master passion. We need not impute
conscious dishonesty to Wordsworth or to any of the
Lakists. They were the sincere and well meaning victims
of that self-deception which becomes a virtue during and
just after a great war. At such times, there is no longer
any truth to be spoken: there are only certain useful
things that a patriot must say. No one who did his bit to
make the world safe for democracy should hasten to condemn these poets.

When I said that the Lakists grew up, I should have
added that they became respectable. They were married
and had families; they went into society and met nice
rich powerful people. They ate better, dressed better,
and learned to be polite to bores. The critics gradually
ceased abusing them, so that by the time they had become
almost wholly negligible as artists, they were generally
admired and respected. This gave them a ruinous sense
of responsibility to the nation, a feeling that they should
be sound and wholesome in their sentiments. Southey
became poet laureate in 1813, and Wordsworth succeeded
him on his death in 1843. But long before this honor came
to him Wordsworth had been a semi-official bard. He was
appointed stamp distributor for Westmoreland in 1813,
and received a state pension in 1842.

The factors contributing to Wordsworth's loss of
poetic sensuousness contributed equally to his conservatism. The death of his brother is reflected in *Elegiac
Stanzas Suggested by a Picture of Peele Castle* (1805).
Since the painting includes a ship tossing in a storm, it
naturally suggests to him the tragedy of the preceding

year. In earlier days, he says, he could have painted in
verse a beautiful picture of this scene:

> Ah! then, if mine had been the painter's hand,
> To express what then I saw; and add the gleam,
> The light that never was, on sea or land,
> The consecration, and the poet's dream;
>
> I would have painted thee, thou hoary pile,
> Amid a world how different from this!
> Beside a sea that would not cease to smile;
> On tranquil land, beneath a sky of bliss.
>
> .   .   .   .
>
> Such, in the fond illusion of my heart,
> Such picture would I at that time have made:
> And seen the soul of truth in every part,
> A steadfast peace that might not be betrayed.
>
> So once it would have been, — 'tis now no more;
> I have submitted to a new control:
> A power is gone, which nothing can restore;
> A deep distress hath humanised my soul.
>
> Not for a moment could I now behold
> A smiling sea, and be what I have been:
> The feeling of my loss will ne'er be old;
> This, which I know, I speak with mind serene.

This poem resembles *Dejection* in the idea that the
poet has lost the power to impose significance on what
he beholds. It differs from Coleridge's ode, however, in an
essential respect. Whereas Coleridge at present can see no
remedy for the loss of his "shaping spirit of imagination,"
Wordsworth seems determined to make his sorrow a
source of spiritual discipline. This "deep distress" has

"humanised his soul"; his mind is "serene"; he has "submitted to a new control."

Wordsworth had never been a lover of outright wildness; he had always appreciated the importance of discipline and restraint. At the height of his naturalistic enthusiasm, however, he felt that nature herself had power to discipline the human spirit. In *Three years she grew*, Nature says of her relations with Lucy:

> Myself will to my darling be
> Both law and impulse; and with me
> The girl, in rock and plain,
> In earth and heaven, in glade and bower,
> Shall feel an overseeing power
> To kindle or restrain.

But Wordsworth gradually comes to believe that one looks to nature in vain for the necessary law and restraint. A poem of 1845, *The Westmoreland Girl*, shows how differently he feels in his old age. The Westmoreland girl bears all the earmarks of the Lucy type. The first part of the poem describes her rearing among the mountains and relates an incident in which she rescues a lamb from a flooded stream. But in the second part of the poem Wordsworth insists that so promising a child should not be

> Left among her native mountains
> With wild Nature to run wild.
>
> .   .   .   .
>
> What then wants the child to temper,
> In her breast, unruly fire,
> To control the froward impulse,
> And restrain the vague desire?

> Easily a pious training
> And a steadfast outward power
> Would supplant the weeds, and cherish
> In their stead each opening flower.

So in the end Lucy is to be sent to Sunday School, for nature seems better at kindling than at restraining.

A symptom of this change is the sonnet beginning *Nuns fret not at their convent's narrow room*. It was published in 1807. We do not know when it was written, but Wordsworth began to cultivate the sonnet in 1802. One might guess that it was written in 1805, the year of the *Peele Castle* stanzas, for it uses the restrictions of the sonnet form to symbolize the "new control" to which Wordsworth has submitted:

> Nuns fret not at their convent's narrow room;
> And hermits are contented with their cells;
> And students with their pensive citadels;
> Maids at the wheel, the weaver at his loom,
> Sit blithe and happy; bees that soar for bloom,
> High as the highest peak of Furness-fells,
> Will murmur by the hour in foxglove bells;
> In truth, the prison unto which we doom
> Ourselves, no prison is; and hence for me,
> In sundry moods, 'twas pastime to be bound
> Within the sonnet's scanty plot of ground;
> Pleased if some souls (for such there needs must be)
> Who have felt the weight of too much liberty,
> Should find brief solace there, as I have found.

It should be noted that from about 1802 to about 1807, just when Wordsworth begins poignantly to feel that his joy in nature must pass away, he has an opportunity to become a great poet, not of the exuberance of nature, but of the discipline of moral and religious law. One sees clear hints of this possibility in the austere stoicism of *Michael* (1800), that most classical of romantic poems, in the sonnet *Nuns fret not*, and in *Character of the Happy Warrior* (1806). But the clearest explanation of what he means by saying in *Peele Castle* that he has "submitted to a new control" is the *Ode to Duty* (1805). This is the key passage:

> I, loving freedom and untried,
> No sport of every random gust,
> Yet being to myself a guide,
> Too blindly have reposed my trust:
> And oft, when in my heart was heard
> Thy timely mandate, I deferred
> The task, in smoother walks to stray;
> But thee I now would serve more strictly, if I may.
>
> Through no disturbance of my soul,
> Or strong compunction in me wrought,
> I supplicate for thy control;
> But in the quietness of thought:
> Me this uncharted freedom tires;
> I feel the weight of chance desires:
> My hopes no more must change their name,
> I long for a repose that ever is the same.

The same note of triumphing over life by submitting to its laws is sounded at intervals as late as 1814, when — not to mention *The Excursion*, in which it is blurred by other themes — he speaks in *Laodamia* of "calm pleasures" and "majestic pains," and makes Protesilaus declare that

> the Gods approve
> The depth, and not the tumult, of the soul.

Some students would trace this Matthew Arnold-like quality on into Wordsworth's later work. Where to draw the line between a nobly stoical philosophy of control and a reactionary and obscurantist conservatism depends on the temperament of the individual student. It seems to me that after about 1814 Wordsworth is definitely on the wrong side of that line. A brief but magnificent struggle to preserve a balance between romantic naturalism and a more or less stoically Christian humanism ends in his becoming soundly, stuffily, Anglican and Tory. He opposes the abolition of the Test and Corporation Acts, extension of the franchise, and most of the other liberal measures of his day. In 1821 he writes to Lord Lonsdale:

When I was young . . . I thought it derogatory to human nature to set up property in preference to person, as a title to legislative power. That notion has now vanished. I now perceive many advantages in our present complex system of representation, which formerly eluded my observation.

He also perceived many advantages in placing on the freedom of the press heavy restrictions which had eluded his observation in the days when he wished to found a journal called *The Philanthropist*. Wordsworth's religious conservatism was noted in the preceding lecture. Professor Harper believes that his final acceptance of Anglican orthodoxy was motivated rather largely by the feeling that it was a civic duty to adhere to the Established Church. The parts of the *Ecclesiastical Sonnets* which relate to Henry VIII and the Reformation are certainly a tragic example of Wordsworth's downfall. An even more tragic example, however, occurs in his *Postscript* to the collected edition of 1835. Here he quotes the beautiful passage from the yet unpublished *Prelude* describing his intention to devote his verse to the lives of those who live close to nature, and solemnly says of it:

The passage is extracted from my MSS. written above thirty years ago: it turns upon the individual dignity which humbleness of social condition does not preclude, but frequently promotes. It has no direct bearing upon clubs for the discussion of social affairs, nor upon political or trade-unions; but if a single workman — who, being a member of one of those clubs, runs the risk of becoming an agitator, or who, being enrolled in a union, must be left without a will of his own, and therefore a slave — should read these lines, and be touched by them, I should indeed rejoice, and little would I care for losing credit as a poet with intemperate critics who think differently from me upon political philosophy or public measures, if the sober-minded admit that, in general views, my affections have been moved, and my imagination exercised, under and *for* the guidance of reason.

Now that *The Prelude* has become a weapon against debating clubs and labor unions, we may glance more briefly at Coleridge. An important factor in his turn toward conservatism was his romantic love of tradition — the quality that we noticed in Edmund Burke. Coleridge had to an eminent degree the feeling that old customs are beautiful and worthy of being preserved, that old ideas are venerable and precious, that old superstitions probably contain much truth. When revolutionary enthusiasm had passed away and Napoleon was threatening to invade England, this Burkian romanticism was strongly stimulated. By 1802, Coleridge was a completely pro-Pitt and anti-Bonaparte patriot and a violent foe of English Jacobinism. This peril he saw everywhere: in 1809 he even opposed as a Jacobin measure a bill for the prevention of cruelty to animals. His fear of foes without

and within the nation caused him to enlist his transcendental philosophy in the service of the Tory party and the
Church of England, so that the British constitution became
first cousin to the categorical imperative, and the Establishment first cousin to the absolute.

Coleridge's path to respectability was less straight and
smooth than Wordsworth's. It was broken by the ups and
downs of opium taking, his estrangement from his wife
in 1804, his sojourn in Malta during the next two years,
his journalistic ventures, and his lecturing. Although he
had been on the side of the angels at least since 1802, it
was not until 1816, when he went to live with the Gillmans at Highgate, that he could settle down in real peace
and dignity as a prophet of transcendental Toryism. The
details of the intervening years are complex, and I must
ask you to dig them out for yourselves.

I shall, however, relate one incident illustrating the
embarrassments which are likely to beset such a convert
as Coleridge. In 1803, he attended a gathering of right
thinking authors and gentlemen. On this occasion Sir
Walter Scott recited from memory a poem whose sentiments he totally disapproved but whose vivid imagery
and powerful rhythm he could not help admiring. The
poem was entitled *Fire, Famine, and Slaughter*, and it
breathed the most savage hatred of William Pitt. Of
those present, only Sir Humphry Davy knew that Coleridge himself had written the poem seven years before.
Coleridge knew that Davy knew. The other guests, less
broad-minded than Scott, were shocked by this wild scream
of radicalism, and abused it strongly. Davy, very uncomfortable, kept his secret. The much more uncomfortable
author launched into a long, metaphysical, hypothetical

defense of the anonymous poet, which curious document you may read in the *Apologetic Preface to "Fire, Famine and Slaughter"* (1817). But as the company still refused to forgive the unknown Jacobin, at last Coleridge exclaimed to Scott:

> I must now confess, sir! that I am the author of that poem. It was written some years ago. I do not attempt to justify my past self, young as I then was; but as little as I would now write a similar poem, so far was I even then from imagining that the lines would be taken as more or less than a sport of fancy. At all events, if I know my own heart, there never was a moment in my existence in which I should have been more ready, had Mr. Pitt's person been in hazard, to interpose my own body, and defend his life at the risk of my own.

If you can credit this after reading *Fire, Famine and Slaughter* together with the bitter sonnet against Pitt which was quoted a few days ago, your credulity is greater than mine. I can manage to believe that Coleridge thought he was telling the truth in 1803, but I cannot believe that he did not loathe William Pitt in 1796. It is somewhat easier to believe that he would have confessed if Sir Humphry Davy had not been present.

Robert Southey was born to become conservative, and he simply went through the normal course of his development. Beginning in 1808, he was a regular contributor to the Tory *Quarterly Review* — writing, for example, against the freedom of the press and in favor of a seditious libel law. In 1813 the laurel crowned his brow. It is impossible to compare the fulsome loyalty of *A Vision of Judgment* with the radical ardor of early work like *Joan of Arc* without feeling that Southey departed far indeed from the principles of his youth.

Students, however, have been too prone to regard the conservatism of these writers in the light of attacks made upon them by the younger generation of romantic radicals. The Lakists were not bribe-taking turncoats or unprincipled partisans of oppression. Factors in their personal lives and in their general environment caused them to turn from naturalistic romanticism to Burkian romanticism, with its almost mystical conception of the state as the sacred flower of an august tradition. They were as dissatisfied with present conditions as the most urgent of the reformers, but they saw in the reform movement a continuation of the eighteenth century radical spirit which they had come to detest. It was rationalistic, utilitarian, secular, and democratic; while their thought was anti-intellectualistic, idealistic, ecclesiastical, and feudal. Necessarily, therefore, Wordsworth, Coleridge, and Southey found themselves opposed to almost every change proposed by the liberal reformers, and were forced into an obstructionism which thwarted their earnest desire to benefit mankind. It must also be granted that they rather ignobly feared the ideas which they opposed, and too eagerly advocated their suppression by official methods.

They believed in a very close connection between church and state, and in as much education for the poor as would give them wholesome and loyal ideas. The division of society into ranks and classes seemed to them a part of the divinely constituted order of things. But hatred of the low for the high, and callous indifference of the high for the low, were alike sinful. The remedy was an abandonment of the evil spirit of competition engendered by democracy, and a return to the genial coöperative spirit of feudalisism, in which everyone proudly knew his place and labored toward the ideal of a state that was a kind of *civitas Dei*. They advocated, therefore, an enlightened paternalism on the part of the upper classes, and a cheerful filial trust on the part of the lower.

The Lakists were so imperfectly understood by most of their contemporaries that they were never wholly comfortable even in the Tory camp, which was the only home they could find. But their thought, for better or worse, was not without influence. Their union of desire for social betterment with keen distrust of democracy, their preference of coöperation to competition, and their emphasis on emotional and imponderable factors in the social sciences enter deeply into Victorian thought. In varying proportions and combinations, their ideas are discernible in Carlyle and Ruskin, in the Oxford Movement, and in the Christian Socialism of F. D. Maurice. Recently, on reading *Coningsby* for the first time, I was struck by Disraeli's evident sympathy with this type of conservative thought. "I wish," declares the hero, "to see a people full of faith, and a government full of duty." "England," Sidonia observes, "is governed by Downing Street; once it was governed by Alfred and Elizabeth." Those remarks perfectly represent the spirit of Wordsworth, Coleridge and Southey after they became romantic Tories.

Since the Lakists inherited from their master, Burke, a distrust of abstract political and social theories, they were able to prick several *a priori* bubbles of reform in a shrewd and profitable way. But their realism was more limited than Burke's, and even more completely motivated by a very non-realistic desire to preserve certain traditional sentiments in the face of inevitable change. Hence they carried into political theory that mixture of hard fact and soft dream which is inherent in romanticism. The value of their contribution to the anti-utilitarian and anti-liberal strain in Victorian social thought must therefore depend upon our attitude toward romanticism, and cannot be stated in objective terms. Limitations of time have forced me to generalize about the conservatism of the Lakists without distinguishing the special views of each member of the group. For more specific information on these matters I must refer you to Alfred Cobban's *Edmund Burke and the Revolt against the Eighteenth Century. A Study of the Political and Social Thinking of Burke, Wordsworth, Coleridge, and Southey.* Mr. Cobban says perhaps a little more than everything that can be said in behalf of the Lake poets. For Southey, by far the most open-minded, practical, and constructive of the group, see also an article by William Haller entitled "Southey's Later Radicalism" (*Publications of the Modern Language Association of America*, Vol. XXXVII, pp. 281-292).

XII

THE YOUNGER GENERATION

Just as our three poets became comfortably respectable, Byron, Shelley, Hazlitt, Leigh Hunt and others began to attack them as turncoats. William Smith arose in the House of Commons with Southey's *Wat Tyler* in his hand as evidence of the earlier opinions of the laureate. Coleridge's Toryism was similarly contrasted with his former radicalism. The bitterness of liberal youth against the supposedly apostate Wordsworth lasted long enough to impel Robert Browning to burst out with "Just for a handful of silver he left us" — an absurdly unjust account of the matter which Browning was later to regret.

Although the fall of Napoleon made the forces of conservatism feel that the world was completely in their power, it also removed the lid from a cauldron of liberal sentiment which had been seething restlessly for several years. Wordsworth, Coleridge, and Southey, having been born early enough to respond directly to the French Revolution, had experienced for themselves the causes of the subsequent conservative reaction. The younger men who now arose to reproach them were mere children during the Revolution, and grew up during the conservative reaction. They breathed an anti-liberal atmosphere without understanding why, and when they came to maturity they began asking questions which older folk supposed had been answered in the 1790's.

What has just been said does not literally apply to

William Hazlitt, the oldest of the post-1814 liberal romanticists, for he was born as early as 1778. Though he was but a lad during the Revolution, his father was a friend of Joseph Priestley, and inculcated the boy with real enthusiasm for democratic principles. In 1795, moreover, the future essayist was an admirer of Joseph Fawcett, the original of Wordsworth's Solitary. But Hazlitt was the sort of man who, once having formed an opinion, sticks to it forever. All his life he was a consistent liberal. In one of the *Round Table* papers he writes, "A person who forgets all the sentiments and principles to which he was most attached at nineteen, can have no sentiments ever after *worth* being attached to." Here he is glancing at Southey, who had declared, "I am no more ashamed of having been a republican than I am ashamed of having been a boy."

As for the other writers who arise to accuse the Lakists, Leigh Hunt was born in 1784, Byron in 1788, and Shelley in 1792. When Southey met Shelley in 1812, the elder poet wrote:

Here is a man at Keswick who acts upon me as my own ghost would do. He is just what I was in 1794.

From now on the Lakists are to be haunted by these ghosts of their own ardent youth.

The political and social controversies of this period enlisted almost all the important writers and had many points of contact both with creative literature and with criticism. Learn to know the *Edinburgh Review's* curious mixture of literary conservatism and political liberalism, the *Quarterly Review's* defense of conservative standards in both literature and politics, and the lively, extravagant, antiliberal scurrility of *Blackwood's Magazine*. Familiarize yourselves with Leigh Hunt's stormy experiences as editor of the *Examiner* and other liberal papers of which Hazlitt was a principal supporter and contributor. Do not neglect the abortive attempt of Byron, Shelley, and Leigh Hunt to publish a magazine called *The Liberal*. All this I must leave to you in order to say something about the radicalism of Byron and Shelley as reflected in their poetry.

I have earlier quoted a thrust at the Lakists from the first canto of *Don Juan*. You may remember that the whole poem is ironically dedicated to Southey, with incidental compliments to his friends:

> Bob Southey! You're a poet — Poet-laureate,
>   And representative of all the race,
> Although 'tis true that you've turned out a Tory at
>   Last, — yours has lately been a common case, —
> And now, my epic renegade, what are ye at?
>   With all the Lakers, in and out of place?
> A nest of tuneful persons, to my eye,
> Like "four and twenty Blackbirds in a pye;
>
> "Which pye being opened they began to sing"
>   (This old song and new simile holds good),
> "A dainty dish to set before the King,"
>   Or Regent, who admires such kind of food; —
> And Coleridge, too, has lately taken wing,
>   But like a hawk encumbered with his hood, —
> Explaining metaphysics to the nation —
> I wish he would explain his Explanation.
>
>   . . . .
>
> You — Gentlemen! by dint of long seclusion
>   From better company, have kept your own

At Keswick, and, through still continued fusion
  Of one another's minds, at last have grown
To deem as a most logical conclusion,
  That Poesy has wreaths for you alone:
There is a narrowness in such a notion,
Which makes me wish you'd change your lakes for ocean.

I would not imitate the petty thought,
  Nor coin my self-love to so base a vice,
For all the glory your conversion brought,
  Since gold alone should not have been its price.
You have your salary; was't for that you wrought?
  And Wordsworth has his place in the Excise.
You're shabby fellows — true — but poets still,
And duly seated on the immortal hill.

                . . . .

Meantime — Sir Laureate — I proceed to dedicate
  In honest simple verse, this song to you.
And, if in flattering strains I do not predicate,
  'Tis that I still retain my "buff and blue;"
My politics as yet are all to educate:
  Apostasy's so fashionable, too,
To keep *one* creed's a task grown quite Herculean;
Is it not so, my Tory, ultra-Julian?

To appreciate the venemous last line one must know that
Southey had based an epic on the story of Julian the
Apostate. In the third stanza quoted, Byron's use of the
word "Gentlemen" is intended to be a severe stroke of
sarcasm. He dislikes the Lake poets not merely because
they are apostates, but because they are solemn, middle-
class, professional scribblers — emphatically not men of
the world. He retains the same snobbery that made Con-
greve pose before Voltaire as a person of quality rather
than a writer. This element in Byron's feeling against the

Wordsworth group is evident in the following lines from
Beppo:

> One hates an author that's *all author*, fellows
>   In foolscap uniforms turned up with ink,
> So very anxious, clever, fine, and jealous,
>   One don't know what to say to them, or think,
> Unless to puff them with a pair of bellows;
>   Of coxcombry's worst coxcombs e'en the pink
> Are preferable to these shreds of paper,
> These unquenched snuffings of the midnight taper.
>
> Of these same we see several, and of others,
>   Men of the world, who know the world like men,
> Scott, Rogers, Moore, and all the better brothers,
>   Who think of something else besides the pen;
> But for the children of the "mighty mother's,"
>   The would-be wits and can't-be gentlemen,
> I leave them to their daily "tea is ready,"
> Smug coterie, and literary lady.

In 1821, the year after the death of George III,
Southey as poet laureate had produced a poem entitled
The Vision of Judgment, portraying the rapturous enthusiasm with which the soul of the dead monarch is wel-
comed by the heavenly hosts. The poem was introduced
by a prefatory essay on *The Satanic School*, a diatribe,
with particular reference to Byron, against the immorality
of contemporary literature. The following year, Byron
published in *The Liberal* his own *Vision of Judgment*. In
this satire the soul of George III gets as far as the pearly
gates, but Satan follows and claims him as his own.

Michael, who is good-naturedly inclined to admit
George, demands witnesses in support of Satan's charges.
After the great anonymous eighteenth century pamphlet-

eer "Junius" has spoken, Southey appears and qualifies
as an expert witness:

> He had written praises of a regicide;
>   He had written praises of all kings whatever;
> He had written for republics far and wide,
>   And then against them bitterer than ever:
> For pantisocracy he once had cried
>   Aloud, a scheme less moral than 'twas clever;
> Then grew a hearty anti-jacobin —
> Had turned his coat — and would have turned his skin.
>
> He had sung against all battles, and again
>   In their high praise and glory; he had called
> Reviewing "the ungentle craft," and then
>   Become as base a critic as e'er crawled —
> Fed, paid, and pampered by the very men
>   By whom his muse and morals had been mauled:
> He had written much blank verse, and blanker prose,
> And more of both than anybody knows.

He then begins to read his *Vision of Judgment*, but the
disgusted angels throw him out. In the confusion George
creeps into heaven,

> And when the tumult dwindled to a calm,
> I left him practising the hundredth psalm.

The arraignment of George III in this poem is typical
of many satiric thrusts at kings, corrupt ministers and
social injustice throughout Byron's works. A more serious
and idealistic spirit appears in such poems as *The Prisoner
of Chillon*, with its introductory sonnet to liberty, "Eternal Spirit of the Chainless Mind." Noble praises of freedom are frequent in *Childe Harold*, from the fourth
canto of which I quote the following:

Can tyrants but by tyrants conquered be,
And freedom find no champion and no child
Such as Columbia saw arise when she
Sprung forth a Pallas, armed and undefiled?
Or must such minds be nourished in the wild,
Deep in the unpruned forest, 'midst the roar
Of cataracts, where nursing Nature smiled
On infant Washington? Has Earth no more
Such seeds within her breast, or Europe no such shore?

But France got drunk with blood to vomit crime,
And fatal have her Saturnalia been
To Freedom's cause, in every age and clime;
Because the deadly days which we have seen,
And vile Ambition, that built up between
Man and his hopes an adamantine wall,
And the base pageant last upon the scene,
Are grown the pretext for the eternal thrall
Which nips life's tree, and dooms man's worst — his second fall.

Yet, Freedom! yet thy banner, torn, but flying,
Streams like the thunder-storm *against* the wind;
Thy trumpet voice, though broken now and dying,
The loudest still the tempest leaves behind;
Thy tree hath lost its blossoms, and the rind,
Chopped by the axe, looks rough and little worth,
But the sap lasts, and still the seed we find
Sown deep, deep even in the bosom of the North;
So shall a better spring less bitter fruit bring forth.

These lines show that George Washington was the child of nature as well as the father of his country. More importantly, they represent the post-Waterloo liberal attitude toward the French Revolution. The excesses of the Revolution have hurt the great cause by encouraging the suppression of liberty as well as of license; but the ideal of freedom exists, and eventually it will prevail over tyranny. Notice the resemblance in symbolism between the concluding lines of this passage and those of Shelley's *Ode to the West Wind*.

When Byron orates about liberty, it is sometimes difficult to give him credit for complete sincerity. In his work as in his life there is a strong element of histrionism. One must remember, however, that Byron actively sympathized with the Carbonari movement in Italy, and that he gave his life for the liberation of the Greeks. Although modern European liberals look upon Byron as a prophet of their cause, how Byron would look upon modern European liberals is another question. His liberalism, like everything else about him, was divided against itself. There are two great kinds of rebellion: that of the many against the tyranny of a few oppressors; and that of the individual against the mob. These two rebellions are quite different, but they frequently become involved with each other. The average intellectual radical devotes his life to clamoring for the rights of people who would make him extremely unhappy if he were forced to associate with them. Though in certain respects Byron was a cad, he had the gentleman's horror of seeing a groom beat a horse. On the whole, however, his radicalism arose more from scorn of the many than from love of mankind. The single oppressed rebel like Prometheus or Bonnivard, the untamed Ishmaelitish tribe like the Albanians, the proud, sorrowful little states of Italy — in these there was something Byronic, and to these Byron's sympathies went out. But those sympathies were imaginative projections of egotism rather than of social idealism. He loved mankind only by personifying that abstraction as a Byronic hero.

He was an aristocrat, an individualist, and something of a cynic. He was just the sort of man most likely to loathe reformers, and just the sort of man who cannot labor long in a great cause and keep a straight face. In *Don Juan* he breaks down and laughs; but after having had his laugh out, he goes and dies for that Byronic nation, Greece. No one has been able to unravel the complexities of this man's character. He has been called a Shelley with feet of clay; he might equally well be called a Jonathan Swift with wings.

As an antidote to the sweetly sticky conception of Shelley entertained by many, *Peter Bell the Third* is valuable. This remarkable satire has been too much neglected. It is grossly unfair, but satire is unfair by definition. There are times when its wild extravagance approaches silliness, but this is at least partly due to Shelley's attempt to parody the fanciful grotesqueness of Wordsworth's poem. Shelley's Peter Bell is of course Wordsworth. Peter Bell the First is the spirit of Peter before he is born. Peter Bell the Second is the human Peter, who dies after selling his soul to the Devil. Peter Bell the Third is Peter's departed spirit going about in hell in performance of the Devil's commands. We should say that he was a living man in London, but we are wrong: Wordsworth is really dead, and London is really hell:

> Hell is a city much like London —
>   A populous and smoky city;
> There are all sorts of people undone,
> And there is little or no fun done;
>   Small justice shown, and still less pity.
>
>   . . . .
>
> There is a Chancery Court; a King;
>   A manufacturing mob; a set

Of thieves who by themselves are sent
Similar thieves to represent;
    An army; and a public debt.

                .   .   .   .

There is great talk of revolution —
    And a great chance of despotism —
German soldiers — camps — confusion —
Tumults — lotteries — rage — delusion —
    Gin — suicide — and methodism;

                .   .   .   .

Thrusting, toiling, wailing, moiling,
    Frowning, preaching — such a riot!
Each with never-ceasing labour
Whilst he thinks he cheats his neighbour,
    Cheating his own heart of quiet.

And all these meet at levees; —
    Dinners convivial and political; —
Suppers of epic poets; — teas,
Where small talk dies in agonies; —
    Breakfasts professional and critical;

                .   .   .   .

And this is Hell — and in this smother
    All are damnable and damned;
Each one damning, damns the other;
They are damned by one another,
    By none other are they damned.

Here is perhaps the best passage relating to Wordsworth's supposed apostasy:

    As troubled skies stain waters clear,
        The storm in Peter's heart and mind
    Now made his verses dark and queer;
    They were the ghosts of what they were,
        Shaking dim grave-clothes in the wind.

Yet the Reviews, who heaped abuse
  On Peter when he wrote for freedom,
So soon as in his song they spy
The folly which soothes tyranny,
  Praise him, for those who feed 'em.

"He was a man, too great to scan; —
  A planet lost in truth's keen rays: —
His virtue, awful and prodigious; —
He was the most sublime, religious,
  Pure-minded Poet of these days."

As soon as he read that, cried Peter,
  "Eureka! I have found the way
To make a better thing of metre
Than e'er was made by living creature
  Up to this blessed day."

Then Peter wrote odes to the Devil; —
  In one of which he meekly said:
"May Carnage and Slaughter,
Thy niece and thy daughter,
May Rapine and Famine,
Thy gorge ever cramming,
  Glut thee with living and dead!"

Coleridge is also introduced in lines of not unsympathetic penetration. Shelley sees his wisdom and his weakness, his misty-mindedness and his genius, and feels the personal magnetism which drew so many young men about him in his later days:

He was a mighty poet — and
  A subtle-souled psychologist;
All things he seemed to understand,
Of old or new — of sea or land —
  But his own mind — which was a mist.

This was a man who might have turned
    Hell into Heaven — and so in gladness
A Heaven unto himself have earned;
But he in shadows undiscerned
    Trusted, — and damned himself to madness.

He spoke of poetry, and how
    "Divine it was — a light — a love —
A spirit which like the wind doth blow
As it listeth, to and fro;
    A dew rained down from God above.

"A power which comes and goes like dream,
    And which none can ever trace —
Heaven's light on earth — Truth's brightest beam."
And when he ceased there lay the gleam
    Of those words upon his face.

I cannot discuss the numerous points of contact between
Shelley's work and actual contemporary conditions as
displayed in prose pamphlets like the *Philosophical View
of Reform* or in pieces of versified propaganda like the
Masque of Anarchy or *Swellfoot the Tyrant*. A good
source of information on these matters is W. E. Peck's
recent life of Shelley. What chiefly concerns us is the way
in which Shelley turned from the broken fragments of the
actual revolution to create an ideal imaginative revolution
of his own. To Wordsworth, in his days of democratic
ardor, the French Revolution was like a glorious dream
come true. The real world assumed "the attraction of a
country in romance." All the notions of ardent young
idealists about natural goodness, natural rights, and universal brotherhood suddenly took on the appearance of
three-dimensional solidity — "not in Utopia . . . but in
the very world." This vision of a realized Utopia faded

from the eyes of Wordsworth and his contemporaries. After the fall of Napoleon, the younger generation of romanticists tried to revive it, and Shelley played his part in this attempt. But he found it hard to reconcile actualities like the Peterloo Massacre with Utopia. For idealism such as his, the real was very refractory material. He worked hard to fill the gap between the real and the ideal, but the gap remained. Hence in his most mature and characteristic work, Shelley adopts the position of the romanticist in whom transcendentalism looms much larger than descendentalism. Since to find the ideal within the real proves impossible, why not do just the reverse — find the real within the ideal? Or rather, why not achieve the desired result through a transposition of terms, assuming that what most people call the real is merely an illusion of our imperfect earthly senses and that what most people call the ideal is the only true and abiding reality? Thus Shelley asserts the reality of his vision, and regards everything which interferes with it as evidence of our human incapacity to see the truth through that "dome of many-coloured glass" that "stains the white radiance of eternity."

The two best examples of Shelley's transcendental revolution are *The Revolt of Islam* and *Prometheus Unbound*. *The Revolt of Islam* (1817) sketches the basic idea of the more famous work — that evil is powerless once men take as their weapons the love and truth that are the spirit of the eternal world. In his preface, Shelley declares that the failure of the French Revolution need not make mankind forsake the lofty ideals of liberty, equality, and fraternity. His ideas are a more hopeful version of Byron's as seen in *Childe Harold*.

The panic which, like an epidemic transport, seized upon all classes of men during the excesses consequent upon the French Revolution, is gradually giving place to sanity. It has ceased to be believed that whole generations of mankind ought to consign themselves to a hopeless inheritance of ignorance and misery, because a nation of men who had been dupes and slaves for centuries were incapable of conducting themselves with the wisdom and tranquillity of freemen so soon as some of their fetters were partially loosened.

For a long while after the Revolution, says Shelley, social idealism was inhibited by disillusionment:

Thus, many of the most ardent and tender-hearted of the worshippers of public good have been morally ruined by what a partial glimpse of the events they deplored appeared to show as the melancholy desolation of all their cherished hopes. Hence gloom and misanthropy have become the characteristics of the age in which we live, the solace of a disappointment that unconsciously finds relief only in the wilful exaggeration of its own despair. This influence has tainted the literature of the age with the hopelessness of the minds from which it flows. . . . But mankind appear to me to be emerging from their trance. I am aware of a slow, gradual, silent change. In that belief I have composed the following poem.

And so the poem sings a new hope arising from old despair. Canto I begins:

When the last hope of trampled France had failed
　　Like a brief dream of unremaining glory,
From visions of despair I rose, and scaled
　　The peak of an aërial promontory,
　　Whose caverned base with the vexed surge was hoary;
And saw the golden dawn break forth, and waken
　　Each cloud, and every wave.

Then comes the story of the revolution led by Laon and Cythna in a vaguely eastern land. Unstained by the hatred and violence of any Reign of Terror, they go about asserting that love is the law of the world. For a time they are successful: chains burst asunder, and the armies of the oppressor come over to their side. But the world is not quite ready for the rule of love: not all of their followers are able to keep hate out of their hearts. A group of wicked kings — suggesting the European coalitions against France — form an alliance against them. Laon and Cythna are forced to take refuge in the wilderness. There — in a manner very characteristic of Shelley, for whom love of mankind and love of woman are inseparable — these two thwarted revolutionists find solace in each other. Finally the lovers are captured and burned at the stake. (Here there is a suggestion of Joan of Arc. Cythna is a compound of Southey's Joan, Spenser's Britomart, Mary Wollstonecraft, and Mary Shelley.) But even in death Laon and Cythna are victorious, for the flames transport them to Shelley's Platonic paradise, where all the great ideals are real. The subtitle of the first edition of this poem was *A Vision of the Nineteenth Century*; but the vision, beautiful as it is, bears small relation to any century which this wicked world has known.

In *Prometheus Unbound* the victory is not that of two noble spirits, but that of enslaved mankind, of abused nature, of the whole hate-ridden universe. Shelley states in his preface that Prometheus "is the type of the highest perfection of moral and intellectual nature, impelled by the purest and truest motives to the best and noblest ends." Jupiter, who has chained Prometheus to the rock, represents that evil which, in the forms of kingcraft and priestcraft, has enslaved the world. The process by which Prometheus liberates himself is extremely simple: he takes back the curse which in earlier days he had delivered against Jupiter. The revoking of the curse means that love has triumphed over hate in the heart of mankind; and the triumph of love over hate necessarily means the downfall of Jupiter and the liberation of Prometheus.

In her valuable note on this poem Mrs. Shelley says:

The prominent feature of Shelley's theory of the destiny of the species was that evil is not inherent in the system of the creation, but an accident that might be expelled. . . . Shelley believed that mankind had only to will that there should be no evil, and there would be none. That man could so perfectionize himself as to be able to expel evil from his own nature, and from the greater part of the creation, was the cardinal point of his system.

Here we should observe the transformation of Godwinian perfectibility into a related but by no means identical theory. Shelley had been greatly influenced by his rationalistic father-in-law. In the early *Queen Mab* (1812), he accepts Godwin's theories of perfectibility and necessity, but he is already seeking to rise above them in order to effect an emotionally satisfying reconciliation between the incongruous ideas that man is perfectible through voluntary reason and is at the same time a helpless cog in a deterministic machine.

By 1819, when *Prometheus Unbound* was finished, he has found his own solution. The world *is* ruled by necessity, but the law which governs all things is not the law of a machine: it is the law of *love*. How then to account for the Jupiter element in the world? That is a mere transitory accident caused by our failure to affirm the law of love. And so man *is* perfectible; indeed, he is perfect already, if he will but think so and say so. He is not, as Godwin would have it, perfectible through reason; he is perfectible through the assertion of his own will to be part of the love that governs the eternal world. How, if the universe is ruled by a necessity which is love, those little hallucinations which we call lust, cruelty and oppression could ever have entered the mind is a question which Shelley is never able to answer. Orthodox Christianity has its explanation; but the author of *The Necessity of Atheism*, though he had more of the spirit of Christ than most men, could hardly be expected to adopt it. The answer of German idealistic philosophy, which became immensely popular during the Victorian period, is that evil is created by our imagination in order to provide exercise for the moral will. We create obstacles for the pleasure and self-improvement derived from knocking them down; this world is a good world because it is a good world to strangle. Shelley, however, is not a Carlyle or a Browning. He simply has a beautiful faith, and sings about it.

No doubt the speech of Demogorgon at the end of *Prometheus Unbound* is the noblest expression of the idealistic aspect of romantic radicalism. The French Revolution may have failed; politicians may take bribes; the poor may be starving; but in the realm of Shelley's imagination man is free and love is the law of the world:

> This is the day, which down the void abysm
> At the Earth-born's spell yawns for Heaven's despotism,
>   And Conquest is dragged captive through the deep:
> Love, from its awful throne of patient power
> In the wise heart, from the last giddy hour

Of dread endurance, from the slippery, steep,
And narrow verge of crag-like agony, springs
And folds over the world its healing wings.

Gentleness, Virtue, Wisdom, and Endurance,
These are the seals of that most firm assurance
    Which bars the pit over Destruction's strength;
And if, with infirm hand, Eternity,
Mother of many acts and hours, should free
    The serpent that would clasp her with his length;
These are the spells by which to reassume
An empire o'er the disentangled doom.

To suffer woes which Hope thinks infinite;
To forgive wrongs darker than death or night;
    To defy Power, which seems omnipotent;
To love and bear; to hope till Hope creates
From its own wreck the thing it contemplates;
    Neither to change, nor falter, nor repent;
This, like thy glory, Titan, is to be
Good, great and joyous, beautiful and free;
This is alone Life, Joy, Empire, and Victory.

That despite the victory of Prometheus hell is still "a
city much like London" in no way detracts from the poetic
beauty of Demogorgon's speech. It is important, however,
to distinguish between the revolutionary enthusiasm of the
Lakists in the early 1790's and the revolutionary enthusiasm of Shelley in 1819. The former believed that their
visions were about to take form "in the very world."
Their liberalism was naturalistic not only in being closely
related to various aspects of the romantic conception of
nature but in implying that the ideal, actually or potentially, lay within the real. After a brief and uneasy attempt to act upon the same belief, Shelley abandons it in

order to share the freedom of Prometheus. His revolution is consummated by "dreaming true" like Peter Ibbetson. It is not naturalistic, but transcendental.

Further consideration of Shelley's political and social idealism, then, would lead us into the third and last of our major romantic tendencies. For this we are not quite ready. Before taking up transcendentalism, we must turn to our second chief manifestation of the romantic spirit — the revival of interest in the past.

XIII

A DEFINITION OF ROMANTICISM

In turning from naturalistic to what might be called retrospective romanticism, one is struck by a renewed sense of the diversity of the romantic movement. What have old ballads and romances, Chatterton and the Spenserian stanza, to do with anti-intellectualism and the good Indian, nature worship and the revolutionary Utopia? We were perhaps able to achieve a unified conception of romantic naturalism by emphasizing the closeness of the relation between its descendental and transcendental elements. Shall we be able to achieve a unified conception of romanticism in general by finding a bond between naturalism and medievalism?

In a very important sense, the revival of interest in the past may be regarded from the viewpoint of the romantic return to nature. It is a return to the nature, to the native genius, of English literature. The supposedly unpremeditated outpourings of early bards and of the ballad-making folk, moreover, seemed much closer to the romantic conception of nature than the glossy couplets of Pope. The relation between philosophical and esthetic primitivism is sketched in the thirteenth chapter of my *Noble Savage* and need not be dwelt on here. The essential point is that the romanticists closely associated poetic ability with the other good gifts of nature, and often regarded earlier English literature in the light of an illusioned naturalism. Often they felt, too, that the men of the Middle Ages and the Elizabethans were closer to nature in other ways than in freedom from Aristotelian rules. These dim, ancestral figures lived before science had chilled and mechanized the mind. They were men of feeling whose sensibility issued forth in Götzistic outbursts which, though sometimes violent, were at a distance mightily picturesque and thrilling. At least their emotions were not withered by scepticism: they dared and strove and believed and let themselves go. They had passion, loyalty, faith, ideals. They saw into the deep heart of things, and had a lively sense of the reality of the unreal. Somehow they were closer to the Golden Age than the sophisticated modern city dweller; in their hearts the primal lessons of nature had not been stifled by the corruptions of civilization. The romantic return to nature and the romantic return to the past, then, are related in several respects. The latter displays much the same fusion of descendentalism and transcendentalism as the former. The Pre-Raphaelites — to glance beyond the boundaries of our field for the sake of a perfect illustration — devoted themselves to realism in the interests of a "higher" unrealism. They were certainly returning to the Middle Ages, but the essence of their original creed was a return to nature.

The exceptions to any general distinctions which can be drawn between these two tendencies are so numerous that again we are reminded no less of the unity of romanticism than of its diversity. On the whole, for example, we may say that medievalism is more frankly a form of imaginative escape than romantic naturalism. The naturalist stands his ground in the present and seriously fights for the illusion that he desires. The medievalist, in a more superficial and playful spirit, dreams back to a time when

illusion was the free gift of life. It must be granted, however, that many expressions of romantic naturalism are
motivated by an escape psychology, and on the other hand
that medievalism is often far more than a dreamy retreat
from the actual. In the long run, both tendencies entail a
withdrawal from something disliked in the hope of finding
something desired. The negative or the positive element
in the process is stressed according to the temperament
of the individual.

The issue is obscured by our habit of chopping literary
history into segments. German romanticists like Herder
began to collect old ballads and to philosophize about the
Middle Ages almost simultaneously, but this is not the
English way of doing things. In England, on the whole,
the writers of the 1780-1830 period looked back to the
Middle Ages without closely analyzing their motives for
doing so. It was rather the Victorian romanticists —
Carlyle in *Past and Present*, Ruskin in *Stones of Venice*,
the Tractarians, the Pre-Raphaelites — who attempted to
answer that question. The roots of Victorian medievalism
are embedded in the romantic period, but the meaning of
those roots is hardly apparent without consideration of
the growths which they produced. Hence in a study confined within the chronological limits of the romantic
period proper, medievalism, as contrasted with naturalism, seems less significant than it really is.

It may be said that the "far away and long ago"
quality inherent in the literature of the medieval revival
produces an effect of magical strangeness not to be found
in expressions of romantic naturalism. Even this distinction, however, needs to be stated with caution. On the one
hand, "magical strangeness" hardly describes the cus-

tomary manner of Sir Walter Scott, and on the, other
hand many expressions of the romantic view of nature
are compact of witchery and glamor. If it be insisted that
medievalism possesses an exotic element not found in
naturalism, we may observe that much naturalistic poetry
uses exotic scenes, and that even a return to the nature of
one's own back yard, when imbued with the spirit of *This
Lime Tree Bower My Prison*, may be an exotic experience.

From the reader's viewpoint, the literary effects of
these two aspects of romanticism are undeniably different.
The difference, however, rises more from diversity of
subject matter than from diversity of psychological motive. The desire for an illusion obtained by interpenetration of the real and the unreal is present in both
medievalism and naturalism; but the material seized upon
for this purpose is different and calls for different atmosphere, imagery, and mode of expression. A still more
important cause of this difference of effect is that medievalism is necessarily more derivative and "literary" than
naturalism. Although a naturalistic work may be strongly
influenced by some other poem and a medievalistic work
may have a large element of direct observation and personal experience, it is in general true that while naturalism
draws upon nature, medievalism draws upon the literature
and art of the Middle Ages. This is one reason for the
close relation between medievalism and estheticism in the
nineteenth century.

Another partly valid distinction between the two tendencies is that romantic naturalism points toward liberalism and romantic medievalism toward conservatism. Faith
in man's innate goodness and in his power to remake the

world if his benevolent impulses were allowed to operate unchecked is bound up with the cult of nature. The cult of the past, on the other hand, encourages a glorification of tradition. As I have already suggested, we see hints of the conservative implications of the medieval revival in Burke's laments over the passing of the age of chivalry. These hints are more fully developed by Wordsworth, Coleridge, and Southey in their post-naturalistic days. Southey, in his *Colloquies with Sir Thomas More*, contrasts the helpful interdependence of medieval society with the bitter competitive individualism of modern society. The other Lakists had much the same feeling. The genial Toryism of Sir Walter Scott was a direct outgrowth of his love for the Middle Ages and of the tradition of feudal loyalty which he inherited from his Border ancestors. It has been said that the feudal elements in the civilization of our Old South were based partly upon the Southern gentleman's enthusiasm for the ideals which he found embodied in the Waverley Novels. Cobbett, criticizing the conditions of modern industry, idealized the Middle Ages in a way which looks forward to Carlyle. This distinction between naturalism and medievalism is especially clear as regards religion. Both tendencies encouraged a religious revival, but the religion of *Tintern Abbey* is not that of *Ecclesiastical Sonnets*.

But although naturalism is normally liberal and medievalism is normally conservative, we must again pause to note exceptions. On the one hand, love of nature often implies a love of some particular locality, which may in turn lead to a conservative nationalism. This is certainly true of Wordsworth and Coleridge. On the other hand, the Middle Ages are often looked upon as a time of natural virtue and untrammeled emotional expression. Nor are the religion of *Tintern Abbey* and the religion of *Ecclesiastical Sonnets* so antithetical as they appear on the surface. As I have already suggested, the latter is an attempt to find in one way that illusion which the former had failed to find in another way.

Moreover, there is one important sense in which medievalism can hardly be called conservative. The revival of interest in the past provided inspiration for most of the changes in theme, form, and technique which sounded the knell of pseudoclassicism. These changes might be regarded as conservative because they entailed a revival of the most venerable traditions of English literature, but generally speaking the revival was accomplished in a free, adventurous, and experimental spirit. So far as subject matter, diction, and craftsmanship are concerned, the revival of interest in the past is more closely related to literary liberalism than to literary Toryism.

We are perhaps justified in saying, then, that naturalism and medievalism are not so utterly alien to each other as to forbid the hypothesis that they are related aspects of something broader and deeper. But what is that something? Ever since I began juggling with the descendental and the transcendental, my conception of romanticism has been an open secret. If I hope to bring naturalism and medievalism under a single head, however, the time has come for an attempt at more explicit definition. During the next few minutes, please believe that although I speak confidently my mind is as full of doubts as I hope yours will be.

We will all agree, perhaps, that man aspires to discover as much as possible of the truth about the universe. Most of us will further agree that the discovery of the truth about the universe generally means the interpretation of the universe in terms of human instincts and of personal emotions and desires. In this wishful interpretation of the universe, man has two things to take into account — what he knows, and what he does not know. In proportion to the latter the former is still very small, and in primitive stages of existence it must have been extremely minute.

But the images which our remote ancestor's senses brought to the storehouse of his mind played curious tricks. In dreams and in waking reveries they broke away from their original contexts to form pictures that were strangely new. Some of these pictures were more terrible, but some of them were far lovelier, than anything directly provided by sense experience. Like a child with his blocks, man began to play creatively with these fortuitous combinations of images. Within certain limits they could be made to come and go, and the hints which they provided could be used in building imaginative structures of his own. To these mental pictures he responded emotionally, and from them, as time went on, he drew inferences. And so his mind became haunted by vague conceptions of a deeper fear and a higher love than were to be found in the known.

Man's creative treatment of his images had been largely unconscious; at least he had no real understanding of what he had done. Had he realized from the first that he himself had manufactured these conceptions out of little fragments of the known, his history would have been very different from what it became. But he knew only that his mind was filled with much finer things than he could see in the world about him. Since these things did not come from the known, they must have come from the unknown. If then the unknown was the source of these impressive conceptions, it must somehow be a more valuable and higher realm than the known. Thus the unknown was transformed into the supernatural, a forest that would echo "God" when man cried, "Dr. Dodd." In the wishful interpretation of life, the unknown was much more useful than the known. Unlike the known, it never told man what he did not wish to hear or suggested that the universe did not operate for his benefit. The perfect short cut to any desired conclusion was not to look for it in the known, but to place it in the unknown and draw it forth again.

Hence man regarded the unknown with awe, and derived a pleasing thrill from its mysteries. He filled it not only with the nameless terrors which he dreaded, but with the beauty, love, and moral guidance for which he hungered. These abstractions, however, were projected into the unknown chiefly in the form of concrete images. For this fact three reasons may be given. First, in the dim ages when this process began, man was almost wholly incapable of expressing abstract thought, and therefore symbolized his ideals by means of the images which had first suggested those ideals. Thus the unknown was equipped with furniture imported from the known. Secondly, man's attitude toward the unknown was strongly emotional, and strong emotion is likely to be expressed in images. Thirdly, at a more advanced level of development the marked discrepancy between the known and the idealized unknown would naturally arouse the desire to bring them into closer harmony. The pretense of being

able to derive real satisfaction from wishing without ex-
pecting the wish to come true is the last resort of disillusioned sophistication. Before reaching that futile stage,
man long endeavors to give the unknown something of
the firmness and tangibility of the known. He not only
fills the unknown with his illusions, but makes those illusions as concrete and specific as possible. He tries, in
other words, to realize the ideal — Coleridge's task in
Lyrical Ballads.

The converse of this process is the idealizing of the
real — Wordsworth's task in *Lyrical Ballads.* Nowadays, despite our ignorance, it is possible for an educated person to have sufficient understanding of the natural
world to be able to live in it without constantly falling
back upon the supernatural for explanations of his
experience. But this was not true of our remote ancestors. At every step they were confronted by some question which could be answered only by the imagination in
the guise of the supernatural. Consequently the known
was penetrated through and through by influences supposed to emanate from the unknown. As time went on
this penetration of the natural by the supernatural could
be used in more conscious endeavors to interpret life in
terms of wishful emotion. It would soften the hard re-
fractoriness of the known by investing it with the mystery and glamor of the unknown, enabling man to think
of the primrose as "something more."

If at this point we consult our own minds, we will probably find that the satisfaction of this impulse to blend the
known and the supernaturalized unknown still gives us
intense pleasure. According to our temperaments this
pleasure may be esthetic, or spiritual, or both at once.

Although the sources of the feeling may lie in the hypothetical process which has just been described, we are not aware that it has any sources at all. We do not think of ourselves as putting the natural and the supernatural together: we simply observe, with a thrill of happiness, that they are one. I do not believe this happiness to be an absolutely primary fact of consciousness, but it is so deeply rooted that it is primary so far as our own powers of introspection are concerned. In a great many people the pleasurable thrill is constant enough to furnish an illusioned view of the whole of life, and in almost everyone the illusion is present at least intermittently. Since this illusion satisfies very deep, strong, and primitive emotional desires, we are instinctively disposed to cherish it.

I venture to suggest that the illusioned view of life which results from the interpenetration of the known and the unknown, or the natural and the supernatural, constitutes the romantic element in human thought. As explained thus far, it is too nearly universal to be regarded as an *ism*. No human being is without it, though some have much less of it than others. Since the dawn of mentality it has played an important part in the fine arts, in religion, in metaphysics, and in at least the first gropings of science. Man has gradually evolved critical standards, theological and philosophical systems, and methods of scientific investigation which by their firm distinctions between natural and supernatural may seem entirely to shut out the romantic impulse. Nevertheless, the impulse remains. It is older and deeper than reason or rational imagination, and it is very dear to man's heart. If we may invent a term, let us call this instinctive romantic trait of the mind, "romanticity."

Under what circumstances does romanticity become romanticism? Romanticity demands an intellectual environment in which the romantic illusion can be enjoyed without the disturbing awareness that it is illusory. When the maintenance of illusion entails a conscious effort which is evasive, defensive, anxious, or defiant, then romanticity becomes romanticism. Any candid person, as he looks about him today, will grant that his impulse toward the romantic illusion is checked by serious obstacles which may be summed up in the word, "science." I do not mean that any particular scientific discovery has made it impossible to retain any particular belief. I mean that the primeval desire to interfuse the natural and the supernatural has been hampered by the study of the universe as the realm of purely natural law, by the study of man as wholly included within that universe, and by the study of the psychological processes which have led man to imagine a different and a higher realm of being. Modern man is torn between the will to know and the will to dream. The former has made him comfortable and efficient, given him some degree of control over natural forces, and freed his mind from many torturing superstitions. But it has gradually forced upon him a conception of life that threatens the enjoyment of romanticity.

How quick we are to accept the practical fruits of science, and how slow to accept its philosophical implications! How eagerly, in this rational twentieth century, we rush toward any loophole of ignorance through which we may wriggle away from reason! Here is the predicament as set forth in Robinson Jeffers' poem, *Science*:

Man, introverted man, having crossed
In passage and but a little with the nature of things
   this latter century
Has begot giants; but being taken up
Like a maniac with self-love and inward conflicts
   cannot manage his hybrids.
Being used to deal with edgeless dreams,
Now he's bred knives on nature, turns them also inward:
   they have thirsty points though.
His mind forebodes his own destruction;
Actæon who saw the goddess naked among the leaves and
   his hounds tore him.
A little knowledge, a pebble from the shingle,
A drop from the ocean: who would have dreamed this
   infinitely little too much?

Slight as it is, however, man's acquaintance with "the nature of things" is of longer standing than "this latter century." The situation has not burst suddenly upon us: the craving for romantic illusion has become progressively thwarted with every advance in our understanding of nature. But since the graph of knowledge is a series of waves rather than a straight ascending line, the necessity for a defensive fostering of the romantic attitude has waxed and waned with the strength of the obstacles which have confronted it at various periods. Without attempting the impossible task of tracing the complete history of the subject, we may seek in the twilight of the Renaissance the more immediate sources of what Arnold calls "this strange disease of modern life." The happy confidence of Elizabethan romanticity grows uneasy in the universe pictured by the new science. Spenser gives place to Donne, *As You Like It* to *Measure for Measure*. Anachronistic as the nineteenth century interpretation of

Hamlet may be in some respects, late Elizabethan melancholy has much in common with Byronic *Weltschmerz*. When Aldous Huxley wants a motto for the title-page of *Point Counter Point*, he finds it in Fulke Greville's *Mustapha*:

> O wearisome condition of humanity!
> Born under one law, by another bound;
> Vainly begot, and yet forbidden vanity,
> Created sick, commanded to be sound;
> What meaneth nature by these diverse laws,
> Passion and reason, self-division's cause?

Huxley might well have quoted on to the grim lines,

> If nature did not take delight in blood,
> She would have made more easy ways to good;

or he might have turned back to the less familiar *Chorus of Tartars*, with its address to

> Vast Superstition, glorious style of weakness,
> Sprung from the deep disquiet of man's passion.

O God! I could be bounded in a nutshell and count myself a king of infinite space, were it not that I have bad dreams.

The seventeenth century, though hardly conscious of the real issues involved, adopted various methods of shaking off those bad dreams: Cavalier frivolity, "metaphysical" ardor, Puritan fundamentalism, the Miltonic attempt to reconcile Puritanism with the great Renaissance tradition. Meanwhile science moved on. As the century drew near its close, the romantic spirit was at low tide. The tremendous practical benefits of science won the gratitude of men, and its harsher general implications were softened by being absorbed into the system of geometrical rationalism. That rationalism may be interpreted as a compromise between science and antiscience; for despite its machinery of logic it had a wishful and *a priori* element large enough to shield its devotees from undesirable facts. For almost fifty years, the system provided peace and quiet, confidence in material and intellectual progress, urbanity, common sense, pseudoclassicism. Romanticity slumbered, but stirred restlessly in its broken dreams.

The rationalistic compromise was doomed to failure. It was an artificial and bloodless mean between two great, vital extremes. As the eighteenth century went on, those extremes became increasingly independent and militant. Science shook off the bonds of scholasticism and assumed its true character. Romanticity, its vague discomfort clarified by the confrontation of a definite enemy, strode forth in the offensive and defensive panoply of romanticism.

In speaking of the eighteenth century I have succumbed to the eighteenth century habit of personification. The age of course contained no warriors named Geometrical Rationalism, Scientific Empiricism, and Romanticism. It contained human beings none of whom was the embodiment of a single tendency. The thought of any romanticist of the time would doubtless be tinged with abstract rationalism and with scientific empiricism. Nevertheless, by the middle of the eighteenth century the impulse toward illusion had begun to assume the guise of a philosophical force consciously opposed to science and to the scientific element in rationalism. From that time to this, the romantic spirit of man has engaged, evasively or defiantly, with heartsick despair or with triumphant faith, in an attempt to find some correspondence between reality and desire.

Allow me, then, to propose the following definition: *Romanticism is the endeavor, in the face of growing factual obstacles, to achieve, to retain, or to justify that illusioned view of the universe and of human life which is produced by an imaginative fusion of the familiar and the strange, the known and the unknown, the real and the ideal, the finite and the infinite, the material and the spiritual, the natural and the supernatural.* The foregoing pairs of terms are of course not exactly equivalent in meaning. They represent different ways in which the romantic impulse may manifest itself in different temperaments. Emphasis on the first members of these pairs gives what has been called the descendental element in romanticism; emphasis on the second members constitutes the transcendental element.

It is idle to expect that this or any other definition will account for every work of every author of the 1780-1830 period. Who would undertake to provide a formula for the 1880-1930 period that would cover all its personalities and tendencies? Not every writer of the age that we are studying — witness Crabbe and Jane Austen — is strongly moved by the romantic impulse. There are always persons who are comparatively unromantic — either because they have little awareness of the supernatural or because they are temperamentally disposed to make a sharp distinction between the supernatural and the natural. We need not suppose that even definitely romantic writers are strongly moved by the desire for illusion every time they put pen to paper, or that they are always consciously attacking the forces which have turned romanticity into romanticism. Romanticists are no more invariably romantic than scientists are scientific. One must also recognize different levels of depth and intensity in the romantic impulse, running all the way from Blake's titanic yearning for the marriage of finite and infinite to Charles Lamb's gently whimsical disposition to impose glamor upon the familiar. But when all the exceptions and qualifications have been granted, the fact remains that the desire to preserve some aspect of the romantic illusion in the face of obstacles presented by rationalism and empiricism is so prevalent as to be a distinguishing feature of the literature of the 1780-1830 period.

The definition that has been proposed seeks to dive beneath the various definitions which emphasize a single side of romanticism: the return to nature; the revival of interest in the past; liberalism in literature; the renascence of wonder; the predominance of imagination in literature, and so on. In order to find a source to which all these might be related it has been necessary to define in terms of psychological motive rather than of literary expression; but the form and style of romantic literature are the appropriate outgrowths of romanticism as here defined. Romantic writing is the sort of writing that would be expected of a person who lives, or aspires to live, in the light of the romantic illusion.

In the opinion of a friend, this definition is too broad to be useful, for it makes romanticism cover all art, all religion, and all the higher emotions of man. But we must distinguish between the attempt to bend artistic materials and human conduct toward the fulfillment of an ideal and that confusion of fact and dream which is inherent in romanticism. Doubtless a large romantic element enters into the origins of the ideal creative activities of mind, but those origins are steadily if painfully left behind with the growth of rational civilization. Surely there are now forms of artistic expression which in no way depend upon a confusion of natural and supernatural. Surely not the least noble ideals of modern man involve a rational rather than a sublimatedly superstitious interpretation of human experience. Of religion I speak with less confidence, and should prefer to accept the judgment of those whose religious experience has been richer than mine. It seems to me that popular religion tends to be extremely romantic when it is not merely a system of ethics. Undoubtedly, however, there are philosophies of religion which are unromantic and even antiromantic. To what extent these theologies satisfy instinctive human cravings is a question that others must answer.

Broad as it is, this definition is more specific than those which it seeks to unify. It suggests why and in what mood the romanticists return to nature, revive the literature of the Middle Ages, and add strangeness to beauty. Romanticism can never be defined in a manner satisfactory to everyone. So far as I am concerned, however, this explanation accounts for all the tendencies which can reasonably be regarded as romantic, and yet it does not belie the diversity with which the romantic spirit manifests itself in literature. The Proteus of romanticism, when gripped by the Agamemnon of science, assumes several different forms. The purpose of this course is to study Proteus through three of those forms. But I hope that, having gained some acquaintance with Proteus by this method, you will return to his forms and examine them with proper regard to differences as well as to similarities. If you then feel that these romanticisms, in spite of their diversity, are related to one underlying romanticism, I shall be glad. If not, we must agree to disagree.

Those who are interested by this definition of romanticism but who dislike the somewhat prejudiced viewpoint from which it has been formulated may be assured that the same definition can be adjusted to quite different prejudices. It is possible to feel that the life of any sane inhabitant of the modern world must be based upon the acceptance of an absolutely pure naturalism, and that just when a pure naturalism began to take form romanticism seized upon it and made it so extremely impure that there has been no cleaning it up from that time to this. But it is equally possible to feel that pure naturalism is a curse from which romanticism has helped to save mankind by elevating it and harmonizing it with spiritual ideals. On this matter there is no easy truth to be set down in your notebooks.

One question is so certain to be asked that I may as well try to answer it at once. Does not the science of to-day, despite the mood expressed in the lines quoted from Jeffers and in Mr. J. W. Krutch's *The Modern Temper*, offer plenty of scope for the romantic view of life? That depends, perhaps, upon the sort of science we are considering. Those sciences which deal with man's body and mind, and with the world as it presents itself to our human senses, continue to amass evidence that is extremely hostile to the romantic illusion. The new mathematical physics, on the other hand, has encouraged an idealism which the romanticist can use in support of his will to dream. In fact, the mixture of the physical and the metaphysical in such books as Eddington's *The Nature of the Physical World* is an interesting example of our definition of romanticism. The new physics has not furnished *evi-*

dence for any religious or philosophical theory, but by opening up four-dimensional chasms of mystery it has furnished *opportunity* for the enjoyment of beliefs which were decidedly cramped in the trim little universe of Newton.

Undoubtedly the romanticism of the eighteenth and nineteenth centuries owed its nobilities and absurdities partly to the desire to combat a very imperfect and transitory conception of science. It was feared that science would soon provide a clear, dry explanation of everything. That fear has of course abated. All sciences have grown modest and tentative. The old rigid cleavage between thinking and feeling has broken down, and wonder has found a place even in the laboratory. There is no longer any reason to believe that science will destroy human emotion.

But "emotion" and "romanticism" are not synonymous terms. Beneath the historical changes in science and man's attitude toward science there remains, it seems to me, an irreconcilable hostility between the scientific spirit and the particular kind of illusion which is the essence of romanticism. Science no longer distresses the romanticist by threatening to explain everything. The discomfort of the twentieth century romanticist consists rather in the fear that although science is unable to interpret the universe there is no other means of doing so. We have plenty of mystery, but no valid excuse for being mystical about it. There are an infinite number of things that we do not know; but what we *do* know makes it very difficult to identify the unknown with our conception of the supernatural, and very difficult to relate our conception of the supernatural to our knowledge of the external world.

Hence although no sane person nowadays supposes that science forbids him to fall in love or admire a rainbow, the romantic illusion, it seems to me, is more seriously threatened than ever.

Not everyone, however, will share this view, and indeed the present state of science, philosophy, and religion is too confused to permit us to single out any one mental attitude as generally prevalent. I shall be quite content, therefore, to have you regard my notions about romanticism from a merely historical viewpoint. How men feel at the present moment, and how they will feel in the future, are debatable matters; but that from the close of the Renaissance up to the recent past they felt more or less as I have described seems fairly obvious.

This attempt at definition arose from the wish to find a common source for romantic naturalism and romantic medievalism. The preceding lectures should have made sufficiently clear the relation of romantic naturalism to the proposed definition. The same definition will explain why the romanticists turned admiringly toward an age which freely combined the familiar and the strange, the natural and the supernatural. From the viewpoint here suggested, romanticism is the quest of an illusion. That illusion may be sought in supernaturalized nature. It may be sought in times when romanticity had not yet been forced to become romanticism. Finally, it may be sought in man's own imagination, the true abiding place of the power to make dreams real, and the real a dream.

XIV

THE MEDIEVALISM OF SCOTT

My treatment of medievalism will be brief because I can add almost nothing to the readily accessible authorities who have dealt with this subject. Moreover, since the medievalism of the romantic period proper is of greater artistic than philosophical importance, I shall discuss this aspect of romanticism chiefly from the viewpoint of its influence upon form and expression. To avoid confusion let me say that except when a distinction is required I shall use the term "medievalism" to cover the revival of interest in all that earlier literature — Elizabethan and seventeenth century as well as medieval — which the pseudoclassicists tended to neglect and undervalue.

Scott's devotion to olden times is so free from self-conscious fuss that one is sometimes tempted to call it superficial. It is, on the contrary, free from fuss because it is deep and true. His love of the romantic past was not the result of a deliberate philosophy: it was native and instinctive. In this sense he may be compared with Burns; for just as Burns did not return to nature because he was there already, so Scott did not return to the Middle Ages because he was there already. The descendant of an old Scottish Border clan, he was brought up on old ballads and tales of border warfare and on the reminiscences of his grandmother, whose memory went back to a past which had already become romantic. From his father he inherited Jacobite leanings which made feudal loyalty far more than a merely bookish tradition. As he grew older, he became the man of letters and the scholarly antiquarian; but his writing and his scholarship were normal outgrowths of his ancestry and environment, not exotic specialties cultivated for some theoretical reason.

The fact that Scott was an accomplished scholar will remind us that the romantic movement has sometimes been credited with the development of the historical method in scholarship and criticism. This point requires discrimination. Since history is in some measure a science, the relations between romanticism and history are much like those between romanticism and science. In an earlier lecture it was said that the romantic naturalist is sometimes attracted toward science by the attention it devotes to nature, but that he is repelled when he realizes that scientific naturalism is hostile to the illusion which he seeks. Similarly, the romantic medievalist is attracted toward history by its devotion to the past, but he is repelled when he realizes that history is fundamentally scientific in spirit and that it must eventually destroy his retrospective illusion. This realization, however, is often delayed or obscured by non-scientific elements in history which offer considerable scope to the romantic attitude — subjective interpretation and literary form. History provided facts on which romanticism could base its dreams; romanticism provided dreams which sweetened the search for facts. The inevitable divorce occurred in the nineteenth century, when history was almost completely dominated by the aims and methods of evolutionary science. But while it lasted, the union was fruitful for both scholarship and literature. Although we must not ascribe the rise of the historical attitude wholly to the influence of the romantic movement, we may say that romanticism provided much of the emotional impetus which that attitude needed for its development.

But to return to Scott. The eighteenth century ballad revival reached its climax in 1765 with Bishop Thomas Percy's *Reliques of Ancient English Poetry*. This was a collection of old popular ballads — genuine, but touched up by the editor — mingled with a good many of the later minstrel and broadside ballads and with a few definitely modern poems by artificially artless writers like Shenstone. Scott's boyhood fondness for ballads was deepened by his reading of the *Reliques*. At the beginning of the 1790's he was already a student of border folklore and minstrelsy. In 1792, however, an especially strong impulse came to him from the German revival of interest in early poetry, a movement which itself owed much to Percy.

The first partial German translation of the *Reliques* appeared in 1767; the first complete translation, in 1790. Herder, a prominent figure in early German romanticism, became greatly interested in German folk poetry, made collections in emulation of Percy, and aroused the enthusiasm of Schiller and Goethe. Eventually this movement exerted a wholesome influence on German poetry, but in its first stages it was marked by a good deal of crudeness and absurdity. The poet Bürger became the leader of a group in whose work ghostly thrills and charnel-house horrors abounded. The best example of this type of ballad is Bürger's own *Lenore*. Lenore's lover is killed in battle, but because of some blasphemous words which she utters in her despair his ghost returns and takes the maiden on a wild, spooky ride which ends in the graveyard, where he espouses her amidst the gibbering of wraiths and demons.

Various early manifestations of the romantic spirit, of course, cultivate some sort of Gothic goose flesh. This *penchant* for horrors can quite easily be related to the definition of romanticism proposed in the foregoing lecture, since it is associated with the most primitive level of the romantic illusion. Doubtless the sense of the fusion of natural and supernatural terrified man long before it gave him spiritual delight, just as the mountains gave young Wordsworth fear before they gave him love. In the eighteenth century, goose flesh appeared to be an aspect of romanticity well worth defending against the encroachments of common sense. After some years of reading "what oft was thought, but ne'er so well expressed," people were delighted when the unearthly invaded the everyday world, and at unexpected moments popped out and cried "Boo!"

In England the German spook balladry combined with the well established native "graveyard" tradition and had a considerable vogue. Of several English translations of *Lenore*, the most notable were those produced by Walter Scott, Matthew Gregory Lewis, and William Taylor of Norwich. Lewis is an important figure in this aspect of romanticism. Besides this translation and several imitations of German spook ballads, such as *Alonzo the Brave and the Fair Imogene*, he wrote one of the most famous novels of terror, or Gothic romances, *Ambrosio, or the Monk* (1795). Hence his sobriquet of "Monk" Lewis. Lewis continued his horror mongering in *Tales of Terror* (1799) and *Tales of Wonder* (1801). In the second of these collections of spook ballads Scott was a collaborator. "Apollo's sexton," as Byron called Lewis, imitated the German practice of embodying the Gothic romance in dramatic form. *The Castle Spectre* (1797) is his best known play.

As a translator of *Lenore* and collaborator with Lewis in *Tales of Wonder*, Scott begins his literary career under the influence of the pseudo-medieval German ballad. His relation to the novel of terror will be discussed later. Another instance of German influence upon Scott is his translation of Goethe's *Goetz von Berlichingen* (1799). This work of the young Goethe is one of several early romantic German dramas on themes drawn from medieval history. They indulge rather heavily in gloom, violence, and ranting, but they are more serious and mature, and less laboriously *macabre*, than the spook ballads. Considering Scott's future development, their attention to historical background is also significant. An example of the same stream of influence is Coleridge's translation of Schiller's *Wallenstein* (1800).

But with Scott this period of translating and imitating German literature was of brief duration. In 1799, his appointment as Sheriff-Deputy of Selkirkshire strengthened his roots in the soil of the border, and turned him from artificial thrills to the natural strangeness of his own environment and traditions. His official tours of duty and his unofficial rambles and ballad raids enriched the native element in his literary equipment, added to his store of narrative material, and provided the physical background for much of his later work. The immediate result was *Minstrelsy of the Scottish Border*, which appeared in 1802 and 1803. The collection contained about eighty ballads, forty-three of which had never been published before and almost all of which were genuine folk poems. There were also, however, a number of confessed imitations by Scott and several of his friends.

Scott's studying, collecting, editing, and imitating of the border ballads provide merely the most striking example of the activity of a whole group of men who helped Scott and who in some cases published similar works of their own. The most important members of this group deserve more attention than we have time to give them. John Leyden was a wild Scot who had gone to Edinburgh and there acquired unusual learning. He possessed that combination of trained scholarship and direct contact with native tradition which this revival of popular poetry demanded. James Hogg, "the Ettrick Shepherd," is still a fairly well known poet. He was one of several rustic, home-grown singers who provided the romanticists with evidence that poetic ability is one of the gifts of nature. The contemporary popularity of Burns was of course partly due to the belief that he furnished evidence of this kind. Hogg, who for years was a mere farm hand, had almost no education; but he had a headful of ballads which his mother had sung to him in the cottage, and he had a little spark of poetry in him, too. Joseph Ritson was an eccentric English medievalist. He had no contact with the folk, but he was a good scholar the fruits of whose antiquarian researches are still useful to students. George Ellis of the *Anti-Jacobin* also corresponded with Scott about old ballads and romances. His *Early English Metrical Romances* is still widely used. This collection, which appeared in 1805, did for medieval romance almost what Percy's *Reliques* had done for the medieval ballad.

The next stage in Scott's career is marked by the production of a series of original poems growing out of his studies. These begin in 1805 with *The Lay of the Last Minstrel*, and end in 1817 with *Harold the Dauntless*. The first of the series is based closely on border balladry, but *Marmion* (1808), *The Lady of the Lake* (1810), and the rest draw their inspiration rather from the medieval metrical romances. Scott, however, carries into the romance something of the rugged, vigorous spirit of the minstrel ballad or lay. This crossbreeding did much to preserve the reputation of the medieval romance at a time when imitations of the genuine courtly article could have found favor with but few readers. Scott's tremendous influence as a popularizer of the Middle Ages was due not only to the positive merits of his poems but also to the fact that he exploited chiefly those elements of the past which any normal reader of his own day would have found picturesque and exciting. He introduced the romantic past to thousands who would have recoiled from the queerness of Coleridge's *Christabel*.

In 1813, Byron began to capitalize his recent Mediterranean tour by pouring out a series of romantic verse tales dealing with the adventures of Byronic heroes in the Near East — *The Giaour, The Bride of Abydos, The Corsair, Lara, The Siege of Corinth*. The author was trying to outdo Scott in his own field; and, so far as the taste of his times is concerned, he succeeded. Byron's verse romances exploited fresh exotic territory; they had more fire and more fashionable melancholy than Scott's; and they had much more sex appeal. Both in verse and in prose, Sir Walter generally wrote as if he were the heroine's elderly uncle. Scott, being a good sportsman and an intensely practical person, cheerfully admitted that he was beaten, and began to cultivate the novel. Rummaging through an old desk for some fishing tackle one day, he found a prose manuscript which he had begun some time before but had laid aside. He now completed it, and it appeared in 1814 as *Waverley*. From that time to 1832, the year of his death, the novels gushed forth in an unbroken stream.

So much has been said and written about Scott's novels that general comment on them here would be a waste of time. I shall simply point out the chief respects in which they pertain to the aspect of romanticism now under discussion. They range very widely in time and place from a period shortly after the Norman Conquest to a period almost contemporary with the author, and from Constantinople to Glasgow. To take a few examples, *Ivanhoe* gives us medieval England; *Quentin Durward*, medieval France; *Count Robert of Paris*, the crusades; *Kenilworth*, Elizabethan England; *Old Mortality*, seventeenth century Scotland; *Rob Roy*, mid-eighteenth century Scotland.

Although these novels are assuredly not romantic in the way that *Tintern Abbey* and *Prometheus Unbound* are romantic, they can be related to the essentially romantic program of making the strange real and the real strange. Scott takes historical figures who are mere names to most of us, like Richard Cœur de Lion, Louis XI, or the Earl of Leicester, and makes them seem as real as people whom we know in actual life. Still more often, he invents imaginary characters, places them against a carefully and somewhat laboriously constructed historical background, and sets them to doing such vivid, natural things that the dim past comes alive, and olden glamor is fairly tangible. Realizing the strange, then, is

no doubt the side of romanticism best illustrated by
Scott's novels. But the novels also illustrate, though to a
less extent, the other side of romanticism — the "strange-
ifying" of the real. If you take a human, lively young
Scotchman and put him back in the reign of Louis XI,
you get two results. Primarily, you make the reign of
Louis XI more realistic, but you also give Quentin Durward something of the far-away atmosphere of the reign
of Louis XI. In other words, the reign of Louis XI as
represented by Scott is the more real for having people
like Quentin Durward in it; but Quentin Durward is a
much more glamorous person in the reign of Louis XI
than he would be in that of George III.

In terms of literary history, Scott's blending of the
actual with the strange is a blending of the novel with
the romance. He himself spoke of *Waverley* as a "romance or novel," and indeed his stories partake of the
characteristics of both forms. They suggest the romance
in their more or less remote setting, in their reliance upon
adventures rather than upon a problem arising from
character, and in their frequent indulgence in the strange
and marvelous. They suggest the novel in the stress laid
upon portrayal of character, in the rather complex and
full-bodied scheme of events, in the careful building up of
background and social environment, in the sense of responsibility to fact and the care taken to make even the
marvelous seem possible. If we may let the romance
stand for the strange and the novel for the actual, this
blending of types gives us the romantic fusion.

Scott of course was thoroughly familiar with the eighteenth century novelists, and from them the realistic elements in his prose works are largely derived. It is easy

to see the Fielding and Smollett in him, and when he uses a long series of letters — as for instance in *Guy Mannering* — the technique of Richardson is evident. For the *genre* painting of the less remotely dated Scotch tales he acknowledged his indebtedness to Maria Edgeworth's studies of Irish character.

The romance element in Scott's fiction is derived partly from his own very considerable knowledge of genuine medieval romance and partly from the Gothic romance or novel of terror, a form which runs well back into the eighteenth century. Scott purges the Gothic romance of its absurd horrors, adds a genuine romance element and a genuine historical setting from the stores of his own scholarship, and further adds a realism of technique which owes much to the great unromantic novelists of the eighteenth century.

In 1762 the Reverend Thomas Leland published *Longsword: an Historical Romance.* This is a dull, talky, sentimental tale, but it does not revel in ghosts and it does make a faithful attempt to reconstruct a picture of the reign of Henry III. Leland was trying to do what Scott much later succeeded in doing. He had no immediate successors, for Horace Walpole's *Castle of Otranto*, 1764, is a quite different kind of book.

The Castle of Otranto has only the vaguest temporal setting. The story arises not from any historical circumstances, but from what was supposed to be the emotional atmosphere of medieval architecture. It comes directly from Walpole's own imitation Gothic castle at Strawberry Hill. The close connection between the revival of Gothic architecture and the revival of medieval literature, by the way, deserves your study. The subject is ad-

mirably treated in Kenneth Clark's *The Gothic Revival*.
Walpole thought that he was doing the very thing
which I have tried to persuade you is typically romantic.
In the preface to the second edition he writes:

> It was an attempt to blend the two kinds of romance, the
> ancient and the modern [*i.e.*, the novel]. In the former, all was
> imagination and improbability; in the latter, nature is always in-
> tended to be, and sometimes has been, copied with great success.
> Invention has not been wanting; but the great resources of fancy
> have been dammed up, by a strict adherence to common life.

The author certainly cannot be accused of excessively
"strict adherence to common life." Despite his own assertion, it is hard to see the slightest element of realism in
a story of huge mailed fists flung down from nowhere into
the courtyard and statues that bleed at the nose to predict approaching horrors.

The Castle of Otranto started a whole chain of Gothic
novels. The next important example is Clara Reeve's
The Old English Baron, 1777. The same author's *Progress of Romance*, 1785, attempts to evolve a critical
theory of the type. Charlotte Smith, who later wrote
Jacobin novels, has two or three Gothic romances,
notably *Emmeline, or The Orphan of the Castle*, 1788.
Mrs. Ann Radcliffe was very prolific and influential in
this field, and her *Mysteries of Udolpho*, 1794, is an important book. She gives the type a strong element of
sensibility conveyed chiefly through a love plot. Her
heroines are fond of reading Shakespeare and weeping
against a sylvan background, for she is a sentimental but
rather eloquent scenery worshipper. Her heroes, on the
other hand, bequeath their chief traits to the Byronic
hero. Another of Mrs. Radcliffe's characteristics is to

use what seem for a time to be supernatural elements but to explain them away before the close of the story. Scott often employs the same method of having his cake and eating it too. Thus the bloodstained figure that arises to curse Claverhouse in *Old Mortality* gives the reader all the thrill of a ghost before he is shown to be a wounded Covenanter who has been lying underneath the table.

Matthew Gregory Lewis's *Ambrosio, or the Monk* (1795) has already been mentioned. His chief contribution to the type was a rather crudely sensational emphasis on torture and lust.

The general type undergoes several specific developments. In 1784, William Beckford's *Vathek* transported the novel of terror to an oriental setting and derived thrills from strange, diabolic, eastern cults. In *Caleb Williams* (1794) Godwin concentrated upon the crime and mystery aspects, left out the historical element, provided a modern setting, and substituted the horrors of contemporary jails for the horrors of Gothic dungeons. The mystery story element is an essential feature in Scott: *Guy Mannering*, for example, is fundamentally a tale of crime and detection.

The novel of terror continues even during Scott's period of activity, usually — see Ainsworth and the Misses Porter — with an increased historical realism due to Scott's influence. Shelley's two juvenile tales of 1810, *Zastrozzi* and *St. Irvyne*, are very Radcliffian. His wife, Mary Wollstonecraft Shelley, figures in a later development of the form, for her *Frankenstein* (1817) uses science or pseudoscience as a means of achieving effects of mystery and horror in a way that reminds us of Poe. Charles Robert Maturin's *Melmoth the Wanderer*

(1820) mingles with its horrors a character named Immalee who is a perfect example of the Lucy type.

Do not miss the delicious mockery of the novel of terror in Jane Austen's *Northanger Abbey*. A good book about the novel of terror and "horror-romanticism" in general is Einar Railo's *The Haunted Castle*. Mr. Railo endeavors to bring almost the whole of romanticism within the scope of his topic, but since the same criticism has been made against my *Noble Savage* I am in no position to cast the first stone.

The more one reads in the Gothic romances the more clearly one perceives their relation to Scott's work. One can see him making judicious use of their thrills, tempering their absurdities, infusing them with a more genuinely medieval atmosphere and background and with a satisfying realism derived from the great founders of the novel. But when the indebtedness has been pointed out the gap between Scott's work and all earlier fiction remains so extremely wide that one can leap it only by recognizing that the man possessed a high order of creative genius. The romantic revival of interest in the past provided much of the material on which that genius worked, and to some extent guided the ways of its working.

XV

THE MEDIEVALISM OF WORDSWORTH AND COLERIDGE

The literature of the past seldom furnished Wordsworth with themes, scenes, or characters; but it strongly influenced his theory of poetry and his application of that theory to his own work. Though Wordsworth responded to the fascination of medieval and Elizabethan times, he responded more deeply to the fascination of natural scenes and of humanity amidst those scenes. He felt that his task was not to deal directly with the marvelous as found in chivalric romance, but to extract a quality of strangeness from the life about him. You will remember *The Solitary Reaper*:

> Will no one tell me what she sings? —
> Perhaps the plaintive numbers flow
> For old, unhappy, far-off things,
> And battles long ago:
> Or is it some more humble lay,
> Familiar matter of today?
> Some natural sorrow, loss, or pain,
> That has been, and may be again?

Wordsworth enjoyed reading of "far-off things, and battles long ago," but in his own work he was not often inspired by them. His most congenial themes were "familiar matter of today" made unfamiliar by imaginative insight.

The introductory lines of *The Prelude* contain a pas-

sage that shows us how he feels when, a lover of Milton
and Spenser as well as of nature, he stands at the threshold of his poetic career. In very Miltonic fashion, he
aspires to produce a work of enduring greatness. He has
the necessary equipment, but where shall he turn for a
theme?

> Sometimes, mistaking vainly, as I fear,
> Proud spring-tide swellings for a regular sea,
> I settle on some British theme, some old
> Romantic tale, by Milton left unsung;
> More often resting at some gentle place
> Within the groves of Chivalry, I pipe
> Among the Shepherds, with reposing Knights
> Sit by a fountain-side, and hear their tales.

I have quoted from the 1805-1806 text because Wordsworth later revised these lines to make them suggest that
he had intended to extract from tales of chivalry a moral
illustrating "Christian meekness hallowing faithful
loves."

But Wordsworth suspects that these are "spring-tide
swellings" rather than a "regular sea." We know on what
sea he finally chose to embark, and where it bore him.
He does not draw upon the romantic past for any important work until his naturalism has begun to give place
to conservatism and orthodoxy. Then, notably in *Song at
the Feast of Brougham Castle* and *The White Doe of
Rylstone*, he imposes a diluted and Christianized version
of his philosophy of nature upon romantic verse narrative of the Walter Scott type. The former poem was
composed in 1807, the latter in 1807 and 1808.

In *Song at the Feast of Brougham Castle*, the troubles
of border warfare have caused the young Lord Clif-

ford to be reared amidst the mountains as a shepherd. When at last he is restored to his rights, he is received at the ancestral castle with great rejoicing. A minstrel sings a song of welcome in which he assumes that the young knight will now go forth to war against his foes. This passage from the minstrel's song recalls Sir Walter Scott:

> Now another day is come,
> Fitter hope, and fitter doom;
> He hath thrown aside his crook,
> And hath buried deep his book;
> Armour rusting in his halls
> On the blood of Clifford calls; —
> "Quell the Scot," exclaims the Lance —
> "Bear me to the heart of France,"
> Is the longing of the Shield —
> Tell thy name, thou trembling Field;
> Field of death, where'er thou be,
> Groan thou with our victory!
> Happy day, and happy hour,
> When our Shepherd in his power
> Mailed and horsed, with lance and sword,
> To his ancestors restored,
> Like a re-appearing Star,
> Like a glory from afar,
> First shall head the flock of war.

But the comment that follows is pure William Wordsworth:

> Alas! the impassioned minstrel did not know
> How, by Heaven's grace, this Clifford's heart was framed:
> How he, long forced in humble walks to go,
> Was softened into feeling, soothed, and tamed.
>
> Love had he found in huts where poor men lie;
> His daily teachers had been woods and rills,

The silence that is in the starry sky,
The peace that is among the lonely hills.

In him the savage virtue of the Race,
Revenge, and all ferocious thoughts were dead:
Nor did he change; but kept in lofty place
The wisdom which adversity had bred.

Glad were the vales, and every cottage-hearth;
The Shepherd-lord was honoured more and more;
And, ages after he was laid in earth,
"The good Lord Clifford" was the name he bore.

The child of nature, we see, can be projected back into the Middle Ages. The mingling of a strain of mild piety with the old naturalistic ardor is typical of Wordsworth in the transitional years between the *Ode to Duty* and *The Excursion*.

The White Doe of Rylstone is a longer and more ambitious work. Like *Brougham Castle*, however, it is based upon the legendry of the English side of the Border. One sometimes forgets that the dalesman's environment was permeated not only by the influences of nature but by tales and ballads about "the Percy out of Northumberland" and other turbulent border nobles. One such ballad found by Wordsworth in Percy's *Reliques*, that of *The Rising of the North*, provided the story and even a few lines of the poem; but the white doe itself came from a separate local tradition.

This poem may be interpreted as Wordsworth's attempt to accomplish several things at once: to tell a beautiful old story; to draw a moral from the story; to use that moral as a means of healing his own sorrow at the loss of his brother; and to reconcile conflicting elements in his mind. The dedication to his wife, written shortly before the poem was published in 1815, reminds her of the days when reading the *Faerie Queene* formed one of the joys of their early wedded life. Then, says Wordsworth, came sorrow (John's death), and "for us the voice of melody was mute." But in time they were able to return to Spenser — more thoughtfully now, and with a deeper sense of his import.

> Then, with mild Una in her sober cheer,
> High over hill and low adown the dell
> Again we wandered, willing to partake
> All that she suffered for her dear Lord's sake.

> Then, too, this Song of *Mine* once more could please,
> Where anguish, strange as dreams of restless sleep,
> Is tempered and allayed by sympathies
> Aloft ascending, and descending deep,
> Even to the inferior Kinds; whom forest-trees
> Protect from beating sunbeams, and the sweep
> Of the sharp winds; — fair Creatures! — to whom Heaven
> A calm and sinless life, with love, hath given.

Let me remount my hobby for a moment to point out that the line "Aloft ascending, and descending deep" is a good expression of the descendental-transcendental attitude. In this work of 1807-1808, however, that attitude is adjusted to the demands of religious orthodoxy.

Emily Norton and her brother Francis are the only living Protestant members of a great Catholic family. In their childhood their Protestant mother, who is now dead, had taught them

> To worship in simplicity
> The invisible God, and take for guide
> The faith reformed and purified.

The Anglican poet wishes the reader to admire Francis Norton for refusing to join the Catholic uprising in which the other men of the family become involved. Wordsworth's Protestantism, however, is anything but savage, for his High Church leanings make him respect, though not approve, the ideals of old Norton. His sympathy for the ritualistic and traditional aspect of religion is evident throughout the poem.

At a crucial moment, Emily prays that her mother's spirit may give Francis this warning:

> If hope be a rejected stay,
> Do thou, my christian son, beware
> Of that most lamentable snare,
> The self-reliance of despair!

Here is a significant footnote to the *Ode to Duty* and the *Peele Castle* stanzas. Wordsworth himself is trying to avoid "the self-reliance of despair" by submitting to "a new control."

But there is a despairing reliance on the will of God which, though it can hardly be called a snare, is also lamentable. This is the state in which Emily finds herself when her father and brothers, including the beloved Francis (emotional equivalent of John Wordsworth), have perished. She has been

> brought
> To the subjection of a holy,
> Though stern and rigorous, melancholy.

She clings so devoutly to her burden of sorrow that her condition, holy as it is, is somewhat abnormal. Her eyes are so persistently raised to heaven that she ignores the

heaven-sent sources of consolation which lie all about her.
She is

> Undaunted, lofty, calm and stable,
> And awfully impenetrable.

At last the white doe, her forgotten playmate of other
years, restores her balance. Its beauty touches her; its
devotion renews her capacity to love and to express love
for living things. Their rambles together bring her into
"haunts of a strengthening amity" where nature can per-
form her healing task. Thus Emily

> now was blest
> With a soft spring-day of holy,
> Mild, and grateful melancholy:
> Not sunless gloom or unenlightened,
> But by tender fancies brightened.

Although Emily and her doe are based partly on Una
and her lamb, no effort need be made to allegorize this
poem. It means exactly what it says. God gives peace to
Emily, not through any direct revelation, but through a
beautiful, gentle, loving "natural object." Allowing for
different circumstances, the doe's function is not unlike
that of the ass in *Peter Bell*.

Wordsworth has woven much of himself into this
legend of Elizabethan days. He hopes that in turning to
God to escape from "the self-reliance of despair" he may
yet retain his contact with nature — a nature in which
the supernatural element is derived not so much from a
possibly heretical world-spirit as from the Deity invoked
on Sundays. Except in a few brisk Scott-like passages, the
personal moralizing obscures the romantic story. The
successful use of old literary material demands the ability
to subject the imagination to the color and texture of the

stuff with which one is working. This ability, possessed so triumphantly by Keats, was lacking in Wordsworth. In *Peter Bell the Third*, Shelley says of him:

> He had a mind which was somehow
> At once circumference and centre
> Of all that he might or feel or know;
> Nothing went ever out, although
> Something did ever enter.
>
> He had as much imagination
> As a pint-pot; — he never could
> Fancy another situation
> From which to dart his contemplation,
> Than that wherein he stood.
>
> Yet his was individual mind,
> And new created all he saw
> In a new manner, and refined
> Those new creations, and combined
> Them, by a master-spirit's law.
>
> Thus — though unimaginative —
> An apprehension clear, intense,
> Of his mind's work, had made alive
> The things it wrought on; I believe
> Wakening a sort of thought in sense.

Though this trait constitutes a peculiarity of imagination rather than a deficiency of that faculty, we may agree that Wordsworth could not impart the illusion of dramatic or impersonal emotion. Wherever we open his works, we find ourselves at some stage in the development of that great egotistic mind.

It is not surprising, then, that the medieval revival should have had less influence upon the content of Words-

worth's work than upon his personal theory of poetry. I
refer, not to his exaggerated, soon forsaken notion about
writing in the language of excited rustics, but to his essential and permanent belief that great poetry is a process
entailing direct observation of the subject, genuinely sensuous response to the stimulus, strong and deep emotion,
and expression which sincerely reflects the writer's feeling
and which reveals, instead of obscuring in a mist of
affected verbiage, the heart of the poetic situation. We
have associated this view of poetry with the revival of
interest in external nature; we may now associate it with
the revival of interest in the past. Here is another link
between naturalism and medievalism.

Wordsworth believes that Percy's *Reliques* did much
to restore simplicity and sincerity to poetry. In the *Essay
Supplementary to the Preface* of *Lyrical Ballads*, he
declares:

I have already stated how much Germany is indebted to this
latter work; and for our own country, its poetry has been absolutely redeemed by it. I do not think that there is an able writer
of verse of the present day who would not be proud to acknowl-
edge his obligation to the *Reliques*; I know that it is so with my
friends; and for myself, I am happy in this occasion to make a
public avowal of my own.

Those obligations are plainly evident in the *Lyrical Ballads*. We should not struggle too hard to associate these
poems with the true popular ballad of the Middle Ages.
Wordsworth loved the genuine old folk ballads, but
seldom found them directly useful in his work. Quite early
in the eighteenth century, the street ballads or broadside
ballads of the preceding century, which had only the most
remote connection with traditional folk poetry, began to
win the favor of the growingly numerous lovers of spon-

taneity and artlessness. In response to the cult of simplicity, a good many intentionally naïve and non-literary
poems, then frequently called ballads, were written by
literary people — pure songs like Carey's *Sally in Our
Alley*, half-narrative songs like Gay's *Black-Eyed Susan*,
and verse tales like Goldsmith's *Edwin and Angelina*.
Percy's collection of "ancient" pieces included a good
many of these productions. If you will turn to the *Reliques*
and read the seventeenth century broadside, *The Spanish
Virgin*, or Shenstone's studiedly artless *Jemmy Dawson*,
you will recognize the true ancestry of *Lyrical Ballads*.
Wordsworth is thinking not so much of real medieval
ballads like *Edward* as of the seventeenth century street
ballad as it had been refracted by the eighteenth century
cult of simplicity. Seizing upon this tradition, he interprets it in the light of his own love of nature and of rustic
folk and his own strong reaction against the artificiality of
eighteenth century poetic diction.

But since even so good a scholar as Percy did not pause
to discriminate between various types of ballad, we shall
understand Wordsworth best by adopting the eighteenth
century's hospitality toward everything that sounded artless and old and of the people. Wordsworth, who had
never studied under Professor Child, doubtless supposed
that he was applying the principles of "ancient English
poetry" to his own work. Certainly the *Lyrical Ballads*
would never have been written except for the revival of
interest in the past. In 1803, when Crabb Robinson lent
Herder a copy of the book, he found that the great German medievalist agreed perfectly with Wordsworth's
theory of poetic diction and regarded it as similar to the
views of the best German ballad revivers.

Wordsworth's poems and critical writings touch upon

other aspects of the eighteenth century medieval revival. In *Resolution and Independence*, he writes:

> I thought of Chatterton, the marvellous boy,
> The sleepless soul that perished in his pride.

The young genius who in the 1760's produced the celebrated pseudo-medieval forgeries, the *Rowley Poems*, was an idol to the romanticists. His precocious talent, his poverty, his death by suicide at the age of eighteen, the strange glamor of his poems, made him a most appealing figure. One of Coleridge's earliest compositions was a *Monody on the Death of Chatterton*; and Keats, who was akin to Chatterton in several respects, dedicated *Endymion* to his memory.

If you are not already familiar with *Ossian*, there is a gap in your knowledge which should be filled without delay. I shall only say that in the 1760's James Macpherson published a series of prose works purporting to be translations from the Gaelic of the legendary bard, Ossian. Even today nobody knows exactly to what extent these works were forgeries. As an antiquarian, Macpherson had a certain amount of genuine material to start with. He rewrote this material, adding so greatly to it from the stores of his own imagination that almost all traces of the hazy originals were obliterated. His own imagination was full of sensibility, sentimental primitivism, love of scenery, graveyard melancholy — in short, all the early romantic tendencies. When the 1760's discovered that ancient Gaelic bards felt exactly as they did, they were naturally enthusiastic about *Ossian*. (Notice, by the way, that the 1760's are the great years of the medieval revival. They give us Percy's *Reliques*, Chatterton's *Rowley Poems*, and Macpherson's *Ossian*.) *Ossian* was widely read and extravagantly praised by almost everyone, but its actual influence was greater on the continent than in England. Among writers of the English romantic period proper, Ossianism appears most strongly in second-rate writers like Mrs. Radcliffe and in first-rate writers before they attain maturity. Two of Coleridge's juvenile works are Ossianic imitations, and the young Byron has plainly thumbed his Macpherson.

It is a testimony of Wordsworth's good taste that in the *Essay Supplementary to the Preface* he attacks Macpherson:

Having had the good fortune to be born and reared in a mountainous country, from my very childhood I have felt the falsehood that pervades the volumes imposed upon the world under the name of Ossian. From what I saw with my own eyes, I knew that the imagery was spurious. In nature everything is distinct, yet nothing defined into absolute independent singleness. In Macpherson's work, it is exactly the reverse; everything (that is not stolen) is in this manner defined, insulated, dislocated, deadened, — yet nothing distinct. It will always be so when words are substituted for things.

Despite this seemingly conclusive evidence, Mr. John Robert Moore, in a paper entitled *Wordsworth's Unacknowledged Debt to Macpherson's Ossian* (*Publications of the Modern Language Association of America*, Vol. XL, pp. 362-378), offers the following thesis:

Although Wordsworth professed contempt for Macpherson's "translation" as a worthless forgery, it can be shown that he was familiar with the subject-matter, the spirit, and, in places the exact phraseology of *Ossian*; that he borrowed an Ossianic word or two when he needed it; that many of his poems deal with themes relating to the Ossianic poems, or present images or lines to which parallels may be found in *Ossian*; and that in his passionate love of the mountain wilderness he came very near the spirit of the blind bard of Selma.

Form your own judgment of Mr. Moore's article. Much of it, in my opinion, belongs to the "salmon in both rivers" school of criticism. Of course no one will deny that Wordsworth knew *Ossian* and passionately loved the mountain wilderness; those are facts no less valid than familiar. And Wordsworth's tours in Scotland made it natural to use Ossianic allusions in poems based upon those experiences. Some of Mr. Moore's material, however, does indicate that Wordsworth came to look upon Ossian more kindly than his criticism would lead us to suppose. Macpherson was an impudent forger whose view of nature and whose imagery ran counter to Wordsworth's theory of poetry; but read in moments when that theory was not uppermost in the poet's mind, the inherent fascination of his material, the sense of "old, unhappy, far-off things," must have exerted some appeal. The poem *Written on a Blank Leaf of Macpherson's Ossian* (1824) begins:

> Oft have I caught upon the breeze,
> Fragments of far-off melodies,
> With ear not coveting the whole,
> A part so charmed the pensive soul.

Thus the forgeries bring from the past messages which garbling has not always obliterated. Macpherson was contemptible, but the blind bard Ossian may well have been a sublime poet.

Wordsworth is the more willing to credit the legendary Ossian with genius because of his belief — not untinged

with the primitivism which characterizes so many romanticists — that in the dawn of inspiration poetry was free
from affected artifice:

The earliest poets of all ages generally wrote from passion excited by real events; they wrote naturally, and as men: feeling
powerfully as they did, their language was daring, and figurative.
In succeeding times, Poets, and Men ambitious of producing the
same effect without being animated by the same passion, set themselves to a mechanical adoption of these figures of speech, and made
use of them, sometimes with propriety, but much more frequently
applied them to feelings and thoughts with which they had no
connection whatsoever. . . . It is indeed true, that the language of
the earliest Poets was felt to differ materially from ordinary language, because it was the language of extraordinary occasions, but it
was really spoken by men, language which the Poet himself had
uttered when he had been affected by the events which he had described, or which he had heard uttered by those around him.

As compared to the scribblers of the age of Pope — I
speak from Wordsworth's viewpoint — medieval and
Elizabethan poets had preserved something of this pristine truth of utterance. Anyone familiar with the literature of courtly love or with Elizabethan sonnets knows
that some of our earlier poetry is in its own way so conventional as to make Alexander Pope sound like Carl
Sandburg. But except for a few rigid traditions, the diction of the older writers is doubtless a more direct outgrowth of personal emotion than that of the pseudoclassicists. The best medieval ballads and songs, Chaucer and
Spenser at their highest, the Elizabethan and Jacobean
song writers, Shakespeare and his fellow dramatists —
these deal so masterfully with the conventions of their
own times that they seem to be perfectly free and "nat-

ural." Even when they are conventional, their conventions are not recognizable as such until one has become thoroughly acquainted with them. Thus Wordsworth felt that practically the whole body of English literature up to the Restoration supported his demand that real feeling should rise from real perception, and real words from real feeling.

The glory of the best pseudoclassic literature is beautiful precision of statement. Since its ideal is clarity, it seldom suggests more than it says; it is not rich in emotional overtones. Romantic literature, on the other hand, is no less concerned with connotation than with denotation; it sets up suggestive reverberations which are an essential part of the poem. This effect can be gained either through unusual richness or unusual economy of expression, and both methods are abundantly illustrated by medieval and Elizabethan literature. (Perhaps you are beginning to realize that the great value of the past lies in its ability to provide anything that one happens to want.) The latter method appealed to Wordsworth much more strongly than the former. Believing imagination to be necessary for the spiritual health of man, he deliberately wished to train the reader in the use of that faculty. He therefore admired the frequent suggestive simplicity of the older literature rather than its frequent elaborate richness. "Cover her face. Mine eyes dazzle. She died young," represents the quality he aspires to restore to poetry. This quality is strong in the medieval ballad, whose authors, being compelled by their limitations to leave much unsaid, thereby often unconsciously serve the highest ends of art. Then, too, the genuine traditional ballad is composed in a community which knows the story and which therefore takes a good many circumstances for granted, so that the modern reader is thrilled by mystery where a member of the original group would feel that everything was quite obvious.

In *Lyrical Ballads*, Wordsworth wishes to give this impression of meaning more than the words say. In fact, we can sometimes see too plainly his anxiety that the reader should coöperate with him in bringing out the total effect. Thus in *Simon Lee*, the poet suddenly interrupts a rather unexciting account of the old huntsman's varicose veins by turning upon the reader and telling him to set his own imagination to work:

> My gentle Reader, I perceive
> How patiently you've waited,
> And now I fear that you expect
> Some tale will be related.
> O Reader! had you in your mind
> Such stores as silent thought can bring,
> O gentle Reader! you would find
> A tale in every thing.
> What more I have to say is short,
> And you must kindly take it:
> It is no tale; but, should you think,
> Perhaps a tale you'll make it.

The line between the simplicity of suggestive restraint and the simplicity of empty flatness is not easy to draw, and the *Lyrical Ballads* furnish some notorious illustrations of that fact. But sometimes in *Lyrical Ballads*, and frequently in later poems which are less laboriously devoted to the enforcement of a thesis, Wordsworth quite triumphantly succeeds in making a few simple words reverberate after they have entered our minds. In such cases, the suggestive power of the phrase or line is generally derived from the support of the whole poem. The line, "Into the middle of the plank," hardly sounds like poetry; but if you will join the parents of Lucy Gray and follow her footprints over the snow you may feel differently about it:

> Then downwards from the steep hill's edge
> They tracked the footsteps small;
> And through the broken hawthorn hedge,
> And by the long stone-wall;

> And then an open field they crossed:
> The marks were still the same;
> They tracked them on, nor ever lost;
> And to the bridge they came.

> They followed from the snowy bank
> Those footmarks, one by one,
> Into the middle of the plank;
> And further there were none!

In itself, "The difference to me" is not particularly impressive, yet how it moves us when we come upon it at the end of *She dwelt among the untrodden ways!* But perhaps the best example is the line in *Michael*, "And never lifted up a single stone." That is one of the saddest lines in all poetry to those who know the shepherd Michael's love for his son Luke, how when Luke went away to the city Michael took him out to the unfinished sheepfold and covenanted with him there like a Biblical patriarch, and finally how when the boy went wrong in the city the old man tried to finish the sheepfold but was too heartsick for the task:

> I have conversed with more than one who well
> Remember the old man, and what he was

Years after he had heard this heavy news.
His bodily frame had been from youth to age
Of an unusual strength. Among the rocks
He went, and still looked up to sun and cloud,
And listened to the wind; and, as before,
Performed all kinds of labour for the sheep,
And for the land, his small inheritance.
And to that hollow dell from time to time
Did he repair, to build the Fold of which
His flock had need. 'Tis not forgotten yet
The pity which was then in every heart
For the old Man — and 'tis believed by all
That many and many a day he thither went,
And never lifted up a single stone.

Although this quality of simple, restrained suggestiveness should not be ascribed wholly to the revival of interest in the past, it was greatly encouraged by that movement.

Aspiring to be the master poet of his age, Wordsworth turned to the master poets of the past. We are told in the *Memoirs*:

When I began to give myself up to the profession of a poet for life, I was impressed with a conviction that there were four poets whom I must have continually before me as examples — Chaucer, Shakespeare, Spenser and Milton. These I must study, and equal *if I could*. I need not think of the rest.

Wordsworth's poems are rich in praises and in verbal reminiscences of these writers. His theory of poetic diction is supported by the statement that "the affecting parts of Chaucer are almost always expressed in language pure and universally intelligible even to this day." Number XXXI of Part II of *Ecclesiastical Sonnets* compares pious young Edward VI to the little boy in the *Prioresse Tale* and hails Chaucer as a precursor of the Reformation. Wordsworth rendered into modern English verse the entire *Prioresse Tale*, together with *The Cuckoo and the Nightingale*, now consigned to the Chaucerian apochrypha, but then regarded as authentic. He also modernized that portion of *Troilus and Criseyde* which contains the lament of Troilus when Criseyde has deserted him. It is perhaps too fanciful to connect the choice of this particular passage with the Annette Vallon situation. The work was composed in 1801, the year before he married his cousin.

In *Personal Talk*, Wordsworth declares that he is not at all interested in chatter about the everyday affairs of friends and relations, but that he is profoundly interested in the lives of those whom he meets in great literature:

> There find I personal themes, a plenteous store,
> Matter wherein right voluble I am,
> To which I listen with a ready ear;
> Two shall be named, preëminently dear, —
> The gentle lady married to the Moor;
> And heavenly Una with her milk-white lamb.

As for Shakespeare, we have already noticed the indebtedness of *The Borderers* to *King Lear*. Elsewhere the diction and movement of Wordsworth's verse often reflect Shakespeare's influence.

Remembering the dedication of *The White Doe of Rylstone*, we may say that the ethical side of Spenser appealed to Wordsworth more strongly than to most of his contemporaries. That rich, dreamy exuberance of imagery for which the *Faerie Queene* was chiefly prized by other romanticists was prized also by Wordsworth, but not as a quality to be emulated in his own works. One finds plenty of Spenserian allusions and echoes, but very seldom the true Spenserian manner. Occasionally, however, he uses the *Faerie Queene* stanza, which had been revived during the eighteenth century as part of the general emergence of old forms against the dominance of the heroic couplet.

To Wordsworth, Milton represents the union of the esthetic and ethical elements of poetry at the highest possible level of each. The desire to achieve Miltonic sublimity is evident in Wordsworth's most serious and elevated poems. From the technical viewpoint, too, Wordsworth emulates Milton's treatment of blank verse and the sonnet. Like the Spenserian stanza, these forms were neglected in the age of Pope but regained their popularity as the eighteenth century went on. Blank verse never came anywhere near disappearing, but the romantic movement restored it to the preëminence which it had once enjoyed. And while we are speaking of poetic form, we may observe that Wordsworth, like the other romanticists, illustrates the triumph of all those free lyrical stanza-patterns the use of which in serious verse was so greatly encouraged by the renewed interest in medieval, Elizabethan, and seventeenth century lyrics.

Though Wordsworth said that he "need not think of the rest," he thought of them a good deal. Dorothy's journals show that he browsed widely in the Elizabethan and seventeenth century poets. In *Biographia Literaria*, Coleridge compares him to Samuel Daniel. He has indeed something of Daniel's purity of style, moral elevation, and steady, sober, glow of thought. Even closer, however, is his kinship with such poets as Herbert and Vaughan. The similarity of the *Immortality Ode* to Vaughan's *The Retreat* has often been pointed out, but

perhaps not all of you have noticed the more remarkable
resemblance between Wordsworth's poem and Traherne's
Wonder:

> How like an angel came I down!
>   How bright are all things here!
> When first among his works I did appear,
>   Oh, how their glory did me crown!
> The world resembled his eternity
>   In which my soul did walk;
> And everything that I did see
>   Did with me talk.
>
>   .   .   .   .
>
> A native health and innocence
>   Within my bones did grow,
> And while my God did all his glories show,
>   I felt a vigor in my sense
> That was all spirit; I within did flow
>   With seas of life like wine;
> I nothing in the world did know,
>   But 'twas divine.

Since no Traherne manuscripts were published before
1903, the parallel can be explained only in terms of natural affinity between Wordsworth and the seventeenth
century religious poets.

Incomplete as they are, these remarks may serve to
show that Wordsworth returned not only to nature but
to the past. The same is obviously true of Coleridge.
Indeed, the fame of *The Ancient Mariner* and *Christabel*
almost tempts one to exaggerate his indebtedness to the
revival of interest in the past. Coleridge's medievalism
was vague and atmospheric, the outgrowth of a passion
for strangeness which found satisfaction in picking up

bits of the marvellous wherever he could find them. Professor Lowes' *The Road to Xanadu* shows both the tremendous range and the fragmentariness of Coleridge's reading. Although well saturated in medieval, Elizabethan and seventeenth century literature — philosophy and theology as well as poetry and drama — he explicitly disclaims the possession of the historic sense. His poems are constantly reminiscent of earlier works; but they do not, like Wordsworth's, send deep, strong roots into the soil of a great tradition.

Coleridge's first volume of verses, the *Poems on Various Subjects* of 1796, testifies that Ossian, Spenser, Chatterton, and Schiller mingled early with his love of nature, his hopes and fears for society, and his religious ferment. *Imitated from Ossian* and *The Complaint of Ninathoma* may be dismissed as juvenile reflections of Macpherson's influence. *Lines in the Manner of Spenser* is a sentimental vision of Sara Fricker. The stanza is that of the *Faerie Queene*; otherwise Spenser's "manner" is suggested only by such things as "false and recreant wight" and "One quill withouten pain yplucked might be." I have already referred to the *Monody on the Death of Chatterton*. Its theme is the woes of genius. Chatterton is called "Nature's genial child," and is informed that if he were now alive he would be a good pantisocrat. *To the Author of 'The Robbers'* hails Schiller as having substituted the deep, human horror of a "famished Father's cry" for the superficial horror of Bürger's goblins:

> Ah! Bard tremendous in sublimity!
> Could I behold thee in thy loftier mood
> Wandering at eve with finely-frenzied eye
> Beneath some vast old tempest-swinging wood!

> Awhile with mute awe gazing I would brood:
> Then weep aloud in a wild ecstasy!

Evidently when Coleridge wrote this sonnet in 1794 he had read not only *Die Räuber*, but *Midsummer Night's Dream*.

The suddenness of Coleridge's artistic development after the beginning of his close association with Wordsworth in 1797 is amazing. One would give much to have a stenographic transcription of their conversations, but even without such a record one may feel sure that Wordsworth directed his friend toward a purer, sincerer, less immaturely "bardic" style. To speak only of poems relating to the medieval revival, the years 1797-1800 give us *The Rime of the Ancient Mariner, Christabel, Love, The Ballad of the Dark Ladie*, and *The Three Graves*. Observe that the high tide of Coleridge's medievalism coincides with the high tide of his naturalism, and that *The Ancient Mariner*, while medieval in form, is naturalistic in theme.

In *Biographia Literaria*, as we remember, Coleridge says that his contributions to *Lyrical Ballads* were to give supernatural things the appearance of reality. This desirable romantic quality is prominent in medieval ballad and romance, where impossibilities are accepted with a naïve literalness mightily thrilling to a person who "knows better." In *The Ancient Mariner*, Coleridge seizes upon this quality of the ballad and consciously develops it, so that the poem is perhaps the finest example in English literature of the realizing of the strange.

> And every soul it passed me by,
> Like the whizz of my cross-bow.

All good medievalists try to get this effect, from Coleridge to Rossetti, whose Blessed Damozel watches the souls going by her "like thin flames," and whose bosom warms "the gold bar of heaven."

Coleridge's great poem depends for its form and style more directly upon the genuine popular ballad than do Wordsworth's contributions to the 1798 volume. A few slightly self-conscious touches of gruesome wierdness, however, show that Coleridge also has at least half an eye on the modern German horror ballads which I mentioned in connection with Scott. In the form in which the poem was first printed, this spook ballad element was considerably stronger, so strong as to make Southey call the poem "a Dutch attempt at German sublimity." Such passages as the following were wisely omitted in later versions:

> His bones were black with many a crack,
> All black and bare, I ween;
> Jet-black and bare, save where with rust
> Of mouldy damps and charnel-crust
> They're patched with purple and green.
>
> . . . .
>
> A gust of wind sterte up behind
> And whistled through his bones;
> Through the holes of his eyes and the hole of his mouth,
> Half whistles and half groans.

The never-finished *Christabel* has not quite the same sharpness of outline as *The Ancient Mariner*. The associations of the writer are held more loosely, and produce a shadowy wierdness, pierced at intervals by serpent thrusts of startlingly realistic illusion. I speak of this uneven poem at its magical best; at its worst it is clap-

trap. Both its best and its worst, one may imagine, are
connected with laudanum.

When *Christabel* was published sixteen years after it
had been laid aside in 1800, Coleridge expressed the fear
that this romantic verse tale would be branded as an imitation of Scott and Byron. Even if chronology permitted
such a charge, other considerations would forbid it. If
Scott should tell the story of *Christabel*, there would be
more riding about and fighting, much more of "Sir Leoline, the Baron rich," and ever so much more description
of the local antiquities. But he would be primarily interested in the narrative values, and would try to make
all other elements of the poem enhance those values.
Byron would transform Bard Bracy into one of his
blighted heroes, and would introduce a tragic love affair;
but he also, in this *genre*, would tell the story for the
sake of the story. Does anyone regard as a story the
Christabel written by Coleridge? Even if the poem had
been completed, we should still think of it as a dream of
strange music and imagery. Coleridge was not trying to
spin a good yarn: the narrative material was a mere occasion for enjoying and passing on to the reader the
thrill of witchcraft. The poem is full of that quality
which we try to express when we speak of romanticism as
"the renascence of wonder." The following lines will
bear witness, though their magic diminishes when they
are torn from their context:

> A snake's small eye blinks dull and shy;
> And the lady's eyes they shrunk in her head,
> Each shrunk up to a serpent's eye,
> And with somewhat of malice, and more of dread,
> At Christabel she looked askance! —

One moment — and the sight was fled!
But Christabel in dizzy trance
Stumbled on the unsteady ground
Shuddered aloud, with a hissing sound;
And Geraldine again turned round,
And like a thing that sought relief,
Full of wonder and full of grief,
She rolled her large bright eyes divine
Wildly on Sir Leoline.

Coleridge found nothing quite like this in medieval literature, but he found hints for it there; and hints are all that a poet needs.

Christabel exemplifies another important element of romantic medievalism. In his preface the author says that the metre of the poem

is not, properly speaking, irregular, though it may seem so from its being founded on a new principle: namely, that of counting in each line the accents, not the syllables. Though the latter may vary from seven to twelve, yet in each line the accents will be found to be only four. Nevertheless, this occasional variation in number of syllables is not introduced wantonly, or for the mere ends of convenience, but in correspondence with some transition in the nature of the imagery or passion.

We so deplorably neglect poetic form in our study of literature that Coleridge's statement may need to be clarified. If you will analyze the following lines, you will see what Coleridge means by saying that the rhythm depends, not upon the number of syllables in the line, but upon the number of accents. The four-stressed beat remains constant, but there is great liberty as regards the number of unstressed syllables:

Aňd thus| the lŏf|tў lā|dў spāke,
All they | who live| iň the ūp|pěr sky,
Thĭs mārk | ŏf mў shāme, | thĭs sēal | ŏf mў sōr|rŏw,
Iň the tōuch | ŏf thĭs bō|sŏm thěre wŏr|kěth ǎ spēll.

Since all the lines have four stresses, they are all rhyth-
mically equivalent despite the unequal number of syllables,
as you can see by reading these lines one after the other as
if they formed a consecutive passage.

The versification of *Christabel*, however, is *not*
"founded on a new principle"; the principle is that of all
Teutonic metre. Coleridge is not even the first to revive
that principle; for after English metre reaches the height
of syllabic exactness in Pope, it begins to regain flexibil-
ity during the eighteenth century. Coleridge is, however,
an important figure in the restoration of the constitutional liberties of English verse. Wordsworth, Scott,
Shelley, and Keats learned much of him in this respect;
and the tradition has come down through Swinburne to
our own time.

Except for the revival of interest in the past, metre
might never have been liberated from syllable counting.
The metre of the romantic poets is based on the varied
sweep and flow of Milton's blank verse; on recognition of
the fact that the rhythm of Shakespeare's early plays is
stiff and wooden like a set of bureau drawers, while the
rhythm of his later plays is free and flexible; on the natural singing movement of Elizabethan lyrics; and on the
accentual cadences of such medieval poetry as had not
been dominated by the syllabic verse of the romance
languages. If you will read aloud, in rapid succession, the
opening lines of *Piers Plowman*, of Pope's *Essay on
Criticism*, and of Shelley's *The Cloud*, you will gain more

understanding of what happened than hours of lecturing could impart.

Let me interrupt myself to warn you against a confusion to which I have here, and perhaps elsewhere, rendered you liable. To speak of the "liberation" of poetry from pseudoclassic standards is to adopt an attitude which is romantic, or at least not pseudoclassic. The versification and, for that matter, the diction of the poetry of the age of Pope were admirably suited to the ideals of pseudoclassic literature and helped that literature to achieve its own special kind of excellence. It is hard not to feel that those ideals were at best extremely limited, but unless we wish to claim the possession of absolute critical truth we had better say that romantic standards differed from pseudoclassic standards, and that the "liberation" here glanced at merely implies freedom to employ a form as well suited to Coleridge's esthetic ideals as the measured heroic couplet to Pope's.

Love, first published as *Introduction to the Tale of the Dark Ladie*, tells how Genevieve, a modern maiden, was courted at moonlight beside a ruined tower, and how she was moved to accept her suitor by his recital of a tale about a lovelorn but heroic knight. The tale itself, though lightly sketched, skillfully evokes the atmosphere of chivalry. The fragmentary *Ballad of the Dark Ladie* was intended to be another story told to Genevieve after she has been won. Its incompleteness forestalls criticism; but one feels that while Coleridge made admirable use of medieval superstition, he saw medieval love through a, to us, slightly irritating haze of eighteenth century sentimentality.

The Three Graves — also fragmentary, but approxi-

mately complete — is noteworthy as an invasion by Coleridge of Wordsworth's chosen field of rustic life. In that
invaluable essay, *My First Acquaintance with Poets*, Hazlitt reports a conversation with Coleridge in which the
poet "lamented that Wordsworth was not prone enough
to believe in the traditional superstitions of the place
[Nether Stowey], and that there was a something corporeal, a matter-of-factness . . . in his poetry, in consequence." There you have the complaint of the strongly
transcendental romanticist against the romanticist whose
work has a larger descendental element. In *The Three
Graves*, Coleridge turns from medieval superstition to a
local story of the tragic effect of a loathsome mother's
curse upon her daughter, her son-in-law, and her daughter's best friend. This story is interpreted in terms of
psychology without loss of its essential horror. The curse
preys upon the minds of its victims until at last Edward,
the young husband, dreams of murdering his wife's
mother, and in blurting out his dream to his wife and her
friend makes the situation unbearable for them:

> He sat upright; and ere the dream
>   Had had time to depart,
> "Oh, God forgive me!" (he exclaimed)
>   "I have torn out her heart."
>
> Then Ellen shrieked, and forthwith burst
>   Into ungentle laughter;
> And Mary shivered, where she sat,
>   And never she smiled after.

An interesting example of how the various strands of
romanticism are interwoven is provided by Coleridge's
preface, which explains that he

had been reading Bryan Edwards's account of the effects of the *Oby* withcraft on the Negroes in the West Indies, and Hearne's deeply interesting anecdotes of similar workings on the imagination of the Copper Indians . . .; and I conceived the design of shewing that instances of this kind are not peculiar to savage or barbarous tribes, and of illustrating the mode in which the mind is affected in these cases, and the progress and symptoms of the morbid action on the fancy from the beginning.

The form of *The Three Graves* is that of *The Ancient Mariner*. Its diction, though resembling that of Wordsworth's *Lyrical Ballads* in its complete simplicity, is much more dramatic and realistic. The speech of the old sexton who tells the story is not purged of local peculiarities, as Wordsworth's theory demanded; without being exactly dialectal, it constantly suggests the language of a particular speaker of a particular region. Coleridge, glancing at his friend, is at pains to assure us that the poem

is in no way connected with the Author's judgment concerning poetic diction. Its merits, if any, are exclusively psychological.

To the modern reader, however, it is chiefly important as showing that Coleridge could sometimes find in his immediate environment the values which he found in the Middle Ages.

Then the fountain begins to run dry. That spirited little metrical experiment, *The Knight's Tomb*, would hardly be worth mentioning had not Scott, by adapting its last three lines in *Ivanhoe*, convinced Coleridge of the true authorship of the Waverly Novels. *Alice Du Clos*, a longish ballad, is of uncertain date. The watermarks on the paper of an early, probably a first, draft are 1822 and 1828. The poem has life of a somewhat hollow and mechanical sort, as if Coleridge, not without a desire to emulate Scott, were vainly trying to recapture the old magic.

Measured against the whole body of Coleridge's verse, the poems which have been mentioned — several of them never completed — do not bulk very large. They include, however, some of Coleridge's greatest art; and it would be easy to show that their qualities appear in other poems less obviously related to the revival of interest in the past. The strangeness of *Kubla Khan*, for instance, is akin to that of *Christabel*.

The question of the relation between Coleridge's fondness for medieval glamor and his transcendental attitude toward life in general can hardly be considered without anticipating a later lecture. But it is evident that he was, as Carlyle says of Teufelsdröckh, "a wonder-loving and wonder-seeking man." In his desire to sense the spiritual reality of things beneath their material trappings he was receptive to whatever might, by imposing strangeness upon the familiar, make existence justify his transcendental faith. Even the most primitive superstitions contained a prophetic glimmer of the light that he sought. The letter to Thomas Poole which was quoted in the lecture on "Romantic Anti-Intellectualism" quite seriously states that his early reading of fairy tales had contributed much to his boundless capacity for belief. He never lost interest in fairy tales such as those underlying *The Ancient Mariner* and *Christabel*, and one may conjecture that his yearning for "the Vast" continued to draw sustenance from their magic. If this supposition is valid, Coleridge the poet and Coleridge the philosopher are less divergent than they appear to be, for his total career may be regarded as one more instance of the romantic fusion of the subrational with the supposedly superrational.

Coleridge is associated with the revival of interest in the past in another and a very important connection. He was a leading figure in romantic literary criticism, which drew so much of its atmosphere and ideals from a study of the earlier literature. In particular he did more than any other English writer to establish the conception of Shakespeare that dominated the nineteenth century. To evaluate Coleridge's Shakespeare criticism, however, would lead us so deeply into questions concerning both the Elizabethan and the eternal Shakespeare that we should never be able to return to the romantic movement. Hence at this point I leave a gap which you must fill in the course of your own future studies.

XVI

THE MEDIEVALISM OF KEATS

Before relating Keats to our present topic, we may briefly consider Byron and Shelley. Although generally speaking any writer of the 1780-1830 period is likely to be more strongly influenced by earlier English literature than any writer of the age of Pope, these two poets are not outstanding exemplars of the revival of interest in the past. Byron was an exoticist, but hardly a medievalist. Intensely romantic as he was in some respects, on one side of his character he was an eighteenth century wit. His critical theories in particular were pseudoclassical, whereas the medieval revival served the ends of romantic criticism. You should clarify this point for yourselves by studying the controversy in which Byron defended Pope against the strictures of Bowles.

Byron's juvenilia, however, are tinged with at least a secondhand medievalism. On August 11, 1807, he informs Miss Pigot:

> I mean to collect all the Erse traditions, poems, etc., etc., and translate, or expand the subject to fill a volume, which may appear next spring under the denomination of *The Highland Harp*, or some title equally *picturesque*.

Nothing came of this Ossianesque project, but *Hours of Idleness*, which was published in the same year, contains a few hints of similar interests. *Oscar of Alva* is a longish ballad of Ossianic material and atmosphere with trimmings of Gothic horror. Byron says that the catastrophe, which I have never had the patience to reach, owes something to *Macbeth* and to a tale by Schiller. This union of Ossian, Shakespeare, and *Sturm und Drang* literature is quite typical of the young romantic mind. *The Death of Calmar and Orla, An Imitation of Macpherson's Ossian* is just what the subtitle indicates. Byron catches the rhythms of Macpherson's prose with some skill. The story, curiously enough, is drawn from the episode of Nisus and Euryalus in the ninth book of the *Aeneid*. To Byron's age, a combination of Virgilian content with Ossianic form did not seem incongruous. The young poet more directly paraphrases Virgil's lines elsewhere in *Hours of Idleness*.

In his fondness for being mournful among the mountains, Byron suggests that a little of his boyish Ossianism clung to him even through maturer years. Of other aspects of the medieval revival, the traces are slight. *Childe Harold* is written in the Spenserian stanza. In Canto I a good many archaisms are used to give the poem an antique flavor, but they are gradually abandoned as the hero beomes more closely identified with the author. Byron is intelligently curious about modern survivals of primitive types of poetry. He translates a Spanish version of a Moorish ballad, touches up an Albanian folk song in Canto II of *Childe Harold*, and in *The Island* versifies an explorer's prose paraphrase of a South Sea Island love song. This sympathy with literary primitivism, however is never thoroughly absorbed into Byron's work. As Wordsworth might say, it is not part of his "regular sea," but a survival of "spring-tide swellings."

Shelley is hardly more of a medievalist than Byron. In her notes on *Queen Mab*, Mrs. Shelley says:

He was a lover of the wonderful and wild in literature, but
had not fostered these tastes at their genuine sources — the romances and chivalry of the middle ages — but in the perusal of
such German works as were current in those days. Under the influence of these he, at the age of fifteen, wrote two short prose romances of slender merit.

These tales, *Zastrozzi* and *St. Irvyne*, are full of the
pseudomedievalism of the novel of terror. His juvenile
verse, too, prickles with Gothic goose flesh. These lines
from *Revenge*, a poem of 1809, follow in Monk Lewis's
footsteps. Try not to let them spoil your enjoyment of
'Twas the Night Before Christmas.

> Thy father, Adolphus! was false, false as hell,
> And Conrad has cause to remember it well,
> He ruined my Mother, despised me his son,
> I quitted the world ere my vengeance was done.
>
> . . . .
>
> Now Adolphus I'll seize thy best loved in my arms,
> I'll drag her to Hades all blooming in charms,
> On the black whirlwind's thundering pinion I'll ride,
> And fierce yelling fiends shall exult o'er thy bride —
>
> He spoke, and extending his ghastly arms wide,
> Majestic advanced with a swift noiseless stride;
> He clasped the fair Agnes — he raised her on high,
> And cleaving the roof sped his way to the sky —
>
> All was now silent, — and over the tomb,
> Thicker, deeper, was swiftly extended a gloom.
> Adolphus in horror sank down on the stone,
> And his fleeting soul fled with a harrowing groan.

This sort of nonsense, however, soon gave place to the
influence of Godwin, and that in turn merged with other
tendencies equally unrelated to medievalism. But although

horror romanticism, with an exception later to be noted, drops out of Shelley's poetry, he never quite loses his fondness for it. Peacock's delicious caricature of his friend in *Nightmare Abbey* is doubtless accurate in making Scythrop's temperament include a strain of Gothicism. At Geneva, on August 18, 1816, Shelley, Byron, and Monk Lewis passed a pleasant evening together during which "Apollo's sexton" related five ghost stories. Shelley — see his *Journal* for this date — was a little shocked to find that Lewis did not believe in ghosts. His transcendentalism, like Coleridge's, was not wholly unsupported by superstition; although his maturest art, unlike Coleridge's, did not rely upon superstition for its effects.

The exception hinted at a moment ago is an important one. Although never deeply read in earlier English poetry, Shelley was an admirer of Elizabethan drama; for its contrasts between absolute goodness and absolute wickedness tallied with his own Prometheus-Jupiter view of life. *The Cenci* plainly draws its inspiration from Elizabethan dramas of horror and revenge. The incest theme suggests Ford, but the general tone of the play and the noblewoman-abused-by-bestial-man motive are decidedly Websterian.

What might be called exotic or cosmopolitan medievalism is one of several romantic tendencies which I shall have no time to discuss. I can only say that Shelley is obviously influenced by European literature of the Middle Ages and the Renaissance — Dante, Petrarch, Camoens. When you fill in the outlines of this course, you should study this aspect of romanticism in other writers of the period as well as in Shelley. Consider for example Keats's love of Boccaccio, and Byron's indebtednes to the Italian mock-heroic romance. A forthcoming dissertation by Mr. Roderick Marshall, *Italy in English Literature, 1660-1815*, may be recommended in this connection.

Prometheus Unbound and several other poems establish Shelley as an important figure in the adaptation of classical material to romantic uses. This tendency, however, is even better exemplified by Keats.

Browning's question, "What porridge had John Keats?" may in some degree be answered by saying that of all the romantic poets Keats derives the most nourishment from the beauty of olden things as preserved by the genius of the past. Once he matures his art, everything that he touches becomes his own property; but to the end of his brief career one can tell from his poems what kind of book has recently been exciting him. In *Endymion* we see the voluptuous Elizabethan poems on classical themes; in *The Eve of St. Agnes*, Spenser and Chatterton; in *Isabella*, Boccaccio; in *Hyperion*, Milton; in *The Fall of Hyperion*, Dante; in *The Eve of St. Mark*, the Chaucer of the early vision poems; in *La Belle Dame Sans Merci* and *Meg Merrilies*, two different aspects of balladry.

These influences were partly direct and partly indirect: he read the older writers, and he also read contemporaries who were reading and imitating the older writers. Keats was the one great man who emerged from a whole ferment of literary activity in London and its suburbs — a coterie of excited, middle-class young men who were eagerly stuffing down everything old and strange and lovely that they could lay their hands on. F. E. Pierce gives a good account of the group in his *Currents and Eddies in the English Romantic Generation*. The spirit of these young "Cockneys" was somewhat hectic and superficial, and at times not free from affectation. Both in its virtues and its defects it predicted the esthetic movement which occurred later in the nineteenth century. Its faults were those of too hastily gorging the externals of a tradition the essentials of which have not been made a part of one's personal culture. If reading *Endymion* through from beginning to end gives an effect like that of eating a whole jar of strawberry jam at a sitting, the reason is that Keats had not yet risen above the movement of which he was a part. As he himself, with his uncanny faculty for self-criticism, knew perfectly well, he had to outgrow Leigh Hunt.

To be fair to his contemporaries, however, one must grant that Keats's indebtedness to them is often quite evident even when he goes furthest beyond them. Mr. E. V. Weller, in a book entitled *Keats and Mary Tighe*, has printed the poems of this almost forgotten pseudo-Spenserian Irish poetess with a great many parallel passages from the work of Keats. Some of the parallels are far-fetched, but there are enough good ones to substantiate Mr. Weller's point. It has also been shown that *The Eve of St. Agnes* bears some relation to an episode in Mrs. Radcliffe's *Mysteries of Udolpho*. In short, Keats's interests are shared by so many of his contemporaries that it is sometimes difficult to say whether a given passage should be ascribed to the influence of Spenser or Mary Tighe, Boccaccio or Leigh Hunt. But we can generally say that whatever else it is, it is John Keats.

The poems of Keats show a general progress from excessive reliance on inferior contemporaries and on eighteenth century medievalists to direct personal contact with the works of the great writers of the past. So far as the older writers are concerned, his work passes on from an exaggerated admiration for the luscious and exuberant qualities of Spenser and his school to a more restrained Elizabethan richness, and at last to a severer majesty derived from Shakespeare, Milton, and Dante. This development is comprised within four years. Where he would have ended if fate had given him more time is beyond our knowledge, though unfortunately not beyond the conjectures of the critics.

Some essential features of Keats's medievalism and Elizabethanism may be brought out by contrasting him with Coleridge and Wordsworth. Keats loves strangeness, and is unexcelled in the ability to impart a sense of mystery. He differs from Coleridge, however, in that he turns to the past for sensuous delight rather than for the sublimatedly superstitious thrill which was Coleridge's chief aim. When, as often happens, antique charm includes an element of supernatural or preternatural strangeness, Keats responds to that element as a part of the total esthetic experience; but his quest is primarily for sheer beauty. His romanticism, indeed, is far removed from its primitive psychological basis. It aspires toward a union of the reality of sense experience with the inward ideal of the beautiful. Keats finds the materials for this union in nature, but in the literature of the past he finds the materials already combined.

Keats, like Wordsworth, believes that poetry was seriously corrupted during the age of Pope. In Elizabethan days, we learn from *Sleep and Poetry*, England was the home of imagination — "here her altar shone." Then came the withering rules of the pseudoclassicists:

Could all this be forgotten? Yes, a schism
Nurtured by foppery and barbarism,
Made great Apollo blush for this his land.
Men were thought great who could not understand
His glories; with a puling infant's force
They swayed about upon a rocking horse,
And thought it Pegasus. Ah dismal souled!
The winds of heaven blew, the ocean rolled
Its gathering waves — ye felt it not. The blue
Bared its eternal bosom, and the dew
Of summer nights collected still to make
The morning precious; beauty was awake!
Why were ye not awake? But ye were dead
To things ye knew not of, — were closely wed
To musty laws lined out with wretched rule
And compass vile; so that ye taught a school
Of dolts to smooth, inlay, and clip, and fit,
Till, like the certain wands of Jacob's wit
Their verses tallied. Easy was the task:
A thousand handicraftsmen wore the mask
Of poesy. Ill-fated, impious race!
That blasphemed the bright lyrist to his face,
And did not know it, — no, they went about,
Holding a poor, decrepid standard out
Marked with most flimsy mottoes, and in large
The name of one Boileau!

But now the cloud has lifted. Addressing the great singers of the past, Keats says that thanks to their influence imagination has regained her old freedom:

But let me think away those times of woe:
Now 'tis a fairer season; ye have breathed
Rich benedictions o'er us; ye have wreathed
Fresh garlands: for sweet music has been heard

In many places; — some has been upstirred
From out its crystal dwelling in a lake,
By a swan's ebon bill; from a thick brake,
Nestled and quiet in a valley mild,
Bubbles a pipe; fine sounds are floating wild
About the earth: happy are ye and glad.

In all this, Keats and Wordsworth seem to be in complete agreement. But Wordsworth's chief complaint against pseudoclassicism is its hollow artifice, whereas Keats is in reaction against its metrical monotony and its lack of sensuousness. Wordsworth turns to the past for corrective lessons of sincerity and simplicity, while Keats turns to the past to enjoy its imaginative opulence and its prodigality of sensuous delight. There he found poets who exemplified the advice that he gave Shelley, to "load every rift of your subject with ore."

Spenser was his first love. Keats was a mere schoolboy when Charles Cowden Clarke introduced him to the *Epithalamium* and the *Faerie Queene*. Clarke tells us that

he went through it as a young horse through a spring meadow, ramping. . . . Like a true poet, too, he specially singled out epithets. . . . He hoisted himself up, and looked burly and dominant, as he said, "What an image that is, — sea-shouldering whales!"

The surest symptom of poetic promise in this anecdote is not so much the singling out of epithets as the organic response to them, the being made to feel like a whale by words about whales. Innumerable lines in Pope delight the mind, but very few get into our muscles and make us hoist ourselves up. It took the Elizabethans to do that for Keats. They, with Chaucer, also helped him to establish his mastery of flexible, fluent rhythm. In loosening and softening the structure of the decasyllabic couplet, Leigh

Hunt and Keats were but reviving the form as it had existed before Denham and Waller imposed precision upon it.

Keats was always to be a worshipper of Spenser — not the "sage and serious" Spenser whom Wordsworth had inherited from Milton, but a richly dreamy and sensuous Spenser who taught nothing but beauty. If his love of fragrant bypaths led Keats even more deeply into the works of Giles and Phineas Fletcher, Drummond of Hawthornden, and Browne of Tavistock, he never ceased to love the master of whom these poets were the disciples. Until toward the close of Keats's career, the Middle Ages were steeped for him in a double glamor — that imparted to them by the romantic imagination of his own time, and that imparted to them by the romantic imagination of Spenser. His medievalism first came to him through the Elizabethans. The early *Specimen of an Induction to a Poem* begins:

> Lo! I must tell a tale of chivalry;
> For large white plumes are dancing in mine eye.
> Not like the formal crest of latter days:
> But bending in a thousand graceful ways;
> So graceful, that it seems no mortal hand,
> Or e'en the touch of Archimago's wand,
> Could charm them into such an attitude.

Then, fearing that he may be unequal to the task, he calls upon the spirit of Spenser, supreme teller of such tales:

> Spenser! thy brows are archèd, open, kind,
> And come like a clear sunrise to my mind;
> And always does my heart with pleasure dance,
> When I think on thy noble countenance:
> Where never yet was aught more earthly seen

Than the pure freshness of thy laurels green.
Therefore, great bard, I not so fearfully
Call on thy gentle spirit to hover nigh
My daring steps: or if thy tender care,
Thus startled unaware,
Be jealous that the foot of other wight
Should madly follow that bright path of light
Traced by thy loved Libertas; he will speak,
And tell thee that my prayer is very meek;
And that I follow with due reverence,
And start with awe at mine own strange pretence.

"Libertas" is Leigh Hunt, Keats's early mentor.

Keats saw not only medieval but classical literature through Elizabethan eyes. His sonnet *On First Looking Into Chapman's Homer* is plain evidence of that fact, but the best illustration of his Elizabethan manner of treating ancient material is *Endymion*. It should be thought of in connection with those rather numerous Elizabethan verse narratives which deal with classical legends in an ornate, voluptuous, and somewhat erotic style. Their ultimate model, of course, is Ovid. Keats's source is Michael Drayton's *The Man in the Moone*, but the example of the type most familiar to you will be Shakespeare's *Venus and Adonis*. Marlowe's *Hero and Leander* is also full of the quality that Keats was to inherit from this tradition.

Everyone grants that the poems of the 1817 volume are cloying in their lusciousness; and *Endymion*, published in the following year, is open to the same charge despite its many beauties. Keats's manly and intelligent preface can never be too frequently quoted:

It is just that this youngster should die away: a sad thought for me, if I had not some hope that while it is dwindling I may be plotting, and fitting myself for verses fit to live. . . . The imagination of a boy is healthy, and the mature imagination of a man is healthy; but there is a space of life between, in which the soul is in a ferment, the character undecided, the way of life uncertain, the ambition thick-sighted: thence proceeds mawkishness, and all the thousand bitters which those men I speak of must necessarily taste in going over the following pages. I hope I have not in too late a day touched the beautiful mythology of Greece, and dulled its brightness: for I wish to try once more, before I bid it farewell.

This self-criticism was the result of a deeper, more thoughtful, less boyishly greedy attention which he had recently been devoting, and increasingly continued to devote, to great books. Shakespeare, Milton, and Dante (in Cary's translation) showed him the esthetic superiority of a loftier, more serious, and more firmly controlled imagination. At first he dealt with Shakespeare much as he had done with Spenser, drawing from *Midsummer Night's Dream, Romeo and Juliet,* and *The Tempest* precisely those richly fanciful qualities which his temperament inclined him to exaggerate in his own work. But the great tragedies soon won his admiration, as we may see from the sonnet *On Sitting Down to Read King Lear Once Again*:

> O Golden tongued Romance with serene lute!
>> Fair plumed Syren, Queen of far-away!
>> Leave melodizing on this wintry day,
> Shut up thine olden pages, and be mute:
> Adieu! for, once again, the fierce dispute
>> Betwixt damnation and impassioned clay
>> Must I burn through; once more humbly assay
> The bitter-sweet of this Shakespearian fruit:
> Chief poet! and ye clouds of Albion,
>> Begetters of our deep eternal theme!

When through the old oak Forest I am gone,
    Let me not wander in a barren dream,
But, when I am consumèd in the fire,
    Give me new Phoenix wings to fly at my desire.

Although Keats has dismissed romance, he is not genuinely at ease in the presence of tragedy. He approaches *King Lear* as if it were a purgatorial fire which he hopes will burn away his early poetic sins and transform him into a different kind of poet. A similarly strained and anxious attitude appears in *Lines on Seeing a Lock of Milton's Hair*:

When every childish fashion
    Has vanished from my rhyme,
Will I, grey-gone in passion,
    Leave to an after-time
        Hymning and harmony
Of thee, and of thy works, and of thy life;
But vain is now the burning and the strife,
Pangs are in vain, until I grow high-rife
        With old philosophy,
And mad with glimpses of futurity!

This is so plainly not the mood in which great poetry is written that one wonders whether Keats's admiration for Shakespeare and Milton may not have done him as much harm as good. The question is complicated by the fact that these great poets not only ennobled his taste but made him distrust that delight in pure sensuousness which was the very basis of his art. They seemed to say that a poet should be a philosopher. Hence these lofty models simultaneously inspired him and worried him. To me — you will find that the point is hotly disputed — both the Miltonic *Hyperion, a Fragment*, and the

Dantesque *The Fall of Hyperion: a Dream* are Keats's magnificent attempts to write like someone else, not only in manner but still more in thought. It is significant that both these ventures were abandoned, and that he never really closed the book of "golden tongued Romance." But in the great 1820 volume it is romance with a difference. Shakespeare, Milton, and Dante have not transformed him into the philosopher that he had mistakenly longed to be; but they have made him a better artist of his own particular kind, the true John Keats of the great odes and *The Eve of St. Agnes*. Spenser is not forgotten, but he is seen through the eyes of a great poet, not those of a dazzled boy.

The Eve of St. Agnes is the consummation of Keats's art in its relation to the revival of interest in the past. Extremely rich and gorgeous as it is, it is almost completely free from that lip-smacking self-consciousness which was the curse of the poet's earlier work. Taking his initial hint from Burton, Keats casts a few sidelong glances at Ann Radcliffe and Mary Tighe; then looks back to Chatterton; then back to Spenser, who inspired Chatterton; then back to the Middle Ages, which inspired Spenser. He welds this chain of influences and inspirations into a unified work of art, and fixes upon it the stamp of a genius which, though in the truest sense original, has drawn sustenance from the greatest masters.

The mature Keats — if the term may be applied to a man of twenty-three — still loads every rift with ore, though the ore is now of pure gold. But he has also learned the effectiveness of suggestive restraint in gaining effects that profusion of imagery would merely smother. *The Eve of St. Mark*, which is based upon the technique of the Chaucerian vision poems, is a masterpiece of delicate economy even in its unfinished state. *La Belle Dame Sans Merci* creates a more than Coleridgian strangeness by the choice of a few details so adroitly presented to the imagination that they suggest much more than they say:

> I met a lady in the meads
>   Full beautiful, a faery's child;
> Her hair was long, her foot was light,
>   And her eyes were wild.
>
> I set her on my pacing steed,
>   And nothing else saw all day long;
> For sideways would she lean, and sing
>   A faery's song.
>
> I made a garland for her head,
>   And bracelets too, and fragrant zone;
> She looked at me as she did love,
>   And made sweet moan.

Amy Lowell is right in saying that this poem points directly forward to the work of the Pre-Raphaelites. Notice also how far it soars above its slight indebtedness to the spook balladry of the 1790's. Just one telltale Monk Lewis touch remains, and even that is almost turned into gold:

> I saw their starv'd lips in the gloam
>   With horrid warning gaped wide.

La Belle Dame betokens a more direct approach to the Middle Ages than was characteristic of Keats in the days when he could see them only through Elizabethan eyes. Similarly, Chapman, Drayton, Marlowe, and the young Shakespeare are no longer his only interpreters of the

Greek spirit. Though never a master of the ancient tongues, Keats has learned a purer classicism from Milton, and has embodied it in *Hyperion*. Long contemplation of the Elgin marbles, moreover, has prepared him to write the *Ode on a Grecian Urn*. At his brief and glorious best, then, he is a free artist, tied to no one's apron strings, but responding to each esthetic experience in the way most appropriate to the special quality of that experience.

When I said in the preceding lecture that Wordsworth was restricted in his use of medieval material by his inability to detach his imagination from his personal ideas, I incidentally suggested that he differed from Keats in this respect. The contrast deserves attention. In a famous letter written to Richard Woodhouse on October 27, 1818, Keats says:

As to the poetical character itself (I mean that sort, of which, if I am anything, I am a member; that sort distinguished from the Wordsworthian, or egotistical Sublime; which is a thing per se, and stands alone), it is not itself — it has no self — It is every thing and nothing — It has no character — it enjoys light and shade; it lives in gusto, be it foul or fair, high or low, rich or poor, mean or elevated. — It has as much delight in conceiving an Iago as an Imogen. What shocks the virtuous philosopher delights the chameleon poet. . . . A poet is the most unpoetical of anything in existence, because he has no Identity — he is continually informing and filling some other body. . . . It is a wretched thing to confess; but it is a very fact, that no one word I ever utter can be taken for granted as an opinion growing out of my identical Nature — how can it, when I have no nature.

Like many other passages in Keats's letters, this is a precious document for the student of literary theory. Keats distinguishes two types of poet. One is what he calls "the Wordsworthian, or egotistical sublime." He uses the term "egotistical" without malice, or — considering that Wordsworth had dismissed *Endymion* as "a pretty piece of paganism" — with only a little malice. He means that a poet of this type has a highly developed sense of identity. In reading a poet like Wordsworth, we generally feel ourselves addressed by an individual who is seizing upon things outside of himself as material for the expression of a personal idea. It is impossible for Wordsworth to write *The White Doe of Rylstone* without thinking more about his wife, his brother, the Church of England, the influence of natural objects, and his own spiritual problems than about the material he is dealing with. In fact, he would never have dealt with this material at all if it had not seemed to provide an opportunity to talk in poetry about these personal matters. Please understand that I am not condemning, but distinguishing.

Then there is another type of poet — the type with which Keats rightly associates himself. Such a poet, instead of interpreting life from a fixed personal viewpoint, makes life come alive for us by permeating it with his own imagination. His task is not to judge life explicitly, but to judge it implicitly by tasting, selecting, enjoying, and responding. His mind is like a great sensitized plate, transmitting those qualities in existence which we call beautiful. It is not that his individuality as an artist disappears, but that the individuality is expressed through the material rather than the material through the individuality. Keats almost never has any "message" for us. He does not, like Shelley, yearn to shatter the "dome of many-coloured glass" that "stains the white radiance of eternity." He knows nothing whatever about the white radiance of eternity, and he delights in the many-coloured glass which "threw warm gules on Madeline's fair breast" and thus enhanced the white radiance of her body. This helps to explain why Keats, of all the poets of his age, is most successful in drawing beauty from the older literature. He is willing to let loveliness speak for itself. His freedom from any kind of deliberate spiritual campaign repeatedly enables him to escape from romanticism into a romanticity which seems unconscious of obstacles.

But why should Keats say that this description of himself is "a wretched thing to confess?" Unfortunately, as I have said before, he was haunted by the feeling that "the egotistical sublime" might after all be a worthier kind of poetry than his own. The resultant conflict will be discussed in a later lecture. Today I have merely reminded you of what his porridge was, and how he digested it.

XVII

TRANSCENDENTALISM

This concluding section of the course will deal with transcendentalism in relation to Coleridge, Wordsworth, Byron, and Shelley; and finally with Keats, to whom no tag will be assigned. For some of the facts in these lectures, and for the general idea of the struggle between necessity and transcendentalism, I am indebted to Professor S. F. Gingerich's suggestive *Essays in the Romantic Poets*; but my view of the subject is so nearly antithetical to his that if you will listen to both of us you will have an amusing instance of what diverse conclusions two scholars can draw from more or less the same body of material.

Before I began the actual preparation of these lectures, I had intended to reserve all treatment of transcendentalism for the concluding hours. As you have seen, however, I found myself unable to discuss romantic naturalism without recognizing its transcendental element; and the same difficulty would have applied to romantic medievalism had I not confined myself chiefly to the literary side of that topic. We are now to consider transcendentalism not as a vague emotional attitude, but as a conscious pseudophilosophical formulation of that attitude; not as a more or less important element entering into naturalism or medievalism, but as a third main aspect of romanticism. The overlapping which will remain despite this shift in viewpoint may be regarded as evidence of the fundamental unity of our subject. In fact, it is hardly possible

to discuss any important romantic tendency without cross-
ing the borders of some other romantic tendency.

At this point let us recall my over simple but perhaps
not wholly invalid division of the romantic movement
into three phases: one in which descendentalism is stronger than transcendentalism; one in which descendentalism and transcendentalism are of approximately equal
strength; and one in which transcendentalism is stronger
than descendentalism. Though neither of the two elements is ever wholly absent from truly romantic thought,
the general trend of the movement is away from the
descendental and towards the transcendental. How is this
development to be explained?

Sooner or later, every romanticist whose urge toward
illusion is more than merely superficial discovers that the
desired fusion of natural and supernatural is not to be
sought in any form of social organization, in external
nature, in the Middle Ages, in the redman's wigwam, or
anywhere but in his own imagination. One might suppose
that this discovery would bring the quest to a peaceful
close. The romantic illusion could be indulged in as a
delightful form of mental play which has nothing to do
with actuality and therefore cannot be threatened by reason. Some such compromise represents the attitude of
many intelligent people of today. By frankly recognizing
that the products of imagination are imaginary they avoid
any agonizing conflict between fact and dream, and win
back something of the original pleasure of romanticity by
abandoning all attempt to give that pleasure a rational
justification. But the true romanticist is not content with
this solution. He is unwilling to relinquish the belief that
his vision is not an emotional holiday but a key to the

interpretation of life. Hence he is often discouraged when faced by the realization that the gap between what he wants and what he can get is to be bridged only by "Let's pretend." We see this discouragement in Wordsworth's *Peele Castle* stanzas, in Coleridge's *Dejection*, and in Shelley's *Alastor*. Byron is full of it. It is the source of that melancholy and irony which parallel the romanticist's optimism. It is the seamy side of romanticism.

This predicament is surmounted in an interesting way. The romanticist cannot doubt the truth of his illusion. Therefore, since he has discovered his imagination to be the ultimate source of the illusion, his imagination must have the power of creating a truth which is "higher" than the impressions of sense. Professor Lawrence once requested a student to translate for his class a rather difficult passage in *Beowulf*. "Well," she gushed, "I have this picture in my mind" — and then presented a hodge-podge which had no relation to the passage. "But Miss So-and-so," Professor Lawrence protested, "your pictures must come out of the text." The student was much abashed, like a romanticist disheartened by the gap between reality and illusion. But suppose she had said, "If the picture in my mind does not agree with the text of *Beowulf*, so much the worse for the text. The picture in my mind belongs to a higher order of being than the text. Why should my pictorial mind, my shaping spirit of imagination, be enslaved by the text when it can do so much better?" In that case, the student would have discovered the chief romantic remedy for romantic disillusionment: she would have discovered transcendentalism.

This is the ultimate solution of the romanticist's problem. By shifting from a naturalism or a medievalism which is an uneasy compromise between the descendental and transcendental attitudes to a more or less complete transcendentalism he arises above the obstacles which threaten him. The object of his quest exists in his creative mind, safe from all attack. Blake's insight outstripped that of his contemporaries when he wrote in *The Ghost of Abel*:

Nature has no Outline,
But Imagination has. Nature has no Tune, but Imagination has. Nature has no Supernatural, and dissolves: Imagination is Eternity.

Thus romanticity, which originated in the imagination of primitive man, finds its last stronghold in the imagination of the transcendentalist.

In my eighth lecture I defined transcendentalism as "belief in the dominance of the intuitive and spiritual elements of mentality over sense experience." As a philosophical doctrine, it is an outgrowth of idealism, which teaches that we have no rational grounds for believing in anything but ideas and their relations. In Kantian idealism, the knowledge which is derived *a priori* from the needs of the human spirit transcends the knowledge which is derived from the experience of the senses. Kant himself never asserted that *a priori* knowledge had any *control* over empirical knowledge. He put the two kinds of knowledge into rigidly distinct compartments. The transcendent enjoys the privilege of being "higher" than the empirical by granting to the latter supremacy in its own realm. But the successors of Kant, especially Schelling and Hegel, were not satisfied with their master's assertion of the rights of the moral will to build a home for itself in regions beyond mere understanding. They gave the will a large degree of positive dominance over the whole of existence, material and sensuous no less than spiritual and supersensuous. Hence the term "transcendentalism" comes to imply the power of the mind to reshape, in accordance with the demands of the will, the world depicted by our senses. Professor Gingerich says on page 9 of his *Essays*:

The principle of transcendentalism is closely allied to the principle of Free-will. It lays bare the method, or mode, by which the intellect grows. It reverses the conception that all knowledge is derived from the senses, and asserts that the sense-impressions that stream into the mind from the outer world were meaningless, a mere blotch on the canvas, had not the mind an original, active, organizing principle within itself by which it turns them into knowledge. . . . This constituent force of the mind, which did not come by experience but which renders experience possible, makes the mind an active agent and not merely a passive recipient, implies that the mind is self-determining and the will free.

Most of us will agree that the mind, whatever it may be, is not a passive bucket into which experience is pumped. Somehow or other, we do seem to acquire the power to select, control, and make new units of knowledge out of the stimuli that hit our nerves. We know that our mental states have a strong influence over our sensory experience. It even appears that by adopting a certain mental attitude we can do much to receive impressions that we want and keep out impressions that we do not want. But how far this "constituent force of the mind," as Gingerich terms it, is original, active, and independent of experience, and how far, on the contrary, it is itself a very highly organized product of experience; how far it is free and creative, and how far mechanically determined;

and how far it may be relied upon as a guide to the discovery of truth when perception and logical inference
conflict with what we desire to believe — these are un-
answerable questions in our present state of ignorance. In
any case, however, the transcendentalist values the world
which is created by his imaginative will more highly than
the world of which his senses bring him their crudely
literal reports. To a really good example of the type,
almost no product of the imagination need be regarded
as imaginary.

Throughout this course I have tried not to indulge in
polemics against ideas that I dislike. But the transcendental spree in which certain high priests of the "new
physics" are now indulging irresistibly tempts me to say
something that is perhaps less digressive than it may
appear. Human experience abundantly shows that, no
matter how highly we may value the power of our wills,
if we would avoid disappointment we had better exercise
that power within limits set up by "that false secondary
power by which we multiply distinctions." Some persons
assume that since Newton's three-dimensional universe has
been proved an inadequate picture of reality they may rise
into a perfect intellectual democracy where old-fashioned
reason will be as visionary as nonsense, and nonsense
therefore as valid as reason. The actual business of life
cannot refute such ideals; it simply bears no relation to
them and must act as if they did not exist. No scientific
discovery can ever absolve man from the moral require-
ments of scientific method. Those standards are unrelia-
ble; but they are all that we have, and we must continue
to use them as honestly as we can. Under any abstract
theory of cosmology, some conceptions will be solider than

others in relation to our minds. Whatever picture of the universe we adopt, we shall meet with ideas that are like iron and with ideas that are like mist. No ingenuity of rationalization can give the latter the same reliability and inexorability as the former. Even within a world in which only mathematical formulas are real, there will remain gradations of toughness which man can describe only in terms of impossibility, possibility, probability, and certainty; and man's imagination will continue to breed desires which even the universal dream stuff will coldly deny.

But we must ask how the romanticists made use of transcendentalism. In the period under discussion, there were of course several available philosophies which had transcendental implications. At one time or another, various romanticists found encouragement for their transcendentalism in Plato, the Neo-Platonists, certain medieval and Renaissance mystics, Spinoza, Jacob Boehme, Berkeley, Swedenborg, and Kant and his followers. One might therefore suppose that an adequate treatment of this subject would go deeply into metaphysics. But the poet is almost never a technical philosopher; if he were, he would not be a poet. Even Coleridge had practically ceased to be a poet when he took his metaphysical turn. As an intelligent man, the poet reads and thinks. What he chiefly responds to, however, are the emotional attitudes suggested by various philosophies, rather than the details of philosophical systems. He gets his philosophy mainly from general tendencies pervasive in the air of his environment, the same tendencies from which the philosopher derives his own system in his less obviously emotional way. Nevertheless, acquaintance with the theories of the chief philosophers greatly contributes to one's understanding of the poets' ideas, and without burdening you with technicalities I shall try from time to time to illustrate that fact.

That the transcendentalism of our romanticists was poetic rather than formally philosophical appears in their fondness for drawing analogies between the transcendental faculty and the creative imagination of the artist. To Blake, for example, the rule of Urizen is to be overthrown by recognizing that "a firm persuasion that a thing is so, makes it so;" and repeatedly he identifies this will to believe with the poetic imagination. In the section of *Jerusalem* entitled *To the Christians* he writes:

I know of no other Christianity and of no other Gospel than the liberty both of body and mind to exercise the Divine Arts of Imagination — Imagination, the real and Eternal World of which this Vegetable Universe is but a faint shadow.

You will remember Wordsworth's idea that the instinctive transcendentalism which leads the child to impute love to nature is "the first Poetic spirit of our human life." In Book XIV of *The Prelude* he defines imagination as

> another name for absolute power
> And clearest insight, amplitude of mind,
> And reason in her most exalted mood.

Similarly, Coleridge's "shaping spirit of imagination" is carried over from his poetry to his transcendental philosophy without any essential change.

In Shelley's thought, that exercise of will by which man can expel evil from his nature is closely related to the poetic process:

Most of the errors of philosophers, have arisen from considering the human being in a point of view too detached and circumscribed. He is not a moral and an intellectual — but also, and pre-eminently, an imaginative being. His own mind is his law; his own mind is all things to him.

(Speculations on Metaphysics)

This perfectly accurate statement is used as evidence, not of the subrational weakness of the human mind, but of its superrational strength:

Reason is the enumeration of qualities already known; imagination is the perception of the value of those qualities, both separately and as a whole. Reason respects the differences, and imagination the similitudes of things. Reason is to imagination as the instrument to the agent, as the body to the spirit, as the shadow to the substance.

(Defence of Poetry)

Since he goes on to define poetry as "the expression of the imagination," the poetic and transcendental faculties are for him substantially identical.

Thus to the romantic poet transcendentalism is especially appealing because it seems to give his art a philosophical, almost a religious, dignity. But since it tells him only what he has felt all along, he seldom pauses to study it minutely. He prefers to enjoy the privileges of the transcendental attitude without subjecting himself to the restraints and sceptical distinctions of a thoroughgoing idealism. The idealistic system would enable him to possess the desired illusion within his mind, but would forbid him to discover it anywhere else. Now your true romanticist is seldom willing to relinquish the hope that, after all, things are precious in themselves and not merely as they are regarded. He loves matter so long as he does not have to be materialistic about it. He cannot, in other words, wholly surrender his illusioned descendentalism. The melting away of the objective primrose is a heavy price to pay for the retention of the "something more" which he has imposed upon it. When he grapples with the technicalities of the problem, he finds it hard to reconcile the materialistic implications of his descendentalism with the idealistic implications of his transcendentalism.

Wisely, then, the romanticist interprets transcendentalism in terms of poetic imagination, drawing from the philosophers whatever appears to support such an interpretation. He skips back and forth over the gap between objective and subjective, often thinking himself the champion of an idealism which in reality is based upon a denial that the gap can be crossed at all. He feels that if imagination is an infallible Pope, it should not remain a prisoner in the Vatican of the mind, but should exert its control over "the very world." The ideas of Shelley's Julian would make Kant writhe in his grave, but they have the true spirit of romantic transcendentalism:

> "It is our will
> That thus enchains us to permitted ill —
> We might be otherwise — we might be all
> We dream of happy, high, majestical.
> Where is the love, beauty, and truth we seek
> But in our mind? and if we were not weak
> Should we be less in deed than in desire?"
> "Ay, if we were not weak — and we aspire
> How vainly to be strong!" said Maddalo:
> "You talk Utopia." "It remains to know,"
> I then rejoined, "and those who try may find
> How strong the chains are which our spirit bind;
> Brittle perchance as straw."
>   (*Julian and Maddalo*)

Our romantic poets grow up against a background of eighteenth century thought; and though the early stirings of romanticism in the eighteenth century predict and encourage the transcendental attitude, the dominant philosophy of that era is unfavorable to it. Hence in order to achieve the comforts of transcendentalism, the romanticists were forced either to deny certain popular eighteenth century ideas or to digest those ideas and transform them into something different. On the whole, they did the latter.

The adverse forces with which they had to cope may roughly be summed up in the term "necessity." By this, you will remember, is meant what we should now call determinism — the doctrine that our bodies and minds move at the commands of laws over which we have no control. John Locke and his followers, believing that all knowledge is derived from sensation, regarded the mind as the passive instrument of an experience made up of sense impressions which scratch themselves upon the mind as chalk scratches upon a slate. This theory obviously denies that free will upon which transcendentalism depends.

Professor Gingerich makes the interesting point that the doctrine of necessity held by the sceptical philosophers and the doctrine of predestination held by the Calvinistic theologians are akin in their denial of free will. He might have added, however, that although the tracing of all mental activity back to passively received sense impressions does deny free will, it also discredits the claims of reason as a means of arriving at truth; so that the eighteenth century presents the spectacle of a rationalism which is gradually committing suicide by exposing the futility of its own pretensions. In fact this reduction of mentality to sensation, though entirely unromantic in its origins and motives, plays straight into the hands of romantic anti-intellectualism, and thus indirectly encourages transcendentalism. If Hume had not used his reason to show how very little reason can do, Robert Merry might never have written, in his *Ode to Anna Matilda*:

> Though small the circle we can trace
> In the abyss of time and space,
> Though learning has its limits got,
> The Feelings of the Soul have not!
> Their vast excursions find no end,
> And RAPTURE needs not comprehend!

Ultimately, the discovery that intellect is feeble leads to a glorification of those things that constitute the feebleness of intellect.

But we have generalized long enough. Let us see how the chief romantic poets succeed or fail in substituting for their inherited necessitarianism the transcendentalism which they need in their struggle for illusion.

XVIII

COLERIDGE AND TRANSCENDENTALISM

In speaking of Coleridge's state of mind as it was in 1794, the year of the pantisocratic dream, I said that on the whole he was a fairly typical disillusioned Young Jacobin, and considerably under the sway of Godwin — which is as much as to say that he adhered to the doctrine of necessity. But I also said that Coleridge had too many peculiarities to enable us to put him into any pigeonhole. From boyhood he had a naturally believing mind and a naturally transcendental mind. Since necessity claimed the allegiance of his reason but was repugnant to his temperament, he sought to clarify his mental conflict in the best possible way — by putting his thoughts down on paper. His principal early attempt at self-understanding was *Religious Musings*, begun in 1794 and finished in 1796. This poem bears the same relation to Coleridge's career as *Queen Mab* to Shelley's, for both works display a naturally romantic mind accepting, but endeavoring to surmount, inherited non-romantic ideas.

Religious Musings expresses Coleridge's belief in necessity, a doctrine which he derives, of course, from the Locke — Hume — Hartley — Godwin tradition. But the poem is not necessitarian in any sense of which Godwin, at least in 1796, could have approved without a great many reservations. As the title indicates, it is a definitely religious work. Coleridge converts necessity into a religious conception by combining it with a doctrine of unity.

Everything emanates from a single source of power, and that power is good. The universal whole operates like a machine, but like a beneficent machine which may be worshipped as a God of Love:

> There is one Mind, one omnipresent Mind,
> Omnific. His most holy name is Love.
> Truth of subliming import! with the which
> Who feeds and saturates his constant soul,
> He from his small particular orbit flies
> With blest outstarting! From himself he flies,
> Stands in the sun, and with no partial gaze
> Views all creation; and he loves it all,
> And blesses it, and calls it very good!
>
> .   .   .   .
>
> 'Tis the sublime of man,
> Our noontide Majesty, to know ourselves
> Parts and proportions of one wondrous whole!
> This fraternises man, this constitutes
> Our charities and bearings. But 'tis God
> Diffused through all, that doth make all one whole.

In a letter written at this period Coleridge sums up the combination of unity and necessity which dominates his mind by referring to himself as "a Unitarian Christian, and an advocate for the automatism of man." He draws his theory of unity from various idealistic philosophies, chiefly perhaps that of Plato, who constantly strove to convert the Many into the One, and who regarded the One as something like what Coleridge means by God. The identification of unity with love may come from such Neo-Platonic philosophers as Plotinus, who tried to reconcile Plato with the more mystical portions of the Scriptures. Since Spinoza was a determinist who emphasized the unity of all things and maintained an attitude of religious devotion toward natural law, he also was doubtless an important factor in the young poet's ideas. But as the phrase "a Unitarian Christian" implies, Coleridge derived his idea of unity largely from the late eighteenth century Unitarians. Their chief effort was to harmonize eighteenth century philosophy with the essential spirit of Christianity by rejecting the doctrine of the trinity and many other orthodox tenets, but clinging to the belief that God is love, and that no soul is foredoomed to damnation. In this way they were able to believe in a Christionized kind of necessity and at the same time avoid the acceptance of predestination, the more orthodox form of Christian necessitarianism. When Coleridge's transcendentalism fully emerged, he abjured Unitarianism completely; but at this time he was substantially a Unitarian, preached in Unitarian churches, and in 1797 was on the point of entering the Unitarian ministry when Wedgwood's pension convinced him that his call was not sufficiently compelling. Coleridge's admiration for the great scientist, political liberal and Unitarian theologian Joseph Priestley has been mentioned in connection with pantisocracy. Since Priestley had made an especially close connection between necessity and a loving unity, we may conjecture that the main ideas of *Religious Musings* are derived chiefly from Priestley's forceful reaffirmation of theories which Coleridge had already learned to admire in older philosophers.

Even this early work exhibits clear indications of a transcendental viewpoint in identifying reality with mind and in regarding the external world, with all its vice and misery, as merely a distorted shadow of spiritual truth.

Plato, Spinoza, and Berkeley form the background of such passages as

> Believe thou, O my soul,
> Life is a vision shadowy of Truth;
> And vice, and anguish, and the wormy grave,
> Shapes of a dream! The veiling clouds retire,
> And lo! the Throne of the redeeming God
> Forth flashing unimaginable day
> Wraps in one blaze earth, heaven, and deepest hell.

In *Religious Musings*, however, one finds no trace of that emphasis on the power of the imaginative will which is to assume a major rôle in Coleridge's thought. This element of his transcendentalism is as yet suppressed by the doctrine of necessity.

From 1797, when he begins to be closely associated with Wordsworth, to, let us say, 1802, the year of *Dejection*, Coleridge is attracted by Wordsworth's philosophy of nature. If he himself helped to provide that philosophy with its transcendental element, he also derived from it something of its descendentalism. He became a lover of external nature, and a believer in its power to heal, guide and inspire. This is the stage represented by such poems as *The Nightingale, Frost at Midnight, This Lime-Tree Bower My Prison*, and *Fears in Solitude*. But even at this time he cares much less for objects as objects than Wordsworth. In October, 1797, he writes to John Thelwall, who has been describing to him the beauties of Welsh scenery:

I can at times feel strongly the beauties you describe, in themselves and for themselves; but more frequently all things appear little, all the knowledge that can be acquired child's play; the universe itself — what but an immense heap of *little* things? I can contemplate nothing but *parts*, and parts are all *little*! My mind feels as if it ached to behold something *great*, something one and indivisible. And it is only in the faith of *that*, that rocks or water-falls, mountains or caverns, give me the sense of sublimity or majesty! But in that faith *all things* counterfeit infinity.

What we find in the period of Coleridge's relatively Wordsworthian attitude toward nature, then, is a love of nature to the extent that natural objects can be made to contribute to his sense of the unity of all things. This sense of unity becomes steadily more transcendental: he is less inclined to argue about it than in *Religious Musings*. He is developing a faith in the light of which "all things counterfeit infinity." As this faith strengthens, the grip of the doctrine of necessity weakens, but does not entirely lose its power. In fact *The Ancient Mariner* can be thought of as controlled by necessity. The Mariner *must* tell his story; the ship *must* move or stop as the spirits demand. But the theme of unity is even more important than that of necessity. As an artist, Coleridge regretted having tacked a moral to the end of the poem; but that moral — the unity under God's love of all crea-tion — runs through the whole work. A sin against that unity — the killing of the albatross — brings on the curse; a reaffirmation of that unity — the blessing of the water snakes — causes the curse to lift. The climax of the poem comes at the end of Part IV, when "by the light of the moon he beholdeth God's creatures of the great calm," and suddenly sees those "slimy things" as beau-tiful. It is primarily the moonlight that makes them appear beautiful; but this physical stimulus releases in the Mariner the transcendental power to impose goodness and love on what he beholds. In blessing, he is blest.

You doubtless know that in September, 1798, Wordsworth, Dorothy, Coleridge, and a friend of Coleridge named John Chester went to Germany. Wordsworth was miserable. He huddled up in his chilly lodgings in Goslar and wrote homesick poems about England, whither he and his sister returned in February. Coleridge, however, enjoyed himself extremely despite a few twinges of nostalgia, and remained in Germany until the following June. After some preliminary studies of the language at Ratzeburg, he matriculated at the University of Göttingen and attended lectures there for five months. The idealistic philosophy of Kant and his disciples was in the air, and Coleridge found in it support for his growing transcendental impulses. He did not, however, become directly acquainted with Kant's writings until about a year after his return from Germany.

Let us turn to *Biographia Literaria* for the poet's own account of how his earlier studies prepared him to receive the Kantian gospel. When he was hardly more than a boy, he says,

I began to ask myself; is a system of philosophy, as different from mere history and historic classification, possible? If possible, what are its necessary conditions? I was for a while disposed to answer the first question in the negative, and to admit that the sole practicable employment for the human mind was to observe, to collect, and to classify. But soon I felt, that human nature itself fought against this wilful resignation of intellect; and as soon did I find, that the scheme, taken with all its consequences and cleared of all inconsistencies, was not less impracticable than contranatural.

Here the motivating desire to escape from a distasteful intellectual situation is quite evident. David Hume says somewhere that when reason is against a man he will soon turn against reason.

And so Coleridge began to ransack the older philosophers for evidence of the mind's creative powers very much as he ransacked old literature for glimmering bits of strangeness. *Biographia Literaria* refers to his study of Plato and Plotinus, and, with great enthusiasm, to the inspiration he derived from Giordano Bruno, Jacob Boehme, George Fox, and William Law:

The writings of these Mystics acted in no slight degree to prevent my mind from being imprisoned within the outline of any single dogmatic system. They contributed to keep alive the heart in the head; gave me an indistinct, yet stirring and working presentiment, that all the products of the mere reflective faculty partook of death.

He speaks warmly, but in this context rather vaguely, of Spinoza. Spinoza doubtless helped to spiritualize his ideas of unity and necessity, but does not seem to have contributed much to his Kantianism. It was rather the mystics, and the earlier idealistic philosophers mystically interpreted, who prepared Coleridge to shed over Kant's rock-ribbed categories

> The light that never was, on sea or land,
> The consecration, and the Poet's dream.

Without this mysticizing of his severely rationalistic and agnostic elements, Kant would not have given Coleridge what he needed:

The writings of the illustrious sage of Koenigsberg, . . . more than any other work, at once invigorated and disciplined my understanding. . . . The apparent contradictions which occur, I soon found were hints and insinuations referring to ideas, which Kant either did not think it prudent to avow, or which he considered as consistently *left behind* in a pure analysis, not of human nature in toto, but of the speculative intellect alone. Here therefore [in the *Critique of Pure Reason*] he was constrained to commence at the point of reflection, or natural consciousness: while in his *moral* system he was permitted to assume a higher ground (the autonomy of the will) as a postulate deducible from the unconditional command or (in the technical language of his school) the categorical imperative of the conscience.

Here Coleridge waves aside, as a mere matter of prudence or expository economy, that distinction between empirical and *a priori* knowledge which is essential in Kant's system. The romantic poet prefers "to assume a higher ground" in both spheres of reason, bringing the work of reflective intellect beneath the control of that autonomy of will which according to Kant is supreme only in the realm of morals and religion. In this blurring of Kant's distinctions Coleridge was aided by Kant's much more romantic successors, who adopted toward the phenomenal world that masterful attitude which we now associate with transcendentalism as distinguished from pure idealism. For reasons which do not concern us, Fichte soon disappointed him; but Schelling, who regarded nature as the creation of the ego, was a true kindred spirit — a little more than kin, indeed, for Coleridge was accused of plagiarizing from him. *Biographia Literaria* gives the following explanation:

In Schelling's *Natur-Philosophie*, and the *System des transcendentalen Idealismus*, I first found a genial coincidence with much that I had toiled out for myself, and a powerful assistance in what I had yet to do. . . . All the main and fundamental points were born and matured in my mind before I had ever seen a single page of the German Philosopher; and I might indeed affirm with equal truth, before the more important works of Schelling had been written, or at least made public. Nor is this coincidence at all to be wondered at. We had studied in the same school; been disciplined by the same preparatory philosophy, namely, the writings of Kant; we had both equal obligations to the polar logic and dynamic philosophy of Giordano Bruno; and Schelling has lately, and, as of recent acquisition, avowed that same affectionate reverence for the labours of Behmen [Boehme] and other mystics, which I had formed at a much earlier period.

But the passage in Chapter XII of *Biographia Literaria* which introduces what purports to be Coleridge's own system of metaphysics is drawn without acknowledgment from Schelling's *System des transzendentalen Idealismus.* Similarly, certain very specific debts to Schlegel in Shakespeare criticism were left for others to point out. In order to protect Coleridge's reputation for intellectual honesty, one must sometimes resort to the charitable hypothesis of self-deception. All in all, however, the truth of the matter seems to be that German transcendental idealism corroborated ideas which were already more than half formed in Coleridge's mind, and helped him to arrange those ideas in a system.

After returning from Germany, Coleridge continued to develop his philosophical interests with such success that in March, 1801, he felt able to write to his friend, Thomas Poole:

The interval since my last letter has been filled up by me in the most intense study. If I do not greatly deceive myself, I have not only completely extricated the notions of time and space, but have overthrown the doctrine of association as taught by Hartley, and with it all the irreligious metaphysics of modern infidels — especially the doctrine of necessity. This I have *done*; but I trust that I am about to do more — namely, that I shall be able to evolve all the five senses . . . from one sense, and to state their growth and the causes of their difference, and in the evolvement to solve the process of life and consciousness.

That is a very large order, and one need hardly say that he never accomplished it. But by 1801 he has accomplished enough to satisfy an ordinary man, having through the magic of transcendentalism got rid of associationism, necessitarianism, and "the irreligious metaphysics of modern infidels." Perhaps this letter represents an almost pathological delusion of grandeur. At all events by the following year he has arrived at the state of mind described in *Dejection*. Here he feels that he has lost the "shaping spirit of imagination" just when he has come to recognize its sovereign importance in philosophy as well as in poetry.

Professor Gingerich finds an earlier expression of the attitude expressed in

> O Lady, we receive but what we give,
> And in our life alone does Nature live,

in a poem of 1799, *Lines Written in the Album at Elbingerode in the Hartz Forest*:

> For I had found
> That outward forms, the loftiest, still receive
> Their finer influence from the life within; —
> Fair ciphers else; fair, but of import vague
> Or unconcerning.

But Professor Gingerich might have gone back to 1798, where, in *France: an Ode*, Coleridge "shoots his being through earth, sea, and air, possessing all things with intensest love." He might even have gone back to a poem of 1794, quaintly entitled *Lines on a Friend Who Died*

of a Frenzy Fever Induced by Calumnious Reports, where
Coleridge speaks of his "shaping mind," a phrase looking
forward to *Dejection*. Transcendentalism is latent in Coleridge from his earliest reading of fairy tales. One can only
say that it gradually develops until, stimulated by his
experiences in Germany, it emerges from the eighteenth
century ideas which have partly obscured it.

After *Dejection*, the "shaping spirit of imagination"
returns to Coleridge the poet only in fitful flashes. He is
shaken by opium and by the ailments which had made him
begin to take the drug; his home life is unhappy; and his
native tendency to abstractness draws him further and
further away from the concreteness essential to poetry.
He preserves or wins back, however, enough of the "shaping spirit" to become a transcendental philosopher. In his
final stage, Coleridge is almost completely the metaphy-
sician, employing metaphysics, however, not only for their
own sake, but in support of political conservatism, religious orthodoxy, and romantic literary criticism.

Once he had settled down with the Gillmans at Highgate in 1816, and largely through their care had rendered
himself comparatively free from the opium habit, Coleridge gathered about him a group of young disciples and
deluged them with his wonderful misty talk. In this way
even more than through his inchoate philosophical writings his influence passed on into the Victorian period. One
of the young men who harkened to him in his last years
was Carlyle's friend, John Sterling. Sterling took Carlyle
to hear Coleridge, and Chapter VIII of the *Life of John
Sterling* comprises a remarkable sketch of the philosopher. The following passage suggests that Coleridge's
transcendentalism was in part a wishful device for resist-

ing the encroachments of science, and that it somehow managed to relate Kant's categorical imperative to the Church of England:

The constant gist of his discourse was lamentation over the sunk condition of the world; which he recognized to be given-up to Atheism and Materialism, full of mere sordid misbeliefs, mispursuits and misresults. All Science had become mechanical; the science not of men, but of a kind of human beavers. Churches themselves had died away into a godless mechanical condition; and stood there as mere Cases of Articles, mere Forms of Churches. . . . Men's souls were blinded, hebetated; and sunk under the influence of Atheism and Materialism, and Hume and Voltaire: the world for the present was as an extinct world, deserted of God, and incapable of well-doing until it changed its heart and spirit. . . .

The remedy, though Coleridge himself professed to see it as in sunbeams, could not, except by processes unspeakably difficult, be described to you at all. On the whole, those dead Churches, this dead English Church especially, must be brought to life again. Why not? It was not dead; the soul of it, in this parched-up body, was tragically asleep only. Atheistic Philosophy was true on its side, and Hume and Voltaire could on their own ground speak irrefragably for themselves against any Church: but lift the Church and them into a higher sphere of argument, *they* died into inanition, the Church revivified itself into pristine florid vigour, — became once more a living ship of the desert, and invincibly bore you over stock and stone. But how, but how! By attending to the "reason" of man, said Coleridge, and duly chaining-up the "understanding" of man: the *Vernunft* (Reason) and *Verstand* (Understanding) of the Germans, it all turned upon these, if you could well understand them, — which you couldn't.

Though this is not the time or place to analyze Kant's difficult philosophy, the challenge of Carlyle's last sentence cannot wholly be ignored. I shall try to give a very

compact and simplified account of Kant's ideas in their
bearing on religion. His mind clung to three beliefs: in
God, in immortality, and in free will. He saw that rationalism and science threatened these beliefs either by directly
attacking them or by supporting them in such a way as to
turn them into hollow syllogisms which no honest thinker
could respect and which failed to satisfy religious emotion.
Kant had no desire to join the romantic counterattack
against analytical reason, for he himself was almost in-
humanly rational in everything but religion. How then
could he justify his belief without committing treason
against scientific method?

His solution, in the words of the preface of the *Critique
of Pure Reason*, was "to deny *knowledge* of *God, freedom, and immortality*, in order to find a place for *faith*."
He began with a more destructive analysis of the supposedly rational grounds of religion than the most savage
sceptic had ever presented. Physico-mathematical rationalism and science deal with the phenomenal world as that
world 'exists in our thought. They are therefore perfectly
valid within their own sphere. But the very criteria which
give them validity as means of describing and explaining
phenomena condemn them as invalid guides to the under-
standings of ideas that bear no relation to the phenomenal
world. Rational proof depends upon rational experience.
Since there is no rational experience of God, immortality,
and free will, there can be no rational proof of these
conceptions.

So far, all may seem bleakly agnostic. But observe that
if science is now barred from supporting religion, it is
equally barred from attacking religion. Once religious experience is boldly declared to be non-rational, it cannot

be condemned upon rationalistic grounds unless one assumes that all non-rational experience is illusory. Kant refuses to make this assumption. We have no scientific knowledge of reality; for such knowledge, according to the idealistic theory, can apply only to phenomena. But, says Kant, there is another kind of knowledge, which is not drawn from rational experience and is therefore not restricted to mere appearances. As distinguished from empirical knowledge, it may be called *a priori* knowledge. The criteria of this kind of knowledge are necessity, universality, and detachment from rational experience. If an idea is supported by a strong sense of moral compulsion, if it fulfills a general human requirement, and if it can neither be proved nor disproved by scientific method, then it may be regarded as a part of *a priori* knowledge. Such are the ideas of God, freedom, and immortality. As Kant has proved, they are beyond the scope of science; they satisfy universal longings; and they *must* be believed in. The categorical imperative, that much more robust ancestor of James's "will to believe," forces us to establish these ideas as real through moral volition. Thus man's spirit is fortified by an internal necessity which has a higher sanction than the external, mechanical necessity of the eighteenth century.

Whatever our opinion of Kant may be, we must admit that he played fair. He was no less opposed to the invasion of science by religion than to the invasion of religion by science. If he had been confronted with proof that some element of supposedly *a priori* knowledge could be explained in terms of empirical knowledge, he would manfully have surrendered the prize. The real Kant, in fact, gave small encouragement to romantic illusion.

But Kant's successors, as I have said before, played strange tricks with his philosophy. Whereas Kant had preserved the ideal only by detaching it from the phenomenal, Schelling and his misty brethren exemplified our definition of romanticism by idealizing the phenomenal and phenomenalizing the ideal. They subordinated the understanding to the transcendental will, or reason. Both his natural temperament and his earlier philosophical studies disposed Coleridge to accept this romantic garbling of Kant's ideas. He uses a threefold division of mentality which owes much to German transcendental idealism. I shall not distinguish its pseudo-Kantian from its Kantian elements, but that it is false to Kant's true meaning will be apparent from what has already been said.

The three divisions of mentality are arranged in ascending order like the gradations of the medieval "ladder of being," and the lower divisions are subordinate to the higher. Lowest of all is sense. Coleridge writes in *The Friend*: "Under the term sense I comprise whatever is passive in our being . . .; all that man has in common with animals, in kind at least — his sensations, and impressions."

Above sense is the understanding (*Verstand*). This is simply what unenlightened folk mean by "reason." Coleridge defines it as "a faculty of thinking and forming judgments on the notices furnished by sense." The understanding organizes the work of the senses, but cannot introduce any supersensuous element. Being bound by the laws of cause and effect, it has no genuine freedom.

Above, far above, the understanding is what Coleridge calls reason (*Vernunft*). Reason is the creative imagina-

tion or transcendental faculty. It is the voice of God
within us, or perhaps it is our highest self speaking with
the voice of God. It is free and active, with power to turn
the denials of sense and understanding into affirmations
and thus reinterpret the phenomenal universe in terms of
spirit.

At the conclusion of *On the Constitution of the Church
and State* (1830), Coleridge writes:

Finally, what is Reason? You have often asked me: and this is
my answer:

> Whene'er the mist, that stands 'twixt God and thee,
> Defecates to a pure transparency,
> That intercepts no light and adds no stain —
> There Reason is, and then begins her reign.

But even when he reaches this mystical extreme of transcendentalism, Coleridge cannot quite surrender the descendental longings of the romanticist. His mystical vision
becomes entangled with the facts of the external world.
The reign of Coleridge's reason *begins* with contemplation of the godhead, but it is soon extended until it
suffuses with its mysterious light "the constitution of the
church and state," politics, social and economic problems,
literary criticism, and more or less everything else.

Let us again climb Highgate Hill with Carlyle for a
parting glimpse of the man who had once written *Christabel* and *Kubla Khan*:

Coleridge sat on the brow of Highgate Hill, in those years,
looking down on London and its smoke-tumult, like a sage escaped
from the inanity of life's battle; attracting towards him the
thoughts of innumerable brave souls still engaged there. His express contributions to poetry, philosophy, or any specific province

of human literature or enlightenment, had been small and sadly intermittent; but he had, especially among young inquiring men, a higher than literary, a kind of prophetic or magician character. He was thought to hold, he alone in England, the key of German and other transcendentalisms; knew the sublime secret of believing by "the reason" what "the understanding" had been obliged to fling out as incredible; and could still, after Hume and Voltaire had done their best and worst with him, profess himself an orthodox Christian, and say and print to the Church of England, with its singular old rubrics and surplices at Allhallowtide, *Esto perpetua.* A sublime man; who, alone in those dark days, had saved his crown of spiritual manhood; escaping from the black materialisms, and revolutionary deluges, with "God, Freedom, Immortality" still his: a king of men. The practical intellects of the world did not much heed him, or carelessly reckoned him a metaphysical dreamer: but to the rising spirits of the young generation he had this dusky sublime character; and sat there as a kind of *Magus*, girt in mystery and enigma; his Dodona oak-grove (Mr. Gillman's house at Highgate) whispering strange things, uncertain whether oracles or jargon. . . .

The good man, he was now getting old, towards sixty perhaps; and gave you the idea of a life that had been full of sufferings; a life heavy-laden, half-vanquished, still swimming painfully in seas of manifold physical and other bewilderment. Brow and head were round, and of massive weight, but the face was flabby and irresolute. The deep eyes, of a light hazel, were as full of sorrow as of inspiration; confused pain looked mildly from them, as in a kind of mild astonishment. The whole figure and air, good and amiable otherwise, might be called flabby and irresolute; expressive of weakness under possibility of strength. He hung loosely on his limbs, with knees bent, and stooping attitude: in walking, he rather shuffled than decisively stept. . . . A heavy-laden, high-aspiring and surely much-suffering man. His voice, naturally soft and good, had contracted itself into a plaintive snuffle and sing-song; he spoke as if preaching, — you would have said, preaching earnestly and also hopelessly the weightiest things. I still recollect his "object" and "subject," terms of continual recurrence in the Kantian province; and how he sang and snuffled them into "om-m-mject" and "sum-m-mject," with a kind of solemn shake or quaver, as he rolled along. . . .

Nothing could be more copious than his talk; and furthermore, it was always, virtually or literally, of the nature of a monologue; suffering no interruption, however reverent; hastily putting aside all foreign additions, annotations, or most ingenuous desires for elucidation, as well-meant superfluities which would never do. Besides, it was not talk flowing anywhither like a river, but spreading everywhither in inextricable currents and regurgitations like a lake or sea; terribly deficient in definite goal or aim, nay often in logical intelligibility; *what* you were to believe or do, on any earthly or heavenly thing, obstinately refusing to appear from it. So that, most times, you felt logically lost; swamped near to drowning in this tide of ingenious vocables, spreading out boundless' as if to submerge the world. . . .

His talk, alas, was distinguished, like himself, by irresolution: it disliked to be troubled with conditions, abstinences, definite fulfilments; — loved to wander at its own sweet will, and make its auditor and his claims and humble wishes a mere passive bucket for itself! He had knowledge about many things and topics; much curious reading; but generally all topics led him, after a pass or two, into the high seas of Kantian transcendentalism, with its "sum-m-mjects" and "om-m-mjects." Sad enough; for with such indolent impatience of the claims and ignorances of others, he had not the least talent for explaining this or anything unknown to them; and you swam and fluttered in the mistiest wide unintelligible deluge of things, for most part in a rather profitless uncomfortable manner.

Glorious islets, too, have I seen rise out of the haze; but they were few, and soon swallowed in the general element again. Balmy sunny islets, islets of the blest and the intelligible. . . . Eloquent artistically expressive words you always had; piercing radiances of a most subtle insight came at intervals; tones of noble pious sympathy, recognizable as pious though strangely coloured, were never wanting long. . . . Coleridge was not without what talkers call wit, and there were touches of prickly sarcasm in him, contemptuous enough of the world and its idols and popular dignitaries; he had traits even of poetic humour; but in general he seemed deficient in laughter; or indeed in sympathy for concrete human things either on the sunny or on the stormy side. One right peal of concrete laughter at some convicted flesh-and-blood absurdity, one burst of noble indignation at some injustice or depravity, rubbing elbows with us on this solid Earth, how strange it would have been in that Kantean haze-world, and how infinitely cheering amid its air-castles and dim-melting ghosts and shadows! None such ever came. His life had been an abstract thinking and dreaming, idealistic, passed amid the ghosts of defunct bodies and of unborn ones. The moaning singsong of that theosophico-metaphysical monotony left on you, at last, a very dreary feeling.

XIX

WORDSWORTH AND TRANSCENDENTALISM

Our examination of Wordsworth under this topic will be brief; for since his transcendentalism hardly exists apart from his philosophy of nature, most of the essential facts are already known to us. Little remains but to remind ourselves of those facts and to reconsider their significance from the viewpoint of the last two lectures.

As a disciple of Godwin, Wordsworth is for a short time dominated by the full rigor of necessitarianism. In 1795, however, he begins to rebel against Godwin, and by 1797 his own characteristic views are approaching their final form. We know that Wordsworth's nature philosophy reinterprets Hartley's theory of association in the light of Rousseau's conception of nature, the cult of scenery, the cult of the child, and antirationalistic religious emotion — in other words, that it is a romantic structure erected upon an eighteenth century foundation.

In an early lecture I named Wordsworth — the Wordsworth of 1797-1806 — as the exemplar of that phase of romanticism in which the descendental and transcendental elements are about evenly balanced. He is not, like Coleridge, moved by natural objects merely because they "counterfeit infinity." He loves them in and for themselves; his poetry, both in theory and in practice, is based upon the most devoted attention to the real. On the other hand, he is certainly not a realist: he loves natural objects not only for their visible beauty but for a spiritual beauty of which they seem to be the vehicle.

This fusion of low and high, finite and infinite, matter and spirit, owes its equilibrium to the fact that man is related to nature both passively and actively. Passively, he opens his heart to the impulses that come from the vernal wood; actively, he projects his imagination into the vernal wood and "half creates" the values that he finds there. Neither part of this process is complete without the other: nature cannot work upon man unless he is inwardly attuned to her messages; man's loving imagination cannot do its creative work without fair forms to be made still fairer. Both the outward-inward and inward-outward movements are operations of the divine love which pervades the universe. Love descends into the visible world. It descends also into the naturally good heart of the child and of the man who has preserved the spirit of childhood. Through the ministry of the senses and the imagination these two aspects of universal love interact, thus establishing the union of man and nature.

The imagination or love which Wordsworth sometimes insists upon as essential to a right view of the external world is but another name for the transcendental faculty. Not merely transcendental sentiment, but a more or less technically transcendental theory of the imaginative will is therefore part of Wordsworth's nature philosophy.

It seems to me, however, that although transcendentalism helped Wordsworth to rationalize his feelings about nature, his instinctive temperament pointed rather strongly in the opposite direction. He would never have agreed that "in our life alone does Nature live," and Coleridge surely misinterprets *The Prelude* when he says to his friend:

> Thy soul received
> The light reflected, as a light bestowed.
> (*To William Wordsworth*)

Even in Wordsworth's systematic *thought*, nature's bestowing of light is no less important than its reflection of light; and his non-systematic *feelings* tend to prize the gifts received from the external world more highly than the values imposed upon it by his imagination. His descendentalism, his love for natural objects in themselves, will not allow him to suppose that all their blessings have bounced back to him from his own mind.

> The budding twigs spread out their fan,
> To catch the breezy air;
> And I must think, do all I can,
> That there was pleasure there.
> (*Lines Written in Early Spring*)

Pleasure *there* — not in his imagination, but in the branches of the grove.

It is noteworthy that examples of Wordsworth's transcendental attitude are found almost wholly in long, serious, formal poems in which he is deliberately philosophizing — *Tintern Abbey, The Prelude, The Excursion.* But sometimes even in such poems, and frequently in more spontaneous utterances, Wordsworth either ignores transcendentalism or guards himself against a complete acceptance of it. Eye and ear, after all, only "*half* create" their "mighty world." We must "come forth into the light of *things*," for the best way of dealing with nature is often simply to

> feed this mind of ours
> In a wise *passiveness.*

Moreover, we are sometimes told that imagination itself is nature's gift. Despite the passage on the influence of maternal love in conditioning the child's view of the outer world, the general trend of the early books of *The Prelude* is Lockian; for they represent the boy as plastic clay worked upon by natural agencies until from nature he derives the power to interpret nature. Lucy was no transcendentalist. In Book XII, to be sure, Wordsworth declares that "our first childhood" is the source of those moments which later make us realize that

> The mind is lord and master — outward sense
> The obedient servant of her will.
>
> (220 ff.)

But the two memories which he cites in support of this statement are so strained as to give the impression that he feels obliged to reinterpret his youth in a way not quite representative of his original feelings. And Book XIII of *The Prelude* begins:

> From Nature doth emotion come, and moods
> Of calmness equally are Nature's gift:
> This is her glory; these two attributes
> Are sister horns that constitute her strength.
> Hence Genius, born to thrive by interchange
> Of peace and excitation, finds in her
> His best and purest friend; from her receives
> That energy by which he seeks the truth,
> From her the happy stillness of the mind
> Which fits him to receive it when unsought.

Thus poetic genius, which Wordsworth closely associates with the transcendental faculty, demands active energy and passive receptiveness; but both of these appear to originate in nature. Even if the term "nature" is here, to an extent unusual in Wordsworth, detached from its scenic connotations, we are far from Coleridge's autonomy of the will.

Wordsworth sometimes expresses a transcendental attitude and then withdraws from it as if pulled by some deep instinctive scruple. You will remember the young man in *Ruth* whose internal wildness draws external wildness from American scenery. But the poem continues:

> Yet, in his worse pursuits I ween
> That sometimes there did intervene
> Pure hopes of high intent:
> For passions linked to forms so fair
> And stately needs must have their share
> Of noble sentiment.

In *The Pet Lamb*, the poet feels that he deserves an even share of credit for little Barbara Lewthwaite's speech:

> And it seemed, as I retraced the ballad line by line,
> That but half of it was hers, and one half of it was *mine*.

But he revises this equal division of glory as unjust to Barbara:

> Again, and once again, did I repeat the song;
> "Nay," said I, "more than half to the damsel must belong,
> For she looked with such a look and she spake with such a tone,
> That I almost received her heart into my own."

In Wordsworth's thought, "more than half" belongs to the nature which this child may be allowed to symbolize. What seems to be the poet's part of the song is, to some extent at least, the heart of nature speaking within his heart.

Wordsworth's transcendentalism is restricted not only

by his love of the external world but by what psychologists of the day before yesterday would have called the "self-submissive instinct." Although the term may seem inapplicable to so egotistic a man, the fact remains that his lofty views of human powers, and especially of his own powers, were chastened by the desire to subject himself to some force greater than himself. A pure transcendentalism makes man the master of nature; at heart, Wordsworth wanted nature to be his master. Nature, moreover, was in the good old-fashioned sense Wordsworth's muse, and the Milton of his age perhaps hesitated to assume the existence of an internal Urania. This is not a merely frivolous suggestion: it is traditionally proper for the bard — and Wordsworth was extremely bardic — to be inspired by some great outward power. The poetic or transcendental faculty which illumines nature derives its light from the nature muse. Wordsworth's egotism and self-submissiveness are not, after all, completely irreconcilable, for there is deep pride in being directly controlled by something unspeakably sublime.

Resorting frankly to hypothesis, we may perhaps assume that in 1797 Wordsworth was far from being a transcendentalist. His enjoyment of nature was so intense that it amounted to a religious belief that the supernatural was immanent in the natural. He had not, however, paused to analyze this belief except by rather vaguely justifying it in terms of sensationalism and associationism. As a poet, he was doubtless glad to think that his imagination added subjective values to the objective world; but on the whole he pictured himself as a child of Rousseau's nature, drawing poetic inspiration from her along with other benefits.

Then came the transcendental Coleridge. He had, like Wordsworth, been deeply influenced by the eighteenth century revival of enthusiasm for external nature, and was therefore prepared to be impressed by Wordsworth's instinctive creed. But he had the philosopher's longing to discover or invent reasons for things, and the preacher's longing to push people's minds in one direction or another. Recently he had transformed a mild hankering of Southey's into the pantisocratic vision; he now, with more important results, applied himself to Wordsworth. From his new friend he learned much, both of nature and of art. There were, however, questions which Coleridge felt impelled to ask. Was not Wordsworth's creed, despite its inspiring qualities, still too much enchained by Locke and Hartley? Had Wordsworth successfully reconciled his devotion to material forms with the great truth that all reality is spiritual? Might he not purge his ideas of their excessively passive and determined quality by emphasizing the high prerogatives of the imagination? Finally, had he ever examined his philosophy in the light of certain interesting theories of Plato, Plotinus, Origen, St. Augustine, Duns Scotus, Giordano Bruno, Paracelsus, Cornelius Agrippa, Spinoza, Boehme, Berkeley, William Law, and Joseph Priestley?

Having asked these and many other questions, Coleridge eloquently, persuasively, answered them himself. Wordsworth was stimulated to systematize his feelings. He had already begun to notice that his joy in nature rose and fell according to passing moods. Perhaps a more explicit philosophy would preserve that joy in the form of understanding when it was absent as pure feeling. He noticed, too, that nature gladdened him most when he

retrospectively beheld her through the eyes of his childhood. Perhaps this fact — he thought of Vaughan's *Retreat* — implied a progressive dimming of the light shed
upon him by nature. In that case, it would indeed
be well to think more of the light within his mind.
If the light nevertheless continued to grow dim, he would
at least have the solid satisfaction of understanding so
much of it as lingered. Finally, was it not his duty as a
poet to catch the gleam before it faded and preserve an
intelligible account of it for the benefit of mankind?

Wordsworth was much too independent to adopt Coleridge's ideas bodily, but he could not help being strongly
influenced by his friend's eloquence and learning. He
found, too, that although his feelings were often quite
different from Coleridge's, they assumed a Coleridgean
tinge when he tried to elucidate them on paper. And so he
formulated his philosophy of nature — a temporarily
well balanced compromise between his instinctive descendentalism and a transcendentalism which was more consciously, more laboriously designed to account for his
unaccountable belief that "there is a spirit in the woods."
As I have tried to explain, the two elements are reconciled
in the idea that both passive response and imaginative
creation are parts of a nature so closely unified that, in
theory at least, there can be no distinction between them.

But the psychological basis of the whole structure is the
desire to perceive the infinite within the finite. When love
of external nature is no longer strong enough to support
this feeling, Wordsworth's philosophy has lost the reason
for its existence. Quite possibly, indeed, transcendentalism
helped to weaken the very attitude toward nature which
it was intended to support. When romanticity is turned

into an *ism*, it is slain by the sword with which its cham-
pions seek to defend it. It is one of a very few human
impulses which are so deeply non-rational that they cannot
successfully be rationalized.

As the visionary gleam grows fainter, Wordsworth
vainly tries to keep it alive by means of the transcendental
technique. In Book IV of *The Excursion*, for example, the
Wanderer's address to Solitary abounds in transcendental
ideas. He assures the sceptic that

> Within the soul a faculty abides,
> That with interpositions, which would hide
> And darken, so can deal that they become
> Contingencies of pomp; and serve to exalt
> Her native brightness.

This faculty rises above the cold negations of the understanding:

> Access for you
> Is yet preserved to principles of truth
> Which the imaginative Will upholds
> In seats of wisdom, not to be approached
> By the inferior Faculty that moulds,
> With her minute and speculative pains,
> Opinion, ever changing!

Science is not only powerless to control transcendental
reason, but must be that reason's servant, for

> its most noble use,
> Its most illustrious province, must be found
> In furnishing clear guidance, a support
> Not treacherous, to the minds *excursive* power.

Here is a typically romantic perversion of Kantian doctrine.

But although in *The Excursion* Wordsworth uses the phraseology of transcendentalism more clearly than ever before, his old love of nature is correspondingly moribund. Whatever his theory may be, the imaginative will does not, in practice, furnish the illusion which he had enjoyed when he fed his mind "in a wise passiveness." He is now, if you like, a transcendentalist, but he has little left that is worth transcendentalizing; for the factory system, national education, and the Established Church are not grateful materials upon which to exercise the molding power of the will. During the remainder of his life he sporadically uses transcendentalism as a buttress for his conservative opinions, but this practice is too common in the apologetic thought of the nineteenth century to be of much significance.

In fact it is possible to say that at every stage of his development Wordsworth was chiefly dominated by necessity in various guises. From 1793 to 1796, it is necessity in a more or less purely Godwinian form. From 1797 to about 1805, it is necessity in the guise of nature, sufficiently tinged with transcendentalism to surmount the logical difficulties of his nature worship and to raise it above its foundations in eighteenth century science. After about 1805, his sensuous descendentalism begins to fade and his conservatism begins to grow. Necessity is now Duty, "stern daughter of the voice of God," the "new control" mentioned in *Peele Castle*, but really the old control in a new form.

In its original state the *Ode to Duty* contained a stanza which was cancelled when Wordsworth had grown still more orthodox:

> Yet not the less would I throughout
> Still act according to the voice
> Of my own wish; and feel past doubt
> That my submissiveness was choice:
> Not seeking in the school of pride
> For "precepts over dignified,"
> Denial and restraint I prize
> No farther than they breed a second Will more wise.

This represents a quite natural though somewhat inconsistent desire to preserve the privileges of transcendental freedom without losing the certitude of obedience. Wordsworth is trying to work out a compromise between Christian subjection of personal will to the will of God and transcendental identification of personal will with the will of God. But in the end, control proves stronger than freedom. After the *Ode to Duty*, necessity becomes more and more closely identified with the personal God of orthodox Anglicanism, and one hears little of the imaginative will except when disbelief or radicalism requires a piously superrational rebuke.

If this discussion of Wordsworth seems vague and indefinite, the reason at least partly lies in the inconsistency of Wordsworth himself. His love of freedom, his desire for guidance and control, his egotism, his distrust of that egotism, his passion for the primrose, his longing to believe that the primrose in its very self is "something more," his reluctant knowledge that only transcendentalism can make the real anything more than real — these were never harmonized in the depths of his mind. His struggles to harmonize them resulted in very great poetry, but at last the problem was abandoned rather than solved.

XX

BYRON AND TRANSCENDENTALISM

That Byron never found the peace of transcendentalism must be evident to all who are acquainted with his work. According to Professor Gingerich, who sees transcendentalism as a great spiritual victory, he failed to soar with his contemporaries because he lacked their wisdom — "Lord Byron is a child when he reflects," as Goethe said. But one may justly be irritated by the common assumption that a man who refrains from believing in lofty and inspiring ideas for which there is no evidence whatever necessarily has an inferior mind. Although no one would undertake to prove that Byron was a profound thinker, he possessed a quality which many supposedly profound thinkers lack — a sense of the toughness of facts and an inability to dupe himself about them. It is useless to argue that he had either more or less intelligence than his great contemporaries, but surely he had quite enough intelligence to be a transcendentalist. Perhaps, indeed, he had *too much* intelligence of the realistic sort. Beneath all his protective histrionism, his mind possessed a certain desperate integrity which should command respect.

Like other romanticists, Byron recognized the gap between the real and the ideal, and his inability to be satisfied with any of the fashionable methods of bridging the gap accounts for his wavering between melancholy and irony. That sense of being alone in a world which bears no relation to one's desires is common enough in the romantic movement, but it is especially strong in Byron. In him it takes the extreme form known in Germany as *Weltschmerz* and in France as *mal du siècle*. Mr. William Rose, in *From Goethe to Byron: the Development of Weltschmerz in German Literature*, defines *Weltschmerz* as "the psychic state which ensues when there is a sharp contrast between a man's ideals and his material environment, and his temperament is such as to eliminate the possibility of any sort of reconciliation between the two." This applies perfectly to Byron.

Some students whose enthusiasm for romanticism is much greater than mine speak of romantic melancholy as if it were merely an affected literary fad. Proudly stricken gloom is, to be sure, a fetching pose, and some writers of the period pretended to be melancholy when there was no necessity for gloom or pretended to be more melancholy than they really were. From this affectation, Byron was not wholly free. But we should beware of too hastily branding literary fashions as merely superficial. A fad cannot exist without some relation to the thought and feeling of the age. Once it gets started, superficial writers may make merely superficial use of it, but it can hardly have originated without some basis in the *Zeitgeist*. Thanks to De Musset's *Confessions d'un enfant du siècle*, romantic melancholy is often regarded as a result of the general post-Napoleonic disillusionment. But though this was doubtless a strong influence, the roots of the malady run far back into the eighteenth century. The fundamental cause, I think, is the inevitable conflict of reason with the desire for romantic illusion. On the whole, romantic melancholy deserves to be taken rather seriously. It is natural that the seeker of the romantic illusion should sometimes realize that what he wants has almost no relation to what he can get, and it is natural that this realization should give him pain. Perhaps you have seen the little Blake engraving, representing a child on the top of a ladder which leans against nothing at all. The child is stretching his arms up to the moon, and the title is "I want! I want!" If we want things that we can get, we shall have no occasion to be very melancholy, nor, some would say, to be very happy. But if we want the moon, we must expect some bad quarters of an hour, and people should not call us *poseurs* if we cry out when the ladder collapses. Something like the mood of *Weltschmerz* appears in Wordsworth when he recognizes that the visionary gleam is fading; it appears in Coleridge when he feels that he has lost his shaping spirit of imagination; it appears in *Alastor*, Shelley's most Byronic poem, and returns very strongly toward the end of his life. But in their most characteristic works these poets are able to retain some form of the romantic illusion. In Byron, on the other hand, melancholy is central and pervasive, because, to hark back to Mr. Rose's definition, "his temperament is such as to eliminate the possibility of any sort of reconciliation" between the real and the ideal.

This does not mean that Byron never even attempts a reconciliation. Stanzas 121 and 122 of Canto IV of *Childe Harold* represent a state of mind in which at least an approach to the transcendental attitude is almost a necessity.

> Oh Love! no habitant of earth thou art —
> An unseen seraph, we believe in thee,
> A faith whose martyrs are the broken heart,
> But never yet hath seen, nor e'er shall see

The naked eye, thy form, as it should be;
The mind hath made thee, as it peopled heaven,
Even with its own desiring phantasy,
And to a thought such shape and image given,
As haunts the unquenched soul — parched — wearied
                    — wrung — and riven.

Of its own beauty is the mind diseased,
And fevers into false creation: — where,
Where are the forms the sculptors soul hath seized?
In him alone. Can Nature show so fair?
Where are the charms and virtues which we dare
Conceive in boyhood and pursue as men,
The unreached Paradise of our despair,
Which o'er-informs the pencil and the pen,
And overpowers the page where it would bloom again?

In these lines Byron lays bare the situation which leads
the wishful thinker to assume transcendental powers. We
have cravings which are not a part of things as they are,
and which make the mind "fever into false creation." We
dream a better world, and awake to face the facts.

But after more to the same effect, Byron reaches a
somewhat different point in stanza 126:

Our life is a false nature — 'tis not in
The harmony of things, — this hard decree,
This uneradicable taint of sin,
This boundless upas, this all-blasting tree,
Whose root is earth, whose leaves and branches be
The skies which rain their plagues on men like dew —
Disease, death, bondage — all the woes we see —
And worse, the woes we see not — which throb through
The immedicable soul, with heart-aches ever new.

The phrase "uneradicable taint of sin" suggests the fact

that Byron was burdened not only by rationalistic but by theological necessity in the form of the doctrine of pre-destination. His Scotch Calvinistic background had much to do with the fatalism so apparent in his thought. Shock-ing as the Byronic hero would be to a good Calvinist, he is, in his Radcliffian way, a rather Calvinistic person. He is fated; the mark of Cain is on his brow, and there is very little he can do about it.

The idea that "our life is a false nature," however, has transcendental possibilities. The transcendentalist often deals with the problem of evil by asserting that through lack of faith in the harmony of things man has made his life a kind of cancer which is not a genuine part of the healthy body of the universe. If Byron wishes to tran-scendentalize, he should now assert his faith in the har-mony of things and deny the reality of that false nature which man has allowed his senses to fabricate. He never quite takes this step, but in the next stanza he expresses the hope that human thought may some day be strong enough to bridge the gap:

> Yet let us ponder boldly — 'tis a base
> Abandonment of reason to resign
> Our right of thought — our last and surest place
> Of refuge; this, at least, shall still be mine:
> Though from our birth the faculty divine
> Is chained and tortured — cabined, cribbed, confined,
> And bred in darkness, lest the truth should shine
> Too brightly on the unpreparèd mind,
> The beam pours in, for time and skill will couch the blind.

This comparatively hopeful attitude owes something to the influence of Shelley, whom Byron had met in Switzer-land in the summer of 1816. It is much too exceptional to be representative of Byron's thought. His final answer to Shelley is that which is assigned to him in *Julian and Maddalo*:

> Ay, if we were not weak — and we aspire
> How vainly to be strong!

The *Childe Harold* passage just quoted has clearer transcendental implications than the passage which Professor Gingerich singles out from *Manfred* as Byron's closest approach to transcendentalism. Just before the end of the drama, Manfred says to the demons who have come to bear him away:

> Must crimes be punished but by other crimes,
> And greater criminals? — Back to thy hell!
> Thou hast no power upon me, *that* I feel;
> Thou never shalt possess me, *that* I know:
> What I have done is done; I bear within
> A torture which could nothing gain from thine:
> The mind which is immortal makes itself
> Requital for its good or evil thoughts —
> Is its own origin of ill and end —
> And its own place and time — its innate sense,
> When stripped of this mortality, derives
> No color from the fleeting things without;
> But is absorbed in sufferance or in joy,
> Born from the knowledge of its own desert.

These lines appear to say that after death the immortal mind can be rewarded or punished only by its own knowledge of its goodness or badness. But here there is no dominance of the will over the senses, for when the mind is "stripped of this mortality," there are no senses left to be dominated. Possibly the lines

> Is its own origin of ill and end —
> And its own place and time

may be taken to mean that even on this side of the grave
the mind constructs its own world. If so, Byron is using
a more or less Kantian idea but is not interpreting it in
romantically transcendental fashion. This world of the
mind is an internal, self-absorbed refuge from reality,
without any benignant power to make dreams come true.
Manfred is merely being proud and defiant in the typically
Byronic way, trying to make the best of Astarte's curse:

> I call upon thee! and compel
> Thyself to be thy proper Hell!
> (I, i.)

In his own *Manfred*, Meredith exaggerates, but does not
falsify, the spirit of Byron's drama:

> Projected from the bilious Childe,
> This clatterjaw his foot could set
> On Alps, without a breast beguiled
> To glow in shedding rascal sweat.
> Somewhere about his grinder teeth,
> He mouthed of thoughts that grilled beneath,
> And summoned Nature to her feud,
> With bile and buskin Attitude.

I do not dislike transcendentalism bitterly enough to associate it with this melodramatic ranting.

To Professor Gingerich it seems probable that Byron is
directly indebted to Coleridge for Manfred's speech to
the demons. The somewhat more evident relation of the
passage to lines 249 ff. of Book I of *Paradise Lost* is interesting in view of the sympathetic treatment of Satan in
Byron's *Cain*. Both Satan and Cain are defiant enough:

> The Snake spoke *truth*. It *was* the tree of knowledge;
> It *was* the tree of life. Knowledge is good,
> And life is good, and how can both be evil?

But the necessity which Byron can never escape is ultimately stronger than defiance. Cain is fated as Manfred is fated, and all their haughty oratory cannot remove "this uneradicable taint of sin."

Byron, who is not the man to be deceived by his own bluster, falls back at last upon the irony of *Don Juan*. To take this poem sentimentally would be uncritical, for its author doubtless enjoyed himself extremely when he was writing it. But although Byron would sneer at any one who called *Don Juan* the motley disguise of a tortured heart, the initial impulse to write the poem was not unmingled with pain. Manfred, at the climax of his gloomy Titanism, breaks down and laughs — laughs not only at the world which he scorns, but at himself. He finds relief in the change of mood, but he cannot quite forget that this laughter is only the cynical substitute for tears:

> As boy, I thought myself a clever fellow,
>   And wished that others held the same opinion;
> They took it up when my days grew more mellow,
>   And other minds acknowledged my dominion:
> Now my sere fancy "falls into the yellow
>   Leaf," and Imagination droops her pinion,
> And the sad truth which hovers o'er my desk
> Turns what was once romantic to burlesque.

> And if I laugh at any mortal thing,
>   'Tis that I may not weep; and if I weep,
> 'Tis that our nature cannot always bring
>   Itself to apathy, for we must steep
> Our hearts first in the depths of Lethe's spring,

> Ere what we least wish to behold will sleep:
> Thetis baptized her mortal son in Styx;
> A mortal mother would on Lethe fix.
>
> (IV, 3, 4)

Granting that these lines are not without a touch of histrionism, we may feel that the stagey gesture, as so often happens, expresses a genuine emotion. Aspiration, melancholy, mockery — the history of a mind too idealistic to refrain from blowing bubbles, and too realistic to refrain from pricking them.

Byron's irony is more typical of continental than of English romanticism. The Englishman, on the whole, takes his ideals very seriously. He is solemnly happy when they shine near at hand, and solemnly sad when they recede; but he almost never regards either his happiness or his sadness as absurd. Since the realistic intelligence of the eighteenth century persisted more strongly in France, Germany, and Italy than in England, continental romanticism is marked by a sharper conflict between the heart and head of the writer. From this conflict arise the extremest forms of melancholy and irony. Since Byron possessed a larger share of eighteenth century hard-headedness than his English contemporaries, his response to the romantic dilemma has been recognized by continental writers as closely akin to their own.

The Italian mock-heroic romance is the perfect form for Byron's self-expression. Indeed, with its medley of seriousness and burlesque, idealism and cynicism, it is a symbol of the man's very soul. The spirit of *Don Juan* is summed up in the numerous passages which destroy a dream with mocking anticlimax; for example, the hero's farewell to Spain and Julia in Canto II:

"Farewell, my Spain! a long farewell!" he cried,
    "Perhaps I may revisit thee no more,
But die, as many an exiled heart hath died,
    Of its own thirst to see again thy shore:
Farewell, where Guadalquivir's waters glide!
    Farewell, my mother! and, since all is o'er,
Farewell, too, dearest Julia!" — (here he drew
Her letter out again, and read it through).

"And oh! if e'er I should forget, I swear —
    But that's impossible, and cannot be —
Sooner shall this blue ocean melt to air,
    Sooner shall earth resolve itself to sea,
Than I resign thine image, oh, my fair!
    Or think of anything excepting thee;
A mind diseased no remedy can physic" —
(Here the ship gave a lurch and he grew sea-sick).

"Sooner shall heaven kiss earth" — (here he fell sicker)
    "Oh, Julia! what is every other woe? —
(For God's sake let me have a glass of liquor;
    Pedro, Battista, help me down below).
Julia, my love! — (you rascal, Pedro, quicker) —
    Oh, Julia! — (this curst vessel pitches so) —
Beloved Julia, hear me still beseeching!"
(Here he grew inarticulate with retching).

Burlesque, of course, but burlesque that carries implications. For this is what happens in a world which Byron finds recalcitrant to the transcendental will. Some emotional crisis arises; we strike an attitude and prepare to be masterful — then a button pops, and we must laugh if we do not wish to cry.

It should not be difficult for us to understand the Byron who wrote *Don Juan*. Does not his complete awareness of human frustration predict a mood which is prevalent in the literature of today? Somehow he reminds me of that scene in Aldous Huxley's *Point Counter Point* where two poor damned souls try to find happiness in each other's arms while a parrot is screaming in the corner. They throw a cloth over the cage, but the parrot continues to scream.

XXI

SHELLEY AND TRANSCENDENTALISM

When we glanced at the ideal revolution which is the triumph of Shelley's transcendentalism, we observed that he spiritualized the Godwinian ideas of necessity and perfectibility and that he grappled with the problem of evil through asserting the existence of a perfect universe which becomes truer than brute fact if only we can make our wills powerful enough to affirm its reality. The present lecture will analyze somewhat more fully, though anything but exhaustively, the rise and fall of Shelley's transcendental faith.

Queen Mab was privately published in 1813 and had been written during the previous year, though parts of it may belong to a still earlier period. An enlightening method of studying this poem is first to read the notes for evidence as to the ideas with which Shelley starts out, and then to see what Shelley does with those ideas in the poem. Separately considered, the notes present a fairly complete picture of the Young Jacobin — a free-loving, atheistic, visionary, revolutionary, vegetarian, necessitarian, perfectibilitarian, sentimental rationalist. They reflect the influence of Godwin, Helvétius, Holbach, Volney, Rousseau in his less romantic aspects, and the *philosophe* tradition in general, with some half-baked materialistic notions drawn from scientists like Cuvier and a dash of Lucretius and Spinoza.

But in turning to the poem itself one receives a different

impression, for here Shelley suffuses the doctrine of necessity and its associated ideas with the light of religious emotion. Any mechanical process may be transformed into a spiritual process by being made an object of worship. Hence we are told that

> Throughout this varied and eternal world
> Soul is the only element: the block
> That for uncounted ages has remained
> The moveless pillar of a mountain's weight
> Is active, living, spirit.

This spirit, which is identical with necessity and with nature in the abstract sense of *natura naturans*, is Shelley's God. It is simply a body of operative law, heedless of those ideas of good and evil which man's selfish mind has fabricated. It is the eternal and unchanging reality which guides the shifting appearances of the world of the human senses:

> Throughout these infinite orbs of mingling light,
> Of which yon earth is one, is wide diffused
> A Spirit of activity and life,
> That knows no term, cessation, or decay;
>
> .   .   .   .
>
> But, active, steadfast and eternal, still
> Guides the fierce whirlwind, in the tempest roars,
> Cheers in the day, breathes in the balmy groves,
> Strengthens in health, and poisons in disease;
> And in the storm of change, that ceaselessly
> Rolls round the eternal universe, and shakes
> Its undecaying battlement, presides,
> Apportioning with irresistible law
> The place each spring of its machine shall fill:
> So that when waves on waves tumultuous heap

Confusion to the clouds, and fiercely driven
Heaven's lightnings scorch the uprooted ocean-fords,
Whilst, to the eye of shipwrecked mariner,
Lone sitting on the bare and shuddering rock,
All seems unlinked contingency and change:
No atom of this turbulence fulfils
A vague or unnecessitated task,
Or acts but as it must and ought to act.

     . . . .

Spirit of Nature! all-sufficing Power,
Necessity! thou mother of the world!
Unlike the God of human error, thou
Requir'st no prayers or praises: the caprice
Of man's weak will belongs no more to thee
Than do the changeful passions of his breast
To thine unvarying harmony: the slave,
Whose horrible lusts spread misery o'er the world,
And the good man who lifts, with virtuous pride,
His being, in the sight of happiness,
That springs from his own works; the poison-tree,
Beneath whose shade all life is withered up,
And the fair oak, whose leafy dome affords
A temple where the vows of happy love
Are registered, are equal in thy sight:
No love, no hate thou cherishest; revenge
And favouritism, and worst desire of fame
Thou know'st not; all that the wide world contains
Are but thy passive instruments, and thou
Regard'st them all with an impartial eye,
Whose joy or pain thy nature cannot feel,
Because thou hast not human sense,
Because thou art not human mind.

This hymn of praise to the majestically indifferent processes of nature probably reflects the influence of Spinoza.

Shelley had dipped into this philosopher at Oxford, and in the notes to *Queen Mab* he quotes a passage from the first chapter of the *Tractatus Theologico-Politicus*, beginning, "All things are made through the power of God, for the very reason that the power of God is none other than the very power of nature." Shelley was to begin, though not to complete, a translation of this treatise.

It is hardly an exaggeration to say that Spinoza contributed something to every system of philosophy which appeared after his time. His many-sidedness rendered him liable to the most diverse interpretations. Although the underlying unity of his thought was anything but romantic, we have seen that certain of his ideas could be so interpreted as to give encouragement to Coleridge and Wordsworth. The romanticists were moving from a more or less scientific to a more or less religious conception of nature. Now one peculiarity of Spinoza was that his conception of nature was *both* scientific and religious. He adored the Cartesian physico-mathematical universe with all the passion of a mystic. By showing that it was possible to regard necessity from a viewpoint as warmly emotional as Godwin's was coldly cerebral, he provided the romanticists with a bridge between the ideas they wished to escape and the mood they wished to enjoy. Or, to shift the metaphor, he suggested that if necessity were sufficiently warmed by feeling it might be persuaded to melt.

Thanks to Spinoza, then, Shelley already has a kind of necessity that is at least potentially more romantic than Godwin's. But how are these potentialities to be developed? How is this inhuman world spirit, which denies free will and is absolutely indifferent to good and evil, to be harmonized with perfectibility? The difficulty seems

insuperable, for if perfectibility means anything it means
the perfectibility of man — the fulfillment of certain human aims which to Spinozan necessity are utterly insig-
nificant.

In order to save perfectibility, Shelley mingles with
Spinozan nature a more or less Rousseauistic conception
of nature as a system which from the human viewpoint,
and not purely *sub specie aeternitatis*, is benevolent, but
from which man has separated himself:

> Look on yonder earth:
> The golden harvests spring; the unfailing sun
> Sheds light and life; the fruits, the flowers, the trees,
> Arise in due succession; all things speak
> Peace, harmony, and love. The universe,
> In Nature's silent eloquence, declares
> That all fulfil the works of love and joy, —
> All but the outcast Man. He fabricates
> The sword which stains his peace; he cherisheth
> The snakes that gnaw his heart; he raiseth up
> The tyrant, whose delight is in his woe,
> Whose sport is in his agony.

This is not the nature which Shelley has identified with
necessity. Man cannot be a traitor to nature if his every
thought and action are governed by natural law. Consider
the argument: "Nature is necessity; nature is love; therefore necessity is love." The logical flaw is that the "nature" of the first proposition has nothing to do with love,
while the "nature" of the second proposition has nothing to do with necessity. But Shelley passes over such obstacles. "Every heart," he insists, "contains perfection's
germ," and it is the will of nature that this germ shall
develop until at last

> > happiness
>
> And science dawn though late upon the earth;
> Peace cheers the mind, health renovates the frame;
> Disease and pleasure cease to mingle here,
> Reason and passion cease to combat there;
> Whilst each unfettered o'er the earth extend
> Their all-subduing energies, and wield
> The sceptre of a vast dominion there;
> Whilst every shape and mode of matter lends
> Its force to the omnipotence of mind,
> Which from its dark mine drags the gem of truth
> To decorate its Paradise of peace.

In *Queen Mab* Shelley has lifted Godwin's necessity and perfectibility to a more emotional plane, but he has not succeeeded in reconciling those theories, nor in explaining the presence of evil in a universe of love. We should note, however, the more or less Spinozan distinction between a world of unchanging reality and a phenomenal world of illusory flux. At present Shelley hardly knows what to do with this distinction, but in later years he will take full advantage of it.

Alastor, which is too familiar for detailed analysis, was written in 1815, when Shelley's personal distresses and the social conditions of the age combined to make him gloomy. It represents the tragedy of the poet who supposes that the ideal can actually be found in a human form. Shelley's preface explains that when the poet's desires "point toward objects infinite and unmeasured," he is happy; but that a long and hopeless quest begins when his mind "fevers into false creation," as Byron would say, and imagines a real person who embodies the ideal. Here, then, is a pessimistic view of the romantic endeavor to find the ideal within the real.

But that Shelley was preparing to escape from this dilemma is shown by certain prose fragments which were composed at about the same time as *Alastor*.

I confess [he writes in *On Life*] that I am one of those who am [*sic*] unable to refuse my assent to the conclusions of those philosophers who assert that nothing exists but as it is perceived. . . . The difference is merely nominal between those two closses of thought, which are vulgarly distinguished by the names of ideas and of external objects.

We may already predict that a romantically interpreted idealism is to provide the solution.

In the same fragment Shelley tells us that he was at first inclined toward materialism:

This materialism is a seducing system to young and superficial minds. It allows its disciples to talk, and dispenses them from thinking. But I was discontented with such a view of things as it afforded; man is a being of high aspirations, "looking both before and after," whose thoughts "wander through eternity," disclaiming alliance with transcience and decay. . . . Such contemplations as these, materialism and the popular philosophy of mind and matter alike forbid; they are consistent only with the intellectual system.

This reveals the same wishful type of thinking as Coleridge's discovery that mere perception and inference not only limit the powers of the mind but are "impracticable." Since man is a being of high aspirations, he must somehow acquire a philosophy that will justify those aspirations.

According to Shelley's fragment, "the most clear and vigorous statement of the intellectual system is to be found in Sir William Drummond's *Academical Questions*." If the poet means what he says — and there is no reason to suppose that he does not — Drummond is an important link in the development of Shelley's ideas. This little-known Scotch classical scholar, philosopher, and diplomat was born about 1770 and died in 1820. Volume I of his *Academical Questions* was published in London in 1805. Volume II — on the authority of the Library of Congress — never appeared. This is the more unfortunate since the first volume is chiefly a hostile analysis of all materialistic and mind-and-matter systems, while in the second volume he intended to elaborate his own system. In attacking his enemies, however, he plainly discloses his position.

Locke, when he had traced everything back to sensations, was brought face to face with the question which gives birth to idealism: if we are aware of nothing but internal sensations, how can we claim to have knowledge of an external world? He tried to answer this question in terms of cause and effect: we may infer an external world from the sensations which it produces in our minds. But to a person with a grudge against matter, this solution is unsatisfactory; for, the rebuttal runs, we cannot trace a causal relationship between two things when the very existence of one of those things remains to be proved. From Locke therefore arises not only what Shelley calls "the popular philosophy of mind and matter," but eighteenth century idealism. Berkeley derived his philosophy from his own interpretation of Locke's psychology, and Berkeleyan idealism passes down through many minds until it appears in *Academical Questions*.

I am not well enough versed in the details of eighteenth century professional philosophy to "place" Drummond in relation to his immediate predecessors. There can be no doubt, however, that his philosophy is an extreme idealism derived from pure English, Irish, and Scotch sources. He appears to owe something to his fellow countryman Dugald Stewart, who sought to base his intuitionism upon a severely inductive psychology. But Drummond's conception of the will suggests the influence of Spinoza despite his declared opposition to that philosopher. I believe, too, that Drummond had notions of his own. He blended hard-headed reason and visionary "crankiness" in proportions that might well have appealed to Shelley. In another work, *Oedipus Judaicus*, he interprets the Old Testament as an astronomical allegory with a fantastic erudition that reminds one of Lord Monboddo, that learned Scot who argued for the humanity of the orangutan.

"The intellectual system" has nothing to do with German idealism. In fact Drummond is heavily sarcastic about "a German author of the name of Kant," whom he regards as a pretentious mystagogue. Kant's assertion of *a priori* knowledge conflicts with Locke's denial of innate ideas, and Drummond is as complete a sensationalist as he is an idealist. "I cannot," he declares, "comprehend any thing, which is neither a sensation, nor obtained from one."

Shelley at this time would be impressed by a philosophy which seemed to be firmly rooted in eighteenth century rationalism but which gave him a universe in which mind was the only knowable reality. He could, it appeared, be at once a reasoner and a dreamer. In Drummond, too, he found such echoes of his own temperament as: "Philosophy, wisdom, and liberty support each other; he who will not reason, is a bigot; he who cannot, is a fool; and he who dares not, is a slave." Good material for a pamphlet, surely. And the following excerpt, not from

Academical Questions but from the preface to *Oedipus Judaicus*, is pure Shelley. The author, writing in 1811, has referred to the opposition of religion to philosophy as part of the post-revolutionary conservative reaction. He continues:

It may be hoped, however, that reason and liberality will soon again be progressive in their march; and that men will cease to think that Religion can be really at war with Philosophy. When we hear the timid sons of superstition calling to each other to rally round the altar, we may well blush for human weakness. The altar, of which the basis is established by Reason, and which is supported by Truth and Nature, can never be overthrown. It is before that altar that I kneel, and that I adore the God, whom philosophy has taught me to consider as the infinite and eternal Mind, that formed, and that sustains, the fair order of Nature, and that created and preserves the universal system.

That is the very God of Shelley's quest.

Drummond attacks necessity because that doctrine implies the existence of an external world and the influence of matter upon mind. He recognizes, however, a kind of necessity *within* the mental world, although he refuses to employ a term which carries such materialistic implications. There is no separate faculty of will by which the mind controls its associations:

It is not because the mind previously wills it, that one association of ideas gives place to another. It is because the new ideas excite that attention, which the old no longer employ; and because the mind cannot but give its attention to the strongest sensations and clearest ideas, which offer themselves to its contemplation; and as thus we perceive certain ideas and sensations without our choice, so we constantly attend to them, and their dependent trains, until some new leading sensations, or ideas, attract our notice. . . . Our minds are either tranquil or troubled, either joyful or sorrowful, according to the nature and strength of our sensations.

This would seem to make mind the passive victim of any sensations that come to it heaven knows how from heaven knows where. But watch carefully: a white rabbit is soon to be produced. "Reason," says Drummond, "is only another name for perception," and we perceive nothing but sensations and ideas that arise from sensations. "Is it not possible, that all the subjects of our knowledge may be only different modes of feeling?" Let us suppose that we wish to justify some desirable belief:

There seem to be only two modes by which belief can be said to be produced, namely, by reason and sentiment [*i.e.*, strong feeling]. Whether or not, indeed, the former produces conviction in us in any other way, than by producing in us some distinct perception or sentiment, may well be questioned. If sensation be strong, belief is so likewise; and as belief is always strong in proportion with sensation, so to believe can be nothing else than to feel. . . . The function of reason in producing belief, seems to consist in nothing else than in causing distinct notions to be more accurately perceived by the mind.

Knowledge is perception or feeling; belief is perception or feeling; reason is the means of clarifying perception and hence of strengthening feeling. "Gefühl ist Alles." And in this mind-enclosed world, the statements "seeing is believing" and "believing is seeing" are equally valid. We begin to understand how the intellectual system encourages Shelley's thoughts to " 'wander through eternity,' disclaiming alliance with transcience and decay."

If only man could perceive and feel the right thing! The white rabbit now appears. Though we may not think of the will as a distinct faculty, we may think of it as "the

sentiment of desire which prevails in our minds" — not
desire in general, but desire to attend to some sensation
or idea which we find within us. Hence it is possible to
improve other men by arousing their interest in worthier
sensations and thus changing their "prevailing sentiment."
Similarly, the individual may improve himself. He cannot,
to be sure, lift himself by his own bootstraps: "There is
no power, by which men can create or destroy their feelings. Sensation alone overcomes sensation." But he can
cultivate an already existent desire for the ideas of beauty
and virtue which inexplicably drift across his mind, until
such ideas assume the strength and clarity of belief or
reason and thus constitute a nobler "prevailing sentiment." If you feel that this idea is inconsistent with
Drummond's earlier picture of the mind as the slave of
its sensations, try not to worry. In such a system there is
always an awkward moment when the engines are shifted
from reverse to full speed ahead. Consistently or incon-
sistently, Drummond says that

Moral writers have in vain declaimed upon the government of
the passions, where they have failed to show, that it is only one
sentiment which can subdue another in the human breast. If you
wish to make men virtuous, endeavour to inspire into them the
love of virtue. Show them the beauty of order and the fitness
of things. Seek to elevate the mind to the contemplation of divine
perfection, in which alone is assembled whatever is most excellent
in intellectual nature. Represent vice, as indignant virtue will
always represent it, as hideous, loathsome, and deformed. But do
not hope that your precepts can avail you, if you forget, that will
cannot be changed, while sentiment remains unaltered.

Shelley's whole career might be interpreted in the light
of these words. For him, love was perception, feeling,

belief, knowledge, and reason; it was his "prevailing sentiment." The "intellectual system" justified him in asserting that love was the law of the only real world which his mind could know. He aspired to convince other minds of this truth by expressing it as beautifully as possible. His poetry invited men to enter his world of love in the hope that by winning their attention it might arouse their desire and transfer to them his own "prevailing sentiment." If everyone could be made to perceive love as clearly as he perceived it, love would be universal and perfectibility would be attained.

My only apology for this perhaps disproportionately lengthy treatment of Drummond is that it has presented information of some importance which so far as I know is not elsewhere obtainable. Shelley was soon to arrive at a more mystical idealism and a more boldly transcendental conception of the will; but his later ideas grew from the soil of the "intellectual system" and never ceased to draw some nourishment from that soil. In the preface to *The Revolt of Islam*, a poem in which Shelley's views have reached approximately final form, he condemns the philosophy of the age as gloomy and misanthropic, but appends the footnote: "I ought to except Sir W. Drummond's *Academical Questions*; a volume of very acute and powerful metaphysical criticism."

In 1816 and 1817, Shelley pursued those more serious philosophical studies which gave his mind its final stamp. With persuasive clarity and power, Berkeley revealed to him the sources of Drummond's idealism. Spinoza, now examined more carefully than in college days, justified his desire to believe in the unreality of the finite. But every answer which these and other modern philosophers gave to Shelley's wishes was voiced even more delightfully by Plato. Here at last his heart's creed was expressed in a form which satisfied his esthetic sense:

> Plato exhibits the rare union of close and subtle logic with the Pythian enthusiasm of poetry, melted by the splendor and harmony of his periods into one irresistible stream of musical impressions, which hurry the persuasions onward as in a breathless career.
>
> *(Defence of Poetry)*

Shelley has found his ideal of the philosopher poet. We may say, then, that from about the end of 1816 onward Shelley's transcendentalism, at least as expressed in his poetry, is mainly Platonic. We must remember, however, that Shelley never lost a piece of intellectual baggage which he had at any time collected. Godwin, the *philosophes*, Rousseau, Drummond, Berkeley, Spinoza — all were carried along with him to be reshaped as new ideas were acquired.

To consider the exact relation of Shelley's philosophy to Plato's would entail a closer study of Plato than we are able to undertake. The question is important, and there is still room for a thorough treatment of it. At present your best source of information will be Lilian Winstanley's *Platonism in Shelley* (*Essays and Studies by Members of the English Association, Vol. IV*). But poets, as has already been said, are seldom systematic philosophers, and it is legitimate to call Shelley Platonic without meaning to imply that he subscribed to every detail of Plato's system — especially since there is so little agreement as to what that system was. Unquestionably Shelley knew Plato: he translated the *Symposium*, the *Ion*, parts of the *Republic*, and a part of the *Menexenus*. What is more important for our purposes, he represents the general attitude which people have in mind when they use the term "Platonism" — belief in an eternal realm of being which comprises all our ideals in a kind of intellectual paradise, and of which the things of our unreal world of sense experience are merely imperfect shadows. He differs from Plato, however, in several respects which are important enough to deserve attention even in this hasty sketch.

With Shelley, the world of appearances (which ordinary folk call reality) and the world of the ideas are much closer than they are with Plato. This is what we should expect of a romanticist, under the definition of romanticism which has been suggested: he interfuses the real and the ideal where Plato carefully distinguishes them. This is especially apparent in Shelley's conception of love, which departs from true Platonism in that he can never quite detach his love of love from his love of persons. In the lyric beginning *One word is too often profaned*, Shelley sounds very Platonic:

> I can give not what men call love,
>   But wilt thou accept not
> The worship the heart lifts above
>   And the Heavens reject not, —
> The desire of the moth for the star,
>   Of the night for the morrow,
> The devotion to something afar
>   From the sphere of our sorrow?

But in *Love's Philosophy*, instead of rising into the cosmic love, he makes the cosmic love come down to him and support a personal desire for a personal kiss:

> See the mountains kiss high Heaven,
>   And the waves clasp one another;

> No sister-flower would be forgiven
> If it disdained its brother;
> And the sunlight clasps the earth,
> And the moonbeams kiss the sea:
> What is all this sweet work worth
> If thou kiss not me?

In Plato, the philosopher can rise to some degree of communion with the ideas through contemplation of their most nearly perfect earthly reflections. As the philosopher king, he is then to devote the fruits of his vision to the service of the republic. Shelley, on the other hand, imagines a whole human race of philosopher kings, and makes the upward climb to truth much shorter and easier. It is not really a climb at all, but a stripping away of a veil of appearances that hides the ideal reality — a metaphor which he uses repeatedly. Just strip away the veil through an assertion of the will to love, just break down the "dome of many-coloured glass" that "stains the white radiance of eternity," and the realm of the perfect ideas is all about you. You have been living in it all along, but lacked eyes to see.

I have never found a satisfactory statement as to where Shelley obtained his firm belief in the power of the human will to expel evil and establish the reign of love. Its ultimate basis is doubtless faith in poetic imagination, but one would like to know the process by which this faith is rationalized. The idea is not in itself Platonic. There is no basis for it in Kant. In any case Shelley would not have found it there, for in *Peter Bell the Third* he dismisses the *Critique of Pure Reason* as

> A world of words, tail foremost, where
> Right — wrong — false — true — and foul — and fair
> As in a lottery are shook.

Five thousand crammed octavo pages
  Of German psychologics, — he
Who his *furor verborum* assuages
Thereon, deserves just seven months wages
  More than will e'er be due to me.

I looked on them nine several days,
  And then I saw that they were bad;
A friend, too, spoke in their dispraise, —
He never read them; — with amaze
  I found Sir William Drummond had.

This is precisely the tone which Drummond himself adopts toward Kant. The post-Kantian German idealists made much of the transcendental will, but there is no evidence that they influenced Shelley. If he had known them, he would merely have been bewildered by them. Coleridge is a possibility, but although Shelley was a great admirer of Coleridge's poetry his attitude toward Coleridge's philosophy was borrowed from his friend Peacock, who satirized the English transcendentalist in *Melincourt* and *Nightmare Abbey*.

The following hypothesis is at least conceivable. Spinoza asserts that what men call "will" is really *desire* — the force which determines the vividness and duration of an idea in the mind. But this force controls man instead of being controlled by him. "There is in the mind," declares the *Ethics*, "no absolute or free will; but the mind is determined in willing this or that by a cause which is determined in its turn by another cause, and so on to infinity." The same theory, almost certainly derived directly or indirectly from Spinoza, appears in Drummond's *Academical Questions*. But Drummond, wishing to evade the full rigor of necessity in the interests of perfectibilitarian hankerings, suggests the possibility of

improving men through changing their prevailing sentiments. If I understand him correctly, the will, though not
free in the ordinary sense, can to some extent select the
forces which are to determine its operations. Now in
Plato, the philosopher's prevailing sentiment is the desire
to contemplate the ideas in all their perfection. Shelley,
following Spinoza, identifies this desire with the will. But
according to Spinoza, desire is what makes things vivid
and lasting in the mind; and according to Drummond, the
vividness and duration of an impression are the only
criteria of its reasonableness and credibility. Hence to
desire with the passion of Plato's philosopher is identical
with achieving the thing desired; for in a universe which
is all mind the best way of establishing the truth of an
idea is to keep on paying attention to your impression
of it. Simply as a psychological fact, to will is to desire, to
desire is to perceive vividly, and to perceive vividly is
to possess. Shelley's doctrine of the will, then, is Platonic
aspiration translated into Spinozan terms which are
partly relieved of their mechanistic implications by Drummond or by the system that he represents, and still further
relieved of those implications by Shelley's own faith in
the validity of poetic imagination as a guide to truth.
This, let me say again, is conjectural, and you should
investigate the problem for yourselves.

Now we must return from these misty regions to Shelley's poetry. The *Hymn to Intellectual Beauty*, written
in the summer of 1816, a little less than a year after
Alastor, plainly reflects his devotion to Plato:

> The awful shadow of some unseen Power
> Floats though unseen among us, — visiting
> This various world with as inconstant wing

As summer winds that creep from flower to flower, —
Like moonbeams that behind some piny mountain shower,
    It visits with unconstant glance
    Each human heart and countenance;
Like hues and harmonies of evening, —
    Like clouds in starlight widely spread, —
    Like memory of music fled, —
    Like aught that for its grace may be
Dear, and yet dearer for its mystery.

. . . .

Love, Hope, and Self-esteem, like clouds depart
    And come, for some uncertain moments lent,
    Man were immortal and omnipotent,
Didst thou, unknown and awful as thou art,
Keep with thy glorious train firm state within his heart.
    Thou messenger of sympathies,
    That wax and wane in lovers' eyes —
Thou — that to human thought art nourishment,
    Like darkness to a dying flame!
    Depart not as thy shadow came,
    Depart not — lest the grave should be,
Like life and fear, a dark reality.

. . . .

I vowed that I would dedicate my powers
    To thee and thine — have I not kept the vow?
    With beating heart and streaming eyes, even now
I call the phantoms of a thousand hours
Each from his voiceless grave: they have in visioned bowers
    Of studious zeal or love's delight
    Outwatched with me the envious night —
They know that never joy illumed my brow
    Unlinked with hope that thou wouldst free
    This world from its dark slavery,
    That thou — O awful LOVELINESS,
Wouldst give whate'er these words cannot express.

In that last stanza we see Shelley beginning to use his
Platonic transcendentalism as a means of bringing about
his ideal revolution. Plato would be astounded at the
notion of his ideas swooping down into the phenomenal
world and reforming it at a single stroke, but the leaven-
ing influence of the philosopher king is too slow a process
for Shelley's ardor.

You should read the fragmentary *Prince Athanase* to
see how the poet in *Alastor* would have benefited from
having a friend to read Plato with him, but I can pause
only to quote the significant line, "The mind becomes that
which it contemplates." By 1817, the year in which this
poem was begun and abandoned, faith in the great something or other that Shelley means by "Intellectual Beauty"
has become the driving force of the revolution of Laon
and Cythna in *The Revolt of Islam*. Cythna declares:

> I tore the veil that hid
> Nature, and truth, and liberty, and love.

Nothing need be added to what was said about this
poem in an earlier lecture except a reference to the combat
between the eagle and the serpent in Canto I. The eagle
typifies evil; the serpent, good. Their strife is eternal.
The mysterious woman who interprets the vision says that

> from the depths of ages old,
> Two Powers o'er mortal things dominion hold
> Ruling the world with a divided lot,
> Immortal, all-pervading, manifold,
> Twin Genii, equal Gods — when life and thought
> Sprang forth, they burst the womb of inessential Nought.

This Manichaean conception of life as ruled by two
hostile and equally powerful forces is inconsistent with

the rest of the poem and with Shelley's philosophy in general, for the eagle is no mere error of the senses to be swept away by the will. Shelley, in fact, had an unusually keen awareness of the reality of evil: that is why he strove so hard to convince himself of its unreality. But for all his efforts, his transcendental optimism is often troubled by uneasy thoughts of the eagle and the serpent. The Lucretian theory of love and hate within the atom, picked up by Shelley in his materialistic days at Oxford and glanced at once or twice in *Queen Mab,* was never quite abandoned. Thinking of Drummond, one may say that Shelley desired to change men's prevailing sentiments by stimulating associations of contrast. Drummond had advised the reformer not only to "show them the beauty of order and the fitness of things," but to "represent vice, as indignant virtue will always represent it, as hideous, loathsome, and deformed." Hence in several of Shelley's poems one gets an almost melodramatically black and white contrast between eagle characters and serpent characters: the Tyrant and Laon in *The Revolt of Islam*; Jupiter and Prometheus in *Prometheus Unbound*; Count Francesco and Beatrice in *The Cenci*; the Turks and the Greeks in *Hellas*. But the wish to make men love goodness by making them hate evil will not wholly account for these contrasts. Shelley knows, and cannot always succeed in forgetting, that evil is no more illusory than good.

In 1820, Shelley published *Prometheus Unbound, With Other Poems.* Besides the title piece, the book included *The Sensitive Plant, Ode to the West Wind, To a Skylark,* and *The Cloud.* This volume marks not only the climax of Shelley's poetic genius but the climax of his transcendentalism. *The Sensitive Plant,* to be sure, is tinged with melancholy, but at the end we are reminded that from the Platonic viewpoint the death of the Lady and the decay of the garden are mere errors of sense:

> It is a modest creed, and yet
> Pleasant if one considers it,
> To own that death itself must be,
> Like all the rest, a mockery.
>
> That garden sweet, that lady fair,
> And all sweet shapes and odours there,
> In truth have never passed away:
> 'Tis we, 'tis ours, are changed; not they.
>
> For love, and beauty, and delight,
> There is no death nor change: their might
> Exceeds our organs, which endure
> No light, being themselves obscure.

The garden would bloom forever if only our will to love were strong enough. In *Prometheus Unbound* that will *is* strong enough — strong enough to overthrow Jupiter:

> Love, from its awful throne of patient power
> In the wise heart, from the last giddy hour
>   Of dread endurance, from the slippery, steep,
> And narrow verge of crag-like agony, springs
> And folds over the world its healing wings.

The victory of Prometheus, however, is achieved only within the ideal Platonic realm into which Shelley has projected his imagination. As a romanticist, Shelley cannot be wholly satisfied with this solution. Like the poet of *Alastor*, he wants the ideal to be actualized in the visible and finite. He wants real human beings to love one another, not in Atlantis, but "in the very world." As *Ode to the West Wind*, *To a Skylark*, and *The Cloud* bear witness, he wants to merge his visionary mind with the beautiful objects of sense. It is the dilemma of the romanticist who resorts to transcendentalism in order to protect and justify his illusion, but finds himself so far withdrawn from reality that the fusion of the natural and the supernatural becomes a shadowy philosophical game.

Shelley was never able to forget that the world which lay before his eyes, whether metaphysically "real" or not, was different from the world of his imagination. You could annihilate Jupiter by loving him, but not Viscount Castlereagh. The events of Shelley's life suggested that while love might be the law of the universe, one must beware of acting as if it were. Even between 1816 and 1820, there were moments when Shelley doubted the truth of his vision. Some may call these moments lapses from true spiritual wisdom; I call them flashes of realistic intelligence which might have given him a rational happiness if he had frankly accepted them and used them. As it was, however, they only made him morbid and unhappy. The following sonnet, which was written in 1818, uses one of his favorite metaphors in denial of the faith that it usually symbolizes:

> Lift not the painted veil which those who live
> Call Life: though unreal shapes be pictured there,
> And it but mimic all we would believe
> With colours idly spread, — behind, lurk Fear
> And Hope, twin Destinies; who ever weave
> Their shadows, o'er the chasm, sightless and drear.
> I knew one who had lifted it — he sought,
> For his lost heart was tender, things to love,
> But found them not, alas! nor was there aught
> The world contains, the which he could approve.

Through the unheeding many he did move,
A splendour among shadows, a bright blot
Upon this gloomy scene, a Spirit that strove
For truth, and like the Preacher found it not.

Is this melancholy a mere relic of the *Alastor* mood, soon to be silenced by the optimism of *Prometheus Unbound*? It is silenced, or almost silenced, for a short time; but it soon reappears more strongly than ever. Since Shelley was only thirty when he died in 1822, it is idle to conjecture where his thought would have led him if he had lived longer. One can only say that the poems of 1821 and 1822 seem to suggest a blurring and wavering of the transcendental vision. *Adonais*, of course, contains a beautiful expression of his faith, but the essential melancholy of the poem has been too much neglected. Shelley's self-portrait might almost serve for a sketch of Byron in the depths of *Weltschmerz*:

Midst others of less note, came one frail Form,
A phantom among men; companionless
As the last cloud of an expiring storm
Whose thunder is its knell; he as I guess,
Had gazed on Nature's naked loveliness,
Actæon-like, and now he fled astray
With feeble steps o'er the world's wilderness,
And his own thoughts, along that rugged way,
Pursued, like raging hounds, their father and their prey.

A pardlike Spirit beautiful and swift —
A Love in desolation masked; — a Power
Girt round with weakness; — it can scarce uplift
The weight of the superincumbent hour;
It is a dying lamp, a falling shower,
A breaking billow; — even whilst we speak

Is it not broken? On the withering flower
The killing sun smiles brightly: on a cheek
The life can burn in blood, even while the heart may break.

His head was bound with pansies overblown,
And faded violets, white, and pied, and blue;
And a light spear topped with a cypress cone,
Round whose rude shaft dark ivy-tresses grew
Yet dripping from the forest's noonday dew,
Vibrated, as the ever-beating heart
Shook the weak hand that grasped it; of that crew
He came the last, neglected and apart;
A herd-abandoned deer struck by the hunter's dart.

All stood aloof, and at his partial moan
Smiled through their tears; well knew that gentle band
Who in another's fate now wept his own,
As in the accents of a foreign land
He sung new sorrow; sad Urania scanned
The Stranger's mien, and murmured, "Who art thou?"
He answered not, but with a sudden hand
Made bare his branded and ensanguined brow,
Which was like Cain's or Christ's — oh! that it should be so!

He shakes off this mood toward the end of the poem, where he generalizes the idea that Adonais, in dying, has escaped from the world of shadows into the world of eternal truth; and at last he feels the soul of Adonais calling to him, so that he finds intellectual beauty by dying in his own thought a kind of mystical death.

But this conclusion has its tragic side. Shelley, weary of hoping that the dream will come true on earth, has given in at last to one Platonic idea which he has hitherto avoided — that the only means of attaining complete communion with the ideal is death. In 1821 and 1822 he often heard a voice saying,

Die,
If thou wouldst be with that which thou dost seek.

Trelawny relates that Shelley got out of his rowboat one day and lay down beneath the surface of the shallow water to see what drowning would be like. As the last stanza of *Adonais* prophetically suggests, he was soon to test that experience more fully. It was about this time that he asked Trelawny to obtain for him a supply of prussic acid.

Other poems of these last two years indicate a breaking up. They are either nervously light and inconsequential, or show signs of lassitude and gloom. Something seems to have passed out of him. He wrote a great many fragments, like bits of a comet going to pieces in the sky. Even nature looked different to him. This little poem entitled *A Dirge* was to receive optimistic rebuttal in Pippa's helpful song:

> Rough wind, that moanest loud
>   Grief too sad for song;
> Wild wind, when sullen cloud
>   Knells all the night long;
> Sad storm, whose tears are vain,
> Bare woods, whose branches strain,
> Deep caves and dreary main, —
>   Wail, for the world's wrong!

Everyone knows the beginning of the great final chorus of *Hellas*, visioning the return of that Golden Age which had so often sustained Shelley's hopes for the future:

> The world's great age begins anew,
>   The golden years return,
> The earth doth like a snake renew

Her winter weeds outworn:
Heaven smiles, and faiths and empires gleam,
Like wrecks of a dissolving dream.

But few students seem to have noticed the end of this chorus, where the Greeks repudiate their own ideal with an almost Byronic bitterness:

Oh, cease! must hate and death return?
  Cease! must men kill and die?
Cease! drain not to its dregs the urn
  Of bitter prophecy.
The world is weary of the past,
Oh, might it die or rest at last!

It would be better that the Golden Age should not return if the whole tragic cycle of existence were thereby to begin all over again.

Perhaps the most pathetic evidence of the decay of Shelley's transcendental faith is provided by *When the lamp is shattered* (1822). The first stanza turns from Plato to accept an argument against immortality offered by a sceptical interlocutor in the *Phaedo*. Contrary to the belief of the Platonic Socrates that the music of the lute is more enduring than the lute itself, we are told here that music has no existence apart from the mechanism which produces it, and dies with the destruction of that mechanism. Similarly, light dies when the lamp is broken — where now is "the white radiance of eternity?"

When the lamp is shattered
The light in the dust lies dead —
When the cloud is scattered
The rainbow's glory is shed.
When the lute is broken,

Sweet tones are remembered not;
  When the lips have spoken,
Loved accents are soon forgot.

  As music and splendour
Survive not the lamp and the lute,
  The heart's echoes render
No song when the spirit is mute: —
  No song but sad dirges,
Like the wind through a ruined cell,
  Or the mournful surges
That ring the dead seaman's knell.

  When hearts have once mingled
Love first leaves the well-built nest;
  The weak one is singled
To endure what it once possessed.
  O Love! who bewailest
The frailty of all things here,
  Why choose you the frailest
For your cradle, your home, and your bier?

  Its passions will rock thee
As the storms rock the ravens on high;
  Bright reason will mock thee,
Like the sun from a wintry sky.
  From thy nest every rafter
Will rot, and thine eagle home
  Leave thee naked to laughter,
When leaves fall and cold winds come.

When Shelley died he was engaged upon a poem en-titled *The Triumph of Life.* Its tone is decidedly gloomy, and one hardly sees how it could have been turned about to provide an optimistic conclusion. The life that "tri-umphs" — in the manner of a Roman conqueror with slaves at his chariot wheels — is the imperfect life known to human beings. But the poem is unfinished, and no one can tell how it would have ended. It breaks off with the words, " 'Then, what is life?' I cried." Shelley was drowned shortly after asking this question, and found beneath the waves of the Gulf of Spezia whatever answer there may be.

XXII

JOHN KEATS

"Not one word I ever utter can be taken for granted as an opinion growing out of my identical nature." These words, already quoted from the letter of October 27, 1818, might stand as a warning to anyone who ventures to interpret the thought of John Keats. Unfortunately, this warning has not always been heeded. The "true thought" of a poet who merges his ego in his creations is dangerously easy to find: it may prove to be the thought of the critic, imposed upon the poet's work and drawn forth again as a discovery. Here is a point of comparison between Keats and Shakespeare: both poets are so non-egotistical that we may find in them whatever we desire to find. If, however, we hope to understand such a writer in himself instead of using him for the exploitation of our own personalities, we must tread warily.

When a non-egotistical poet appears to speak in his own person, his utterances are eagerly seized upon. A poet's mental habits, however, are likely to be transferred from one form of composition to another. Even as a sonneteer, Shakespeare is incorrigibly dramatic; and few can now share Wordsworth's belief that the sonnet was the key with which he "unlocked his heart." As an interpretative key, the letters of Keats are much more trustworthy: unquestionably they share with friends the personal thoughts and feelings of the writer. But since a good deal of non-egotistical poetry creeps into the letters of a non-egotistical poet, the warning with which this lecture began is not wholly inapplicable even to Keats's prose. The colors of the "chameleon poet" vary somewhat with the colors of his different correspondents. They vary still more with the mood of the moment. A rise in Tom's temperature, good news from George, a twinge of sexual jealousy, a quiet Sabbath in Winchester, a streak of blood on his handkerchief — such things lie behind the ideas which Keats expresses at various times. This is true of everyone, but it is especially true of a poet who "lives in gusto, be it foul or fair." Even in dealing with the letters, then, we must not be overconfident.

Professor E. E. Stoll, in his contributions to Shakespeare criticism, has tried to cure us of two bad habits: reading between the lines in order to make the plays mean what we want them to mean; and ignoring the simple dramatic values which Shakespeare has placed in his foreground in favor of obscure points which can be twisted to support our notion of Shakespeare's "philosophy." Stoll's realistic attitude may be recommended to students of Keats. A test which is useful in applying this attitude to critical works is to imagine the poet as reading the critic's interpretation of him, and to ask, not if the poet would like the critical portrait, but if he would recognize it as a portrait at all. Imagine, for example, Keats and Shakespeare reading John Middleton Murry's *Keats and Shakespeare*. Or imagine Keats alone reading Clarence Dewitt Thorpe's *The Mind of John Keats*, and learning that when he spoke of beauty he had meant "a subjective conception of truth reached through imaginative perception." When the same test is applied to H. W. Garrod's *Keats*, the results are less startling. The poet would at least feel that the book was about him, and not about Garrod's beautiful soul. Garrod is somewhat meagre and juiceless, and he is unfair to Amy Lowell; but he does not write as if Keats were Dostoevsky. I should gladly express indebtedness to him had not my own very similar views been formed some years prior to the publication of his lectures.

Before students began to peck at interesting phrases in Keats's letters, no one suspected him of being a profoundly philosophical poet. Those early days were not so benighted as one might suppose. Since Keats is a great poet, his poems convey whatever meaning they posses. If his letters should convey a different meaning, that would be the meaning of the letters and not of the poems. Now the poems of Keats proclaim in every line that he was primarily a lover and a creator of sensuous beauty. That is the foreground fact with which all interpretation of Keats as a poet must begin, just as all interpretation of *Hamlet* must begin with the foreground fact that the play is an Elizabethan tragedy of revenge.

Advancing from this starting point, and still considering only the poems, we arrive at other facts. It is obvious that Keats, within the brief space of his career, became a more skilful and intelligent artist. He purged his work of the mawkish and cloyingly luscious qualities of his juvenilia; grew to think more austerely, more nobly, of the senses and their ministry. We may observe, too, that Keats's conception of beauty widened to include not only lovely sights and sounds, but lovely emotions and thoughts. Even this wider beauty, however, is sensuously felt. For him, emotions and thoughts are poetically valuable as being associated with beautiful objects of sense perception in the external world or as stimulating beautiful sensuous imagery within his mind. Ideas as ideas do not greatly interest him. We turn to his poetry not for any revelation of the human heart and brain, but for the pure joy of eye and ear. Unless we think crudely and basely of our senses, this opinion defines but in no way diminishes Keats's greatness.

Although Keats is generally content to create beauty without talking about it, there are times when he seems to hint at something like an explicit philosophy of the beautiful. In doing so he is always modest and tentative, never asserting that he has arrived at an interpretation of the universe or a guide to humanity. It is as if he were saying, "This, in a very perplexing and interesting world, is something that I have found to live by as a man and an artist." Even when his esthetic ideals are not explicit, we are moved by his implicit devotion to them as we read.

When Keats is compared with the other great English poets, it is evident that he seldom responded to purely intellectual beauty. His mind, however, possessed abundant intelligence of a specialized kind. In general speculation, though fitfully brilliant and suggestive, he is unsteady, inconsistent, and lacking in centrality. His intelligence is like that of many great musicians — uncertain enough beyond the sphere of their art, but absolutely commanding within that sphere. He brings the intellect of a great craftsman to bear upon sensuous beauty, not in order to convert it into anything else, but in order to make the most of what it is. Thus in his work sensuous enjoyment is united to intellectual enjoyment.

Personally I should not undertake to distinguish between spiritual experience and the most intense kind of

sensuous experience; but if spirituality implies a rising
above the senses, Keats was not a spiritual man. In speaking of Shelley, however, I observed that one can give anything a spiritual value by worshipping it. Keats seldom
if ever worshipped spiritual beauty in the accepted meaning of that term, but he worshipped sensuous beauty so
intensely that it acquired quasi-spiritual values in his
mind. Thus his work harmonized sensuous enjoyment not
only with intellectual discipline but with an ardor and
elevation that are generally associated with spiritual experience.

It is still true that Keats is primarily sensuous, not
primarily intellectual or spiritual. It is still true that we
read him for the pure joy of eye and ear. But as we read,
that joy is mingled with delicate supersensuous overtones
derived from recognition of his artistic intelligence and
his religious devotion to beauty. This is what makes the
difference between mere titillation of the senses and that
"soul of sweet delight," which, Blake says, "can never be
defiled."

So much may legitimately be inferred from Keats's
poems without a single glance at the letters. But from
the poems we may also infer that Keats was occasionally
influenced by a view of poetry which was alien to his
genius. He was teased by the notion that a really great
poet practises "the egotistical sublime" — gives people a
direct philosophical message, like Wordsworth. This
idea is sometimes confused with his ambition to become
a better artist of his own particular kind.

Sleep and Poetry testifies to his aspirations at the outset of his career:

O for ten years, that I may overwhelm
Myself in poesy; so I may do the deed
That my own soul has to itself decreed.
Then will I pass the countries that I see
In long perspective, and continually
Taste their pure fountains. First the realm I'll pass
Of Flora, and old Pan: sleep in the grass,
Feed upon apples red, and strawberries,
And choose each pleasure that my fancy sees;
Catch the white-handed nymphs in shady places,
To woo sweet kisses from averted faces, —
Play with their fingers, touch their shoulders white
Into a pretty shrinking with a bite
As hard as lips can make it: till agreed,
A lovely tale of human life we'll read.

But the young poet feels an obligation to outgrow these
delights:

And must I ever bid these joys farewell?
Yes, I must pass them for a nobler life,
Where I may find the agonies, the strife
Of human hearts: for lo! I see afar,
O'ersailing the blue cragginess, a car
And steeds with shaggy manes — the charioteer
Looks out upon the winds with glorious fear:

. . . .

The charioteer with wondrous gesture talks
To the trees and mountains; and there soon appear
Shapes of delight, of mystery, and fear,
Passing along before a dusky space
Made by some mighty oaks: as they would chase
Some ever-fleeting music on they sweep.
Lo! how they murmur, laugh, and smile, and weep:
Some with upholden hand and mouth severe;

Some with their faces muffled to the ear
Between their arms; some, clear in youthful bloom,
Go glad and smilingly athwart the gloom;
Some looking back, and some with upward gaze;
Yes, thousands in a thousand different ways
Flit onward — now a lovely wreath of girls
Dancing their sleek hair into tangled curls;
And now broad wings. Most awfully intent
The driver of those steeds is forward bent,
And seems to listen: O that I might know
All that he writes with such a hurrying glow.

The interpretation of this vision is uncertain, but probably the "shapes of delight, of mystery, and fear," are the great poets; the "lovely wreath of girls," very Keatsian muses; and the "broad wings," those of Pegasus.

Keats shakes off the fear that his ambition may be presumptuous:

What though I am not wealthy in the dower
Of spanning wisdom; though I do not know
The shiftings of the mighty winds that blow
Hither and thither all the changing thoughts
Of man: though no great ministering reason sorts
Out the dark mysteries of human souls
To clear conceiving: yet there ever rolls
A vast idea before me, and I glean
Therefrom my liberty; thence too I've seen
The end and aim of Poesy.

Just what is the "vast idea," and what "the end and aim of Poesy"? With all sympathy and admiration, one may feel that Keats himself is not quite sure. He knows that he should refine and dignify his art, but he also feels that he should bring philosophic wisdom to bear upon "the dark mysteries of human souls." The latter has been the function of some great poets, but it was not destined to be that of Keats. His desire to fulfill a nonexistent obligation would have ruined his work if he had not generally managed to forget it.

He was not, however, always able to forget it. Since the following lines form part of a verse epistle enclosed in a letter written to John Hamilton Reynolds on March 25, 1818, to use them here is perhaps to violate our principle of confining ourselves to Keats's poetry; but I shall ask you to admit them as evidence:

> O that our dreamings all, of sleep or wake,
> Would all their colours from the sunset take:
> From something of material sublime,
> Rather than shadow our own soul's day-time
> In the dark void of night. For in the world
> We jostle, — but my flag is not unfurled
> On the Admiral-staff, — and so philosophize
> I dare not yet! Oh, never will the prize,
> High reason, and the love of good and ill,
> Be my reward! Things cannot to the will
> Be settled, but they tease us out of thought;
> Or is it that imagination brought
> Beyond its proper bound, yet still confined,
> Lost in a sort of purgatory blind,
> Cannot refer to any standard law
> Of either earth or heaven? It is a flaw
> In happiness, to see beyond our bourn, —
> It forces us in summer skies to mourn,
> It spoils the singing of the Nightingale.

The conflict is perfectly clear. Keats feels that he should philosophize; does not yet dare to do so; fears that he will never be able to do so; and, with all the force of his instinctive nature, does not wish to do so. The phrase

"love of good and ill" suggests Keats's tendency to associate philosophy with the expression of some helpful
ethical message.

The two uncompleted treatments of the Hyperion
theme are efforts to write philosophical poetry. *Hyperion, a Fragment* is by far the better, since here Keats
indulges more freely in his own kind of beauty — indulges
so freely, indeed, that sheer loveliness, the "material
sublime," smothers the message and forces Keats to abandon the struggle. But we may fear that if the poem had
been completed Apollo would have turned out to be the
poet who helps mankind. His shriek, with which the
fragment breaks off, might almost be regarded as symbolic of Keats's own reluctance to be such a poet.

In *The Fall of Hyperion, a Dream*, Keats, though even
more anxiously determined to serve mankind, is sadly
aware that he is not fitted for the task. He demands of
Moneta:

> "Majestic shadow, tell me: sure not all
> Those melodies sung into the World's ear
> Are useless: sure a poet is a sage;
> A humanist, physician to all men.
> That I am none I feel, as vultures feel
> They are no birds when eagles are abroad.
> What am I then: Thou spakest of my tribe:
> What tribe?" The tall shade veiled in drooping white
> Then spake, so much more earnest, that the breath
> Moved the thin linen folds that drooping hung
> About a golden censer from the hand
> Pendent — "Art thou not of the dreamer tribe?
> The poet and the dreamer are distinct,
> Diverse, sheer opposite, antipodes.
> The one pours out a balm upon the World,
> The other vexes it."

When Keats's poems are regarded as a whole, his tendency to reproach himself for not being a quite different sort of poet cannot be thought of as a factor in his development from boyish talent to genuine greatness. It was a nagging, morbid fallacy which hindered that development by obscuring his true goal and making him doubt his remarkable powers. That it did not, after all, spoil the singing of the nightingale or make the tender-personed Lamia melt into a shade indicates the fundamental strength of his passion for sensuous beauty. To regard his greatest handicap as evidence of a quality that he never possessed is utterly to misunderstand him.

Except to those who insert their own ideas between the lines, the letters of Keats in no way contradict the foregoing interpretation. They clarify that interpretation, however, by revealing glimpses of the mental background from which his art emerged. Let us examine a few important letters in chronological order.

According to Professor Garrod, Benjamin Bailey was largely responsible for Keats's misguided ambition to be a philosophical poet. In the following words addressed to Bailey on November 22, 1817, Keats seems to be defending his true self against the intruding Wordsworthian ideal:

Men of Genius are great as certain ethereal Chemicals operating on the Mass of natural intellect — but they have not any individuality or determined Character — I would call the top and head of those who have a proper self, Men of Power.

This agrees perfectly with the letter written almost a year later to Richard Woodhouse, in which, you will remember, Keats declares that the poet "has no self."

The conclusion of *Ode on a Grecian Urn* has been so

grossly gushed over that "Beauty is truth, truth beauty" has become one of the most nauseating phrases in literature. This passage from the letter to Bailey will help to explain its meaning:

> I am certain of nothing but the holiness of the Heart's affections, and the truth of Imagination. What the Imagination seizes as Beauty must be Truth — whether it existed before or not, — for I have the same idea of all our passions as of Love: they are all, in their sublime, creative of essential Beauty.

The imagination seizes not only upon lovely objects but upon lovely human passions and distills from them the pure essence of the beautiful. If the truth is something solid and satisfying by which man can live, then beauty is the only truth that Keats knows.

Man has no clear conception of the truth which he is seeking, and he never finds it. But he believes that if he ever did find it, it would prove to be completely self-sufficient and final — a pure good in itself. In seeking truth, then, man seeks something that possesses non-instrumental finality. In actual life, however, almost everything is an instrument for doing or getting some other thing. There is always a step above this one, and the end is nowhere in sight. Yet there are certain steps on which we can pause and breathe so happily that we seem for a moment to have reached the top. There are elements of life which can be regarded as good in themselves: play (not professionalized football, but play); love (not propagating the species, but love): science (not applied mechanics, but science); philosophy (not the precepts of Polonius, but philosophy); religion (not teaching poor little boys to play basketball, but religion); and the fine arts (not saying pretty and wholesome things, but the fine arts). At their core these are ends, not means. They may be enjoyed for their own sake, and in this they are like that final truth of which we dream. For Keats, the one great self-sufficient activity is art. When he says "Beauty is truth, truth beauty," he means that esthetic experience shows us what the contemplation of truth would be like if we ever found it. He wisely makes the qualification, "That is all ye know *on earth*"; and then adds, in a thoroughly pragmatic spirit, "and all ye need to know" — meaning that this sense of a correspondence between the esthetic experience and the perception of truth will serve for the working purposes of human beings this side the grave. Although discordant influences sometimes draw Keats away from this position, it represents the only philosophy that he can be said to possess. We may call it estheticism if we remember that it is free from the decadence of Pater's disciples. Keats's veins are filled with blood, not with Pre-Raphaelite ink.

In the Bailey letter, the assertion, "What the Imagination seizes as Beauty must be Truth — whether it existed before or not," points toward a kind of esthetic transcendentalism. The imagination is given the power to create truth by interpreting the world in terms of beauty. But Keats offers this idea with much dubiety. He hopes it is valid, the letter to Bailey continues, because he himself has never been able to arrive at truth in any other way:

I am the more zealous in this affair, because I have never been able to perceive how anything can be known for truth by consecutive reasoning — and yet it must be. Can it be that the greatest Philosopher ever arrived at his goal without putting aside numerous objections? However this may be, O for a life of sensations rather than of thoughts!

Various attempts have been made to sophisticate the frank simplicity of that last sentence, but there is no reason to suppose that it does not mean exactly what it says. Keats instinctively prefers sensations to thoughts. He seizes upon beauty, and hopes that it may prove to be truth. Beauty and truth are akin not merely in that they are self-sufficient and final, but in that the mind responds to them immediately rather than as a result of "consecutive reasoning." Anything to which the mind makes an immediate response is both beautiful and true. We should beware, however, of associating Keats with any elaborate theory of esthetic intuition. It is better to say that he loved feeling better than thinking, but was sometimes impelled to think about feeling in order to rationalize his preference.

Let us turn to a letter written to John Hamilton Reynolds on February 3, 1818. It reads in part:

It may be said that we ought to read our contemporaries, that Wordsworth, etc., should have their due from us. But, for the sake of a few fine imaginative or domestic passages, are we to be bullied into a certain philosophy engendered in the whims of an egotist? . . . We hate poetry that has a palpable design upon us. . . . Poetry should be great and unobtrusive, a thing which enters into one's soul, and does not startle or amaze it with itself, but with its subject.

Here is the true Keats expressing his distaste for the "egotistical sublime." He is not, of course, quite fair to poets of the Wordsworth type, for at their best such poets can express a personal philosophy without preaching at the reader. Keats's inability to respond emotionally to abstract intellectual conceptions is nowhere shown more clearly than in his tendency to associate philosophical poetry with didacticism.

Sixteen days later, Keats writes to the same correspondent in words which recall the last stanza of the *Ode to Psyche:*

Now it appears to me that almost any Man may like the spider spin from his own inwards his own airy citadel — the points of leaves and twigs on which the spider begins her work are few, and she fills the air with a beautiful circuiting. Man should be content with as few points to tip with the fine Web of his Soul, and weave a tapestry empyrean full of symbols for his spiritual eye, of softness for his spiritual touch, of space for his wandering, of distinctness for his luxury.

Although I cannot prove the point, I believe that when Keats uses the word "spiritual" he generally refers to that kind of imagination which draws upon images already steeped in the richness of the poetic mind instead of upon raw impressions just arriving from the external world. Here, for example, spirit is a refined inward sensuousness, luxuriously fingering and feasting its eyes upon a symbolic tapestry of beauty-truth. And in *Ode on a Grecian Urn*, the much-interpreted "Pipe to the spirit ditties of no tone" probably means that the internal poetic senses, "the wreath'd trellis of a working brain," can provide music lovelier than any actual sound.

That Keats's airy citadel rests upon a foundation of scepticism is suggested by a letter written to Benjamin Bailey on March 13 of the same year:

I do not think myself more in the right than other people, and that nothing in this world is proveable. . . . I am sometimes so very sceptical as to think Poetry itself a mere Jack o' Lantern to amuse whoever may chance to be struck by its brilliance. As tradesmen say every thing is worth what it will fetch, so probably every mental pursuit takes its reality and worth from the ardor of the pursuer — being in itself a Nothing. . . . Now, my dear fellow,

I must once for all tell you I have not one idea of the truth of any of my speculations — I shall never be a reasoner, because I care not to be in the right, when retired from bickering and in a proper philosophical temper.

Let us not split hairs over the word "philosophical" in the last sentence: it plainly means no more than "serene." Keats is sure of nothing — not always even of "the truth of imagination." The value of an idea lies only in the intensity of feeling aroused by the pursuit of it. If we sense it as beautiful, we are entitled to suppose that it is as true as anything else in this world where nothing is certain. In the hands of some of Keats's contemporaries, this scepticism might be transformed into an assertion of the powers of transcendental imagination; but he knows that it warrants only the building of an airy citadel.

On the twenty-fourth of the following month, the man who said "I shall never be a reasoner" was writing to John Taylor:

I find earlier days are gone by — I find that I can have no enjoyment in the world but continued drinking of knowledge. I find there is no worthy pursuit but the idea of doing some good to the world. . . . The road lies through application, study, and thought. I will pursue it; and for that end purpose retiring for some years. I have been hovering for some time between an exquisite sense of the luxurious, and a love for philosophy, — were I calculated for the former, I should be glad. But as I am not, I shall turn all my soul to the latter.

Here is the element which is so completely discordant with the real genius of Keats as displayed in his poems and in the letters previously cited. Notice again the harmful association of "philosophy" with "doing some good." Notice also that he still wishes to cultivate the luxurious, but feels drawn in the opposite direction. He is struggling with the first *Hyperion*.

Professor Garrod argues that "doing some good," here and elsewhere in Keats's letters, means speaking out in support of the liberal side of contemporary questions. Although it seems to me that Keats's uneasy feeling of obligation to serve mankind was both broader and vaguer than this opinion would indicate, he was doubtless affected by the romantic humanitarianism of the circle in which he moved. Hazlitt could write a political article as well as an essay on Shakespeare; and Leigh Hunt, the "loved Libertas," was as much at home in a jail as in the garden of the *Decameron*. Such men gave Keats the wistful sense of belonging to "the dreamer tribe." See Garrod's book for evidence on this point and supplement it with stanzas xiv-xvi of *Isabella*, which show that Keats's *forte* was emphatically not the expression of social indignation.

We have not yet finished with that important letter which Keats wrote to Richard Woodhouse on October 27, 1818, distinguishing between his own "poetical character" and "the Wordsworthian, or egotistical sublime." The portion hitherto cited ends with the statement that "not one word I ever utter can be taken as an opinion growing out of my identical Nature — how can it, when I have no nature." But Keats continues:

In the 2nd place, I will speak of my views, and of the life I purpose to myself. I am ambitious of doing the world some good: if I should be spared, that may be the work of maturer years — in the interval I will assay to reach as high a summit in poetry as the nerve bestowed upon me will suffer. . . . All I hope is, that I may not lose all interest in human affairs — that the solitary Indifference I feel for applause, even from the finest spirits, will not blunt any acuteness of vision I may have. I do not think it will. . . . But even now I am perhaps not speaking from myself, but from some Character in whose soul I now live.

It is perhaps not without relief that Keats puts off to "maturer years" the ambition to write a helpful kind of poetry utterly discordant with the "poetical character" described in the earlier part of this letter. Meanwhile he will write as beautifully as he can, hoping that the airy citadel of his imagination will not make him oblivious to the concerns of men. The background of this conflict is a scepticism so complete that Keats even doubts whether he is speaking in his own person.

Who can say what the issue of this conflict would have been if Keats had been allowed the ten years for which he prayed in *Sleep and Poetry?* But I for one am glad that his last significant utterance on the subject of poetry is eloquent of his real, sensuous, esthetic self. It is August, 1820, and he is shortly to sail for Italy and death, when he writes to Shelley:

A modern work, it is said, must have a purpose, which may be the God. An artist must serve Mammon; he must have "self-concentration" — selfishness, perhaps. You, I am sure, will forgive me for sincerely remarking that you might curb your magnanimity, and be more of an artist, and load every rift of your subject with ore.

"Self-concentration" has nothing to do with "the egotistical sublime," nor is it inconsistent with the idea that a poet like Keats "has no self." It is merely the spirit of the artist who aspires toward his own ideal of beauty without any thought of helping mankind. Keats's criticism is all the more striking when one considers that it was addressed to a poet who, although he certainly aspired to "do some good," was almost never crassly didactic, and that it was stimulated by *The Cenci*, the least purposeful of Shelley's major works.

As I said at the outset, these bits of evidence must be used with delicacy. To find in them a steady march of thought upward to the heights of philosophical vision seems impossible. To agree with my interpretation may seem equally impossible to you, but I can only do my best with the clues at my disposal. It seems to me that Keats's most characteristic attitude toward life's problems is a scepticism in which the only certainty is the supreme value of beauty. Even this truth he sometimes doubts, but only in moments of morbidity. His scepticism is not so much the result of searching thought as the result of a subconscious unwillingness to reason analytically. It is a form of romantic anti-intellectualism, a means of guarding Lamia from the eye of Apollonius. Its psychological basis is the desire to build an airy citadel of imaginative luxury. Since he romantically fears that rational certitude would destroy the citadel, he protects it by doubting all things.

Within this fortress of esthetic enjoyment guarded by its wide moat of scepticism, Keats found moments of supreme happiness. But the airy citadel — like those other strongholds of estheticism, the Palace of Art and the Ivory Tower — must draw its provisions from the outer world; and when the lord of the castle goes foraging his imagination recoils from the coarse human stuff on which it must feed. Hence in the thought of any esthete — I use the term in no derogatory sense — art is likely to become not a happy contemplation of life but a desperate refuge from life.

The romantic dilemma as it appears in Keats arises
from this situation. He had in his mind an ideal of beauty
which, though pure and lofty, was never detached from
his sensuous delight in the real. Intensely literary as
Keats was, he constantly pierced through books to the
warm actuality behind them. The esthetic ideal and the
human real, he felt, should be fused: any hostility between art and life was repugnant to him. But happy relations between the airy citadel and the world outside it
were not easy to establish. On the one hand, his appetite
for beauty outstripped reality, and made him hunger for
better bread than can be made of wheat. On the other
hand, the unhappy circumstances of his life gave him
blacker bread than he deserved. And so the song of the
nightingale, instead of illumining the actual with beauty,
arouses a desire to

> Fade far away, dissolve, and quite forget
>   What thou among the leaves hast never known,
> The weariness, the fever, and the fret
>   Here, where men sit and hear each other groan;
> Where palsy shakes a few, sad, last gray hairs,
>   Where youth grows pale, and spectre-thin, and dies;
>   Where but to think is to be full of sorrow
>   And leaden-eyed despairs,
>   Where Beauty cannot keep her lustrous eyes,
>   Or new Love pine at them beyond tomorrow.

Keats, in a way that the author of *Alastor* would have
understood, longed to harmonize his sexual passion with
his ideal of beauty. Had he not been fundamentally sensuous, he would not have dreamed of finding this harmony in the charms of Fanny Brawne. But there, to his
erotic hunger, was beauty; and there, consequently, was

truth. In an age when it was fashionable for a gentleman to assure the beloved that her high moral character was the true reason for his devotion, Keats cries out to Fanny:

Why may I not speak of your Beauty, since without that I could never have loved you? — I cannot conceive any beginning of such love as I have for you but Beauty. There may be a sort of love for which, without the least sneer at it, I have the highest respect and can admire it in others: but it has not the richness, the bloom, the full form, the enchantment of love after my own heart. So let me speak of your Beauty, though to my own endangering; if you could be so cruel to me as to try elsewhere its Power.

(July 8, 1819)

"Though to my own endangering." Knowing that this foreboding proved justified, we may turn with Keats from love in life to love in art. Being "a thing of beauty," the passion depicted on the Grecian Urn is "a joy forever:"

> Bold Lover, never, never, canst thou kiss,
> Though winning near the goal — yet, do not grieve;
> She cannot fade, though thou hast not thy bliss,
> For ever wilt thou love, and she be fair.
>
> . . . .
>
> More happy love! more happy, happy love!
> For ever warm and still to be enjoyed,
> For ever panting, and for ever young;
> All breathing human passion far above,
> That leaves a heart high-sorrowful and cloyed,
> A burning forehead, and a parching tongue.

But it is sad to think of art as infinitely precious because nothing else is worth anything, and sad to think of that bold lover stretching out his arms through the centuries as happier than he who risks the penalty of a human kiss.

Meanwhile Fanny Brawne is innocently flirting with one of her cavaliers.

When the mind feels a conflict between life and art, a thing of beauty is a joy, not forever, but only as long as one looks at it. Sooner or later, one must leave the picture gallery and go out into the sordid streets. *La Belle Dame Sans Merci* offers only a few dreamy moments snatched from life's bewildering flux —

> And I awoke, and found me here
> On the cold hillside.

In *The Eve of St. Agnes*, the warm, bright, tender story is framed in darkness and cold. The poem begins with the "bitter chill" and the half frozen old beadsman; it ends with the lovers going out into the storm. Having briefly experienced beauty-truth, they must experience life. Thus the esthete's joy inevitably has a background of pain. In the *Ode on Melancholy*, Keats tells us that the purest melancholy is to be found not in scenes of horror but in scenes of beauty: "She dwells with Beauty — Beauty that must die."

Since beauty must die, Keats treasures those rare moments when beauty lives in all its richness. The very transitoriness of these moments, the certainty that the real and the ideal will drift apart again and be lost in the flux of things, demands that we wring every drop of value from every second. Hence in the final stage of Keats's development, his esthetic emotion is so intense that it results in oblivion as it reaches its climax. The mind goes blank from the agonized delight of concentrating upon the beautiful object. The esthetic experience of Keats is like a swooning; it is like that failure of the senses which blinds the mystic when he attains to contemplation of the godhead; it is like the consummation of human passion; it is like death.

Severn tells us that Keats repeatedly went to see the Elgin marbles, and would gaze at them for an hour or more in a trance of happiness. How the poet felt in such moments is shown by the sonnet *On Seeing the Elgin Marbles:*

> My spirit is too weak — mortality
> Weighs heavily on me like unwilling sleep.

A particularly revealing instance of the same feeling appears in stanzas 31 and 32 of *The Eve of St. Agnes:*

> "And now, my love, my seraph fair, awake!
> Thou art my heaven, and I thine eremite:
> Open thine eyes, for meek St. Agnes' sake,
> Or I shall drowse beside thee, so my soul doth ache."

> Thus whispering, his warm, unnerved arm
> Sank in her pillow.

Under these circumstances, it seems curious to say, "My soul aches so that I am almost on the point of going to sleep"; but this is the trancelike sleep of one who feels so intensely that he is on the point of not feeling at all.

Some readers have felt that the famous "last sonnet," *Bright star, would I were steadfast as thou art*, is almost unmanly in its softness and limpness. They should re-member that Keats was a very sick man when he wrote it. But quite apart from that fact, the swooning should be interpreted in the light of what has just been said about the quality of Keats's esthetic experience:

> No — yet still steadfast, still unchangeable,
> Pillowed upon my fair love's ripening breast,
> To feel for ever its soft fall and swell,

> Awake for ever in a sweet unrest,
> Still, still to hear her tender-taken breath,
> And so live ever — or else swoon to death.

The implication is that to live forever in this happiness and to swoon to death would be equivalent. On July 25, 1819, he wrote to Fanny:

I have two luxuries to brood over in my walks, your Loveliness and the hour of my death. O that I could have possession of them both in the same minute.

But the supreme example of the esthetic swoon is the *Ode to a Nightingale*. That drugged, painful, ecstatic trance of heartache induced by the bird's song is perfectly characteristic of Keats:

> My heart aches, and a drowsy numbness pains
>   My sense, as though of hemlock I had drunk,
> Or emptied some dull opiate to the drains
>   One minute past, and Lethe-wards had sunk:
> 'Tis not through envy of thy happy lot,
>   But being too happy in thine happiness.

At last, as you remember, the "viewless wings of poesy" carry him into the world of beauty represented by the nightingale's voice. And it is significant that as soon as he reaches this summit of happiness he thinks of death:

> Darkling I listen; and, for many a time
>   I have been half in love with easeful Death,
> Called him soft names in many a musèd rhyme,
>   To take into the air my quiet breath;
> Now more than ever it seems rich to die,
>   To cease upon the midnight with no pain,
>   While thou art pouring forth thy soul abroad
>   In such an ecstasy!
>   Still wouldst thou sing, and I have ears in vain —
>   To thy high requiem become a sod.

But the esthetic experience was not at this time to have
the finality of death. Life called him back from his trance,
as it calls us all back until the very end:

> Forlorn! the very word is like a bell
> To toll me back from thee to my sole self!
> Adieu! the fancy cannot cheat so well
> As she is famed to do, deceiving elf.
> Adieu! adieu! thy plaintive anthem fades
> Past the near meadows, over the still stream,
>   Up the hill-side; and now 'tis buried deep
>   In the next valley-glades:
> Was it a vision, or a waking dream?
> Fled is that music: — Do I wake or sleep?

The ultimate luxury, however, was not long witheld.
He greeted it with: "Severn — I — lift me up — I am
dying — I shall die easy; don't be frightened — be firm,
and thank God it has come."

> Verse, Fame, and Beauty are intense indeed,
> But Death intenser — Death is Life's high meed.

XXIII

CONCLUSION

The governing ideas of these lectures have been stressed so persistently that a summary would be superfluous, and the temptation to apply those ideas to contemporary problems must of course be resisted. If anything I have said raises questions about what to think and how to live, you must either answer those questions for yourselves or seek light from your favorite philosophers and preachers. Those of you who are romanticists deserve thanks for listening so patiently to a statement of views so different from your own. I have no desire to convert you, and I trust that you have no desire to convert me. In one way, I am more afraid of making converts than of not making them, for those of you who are temperamentally disposed to share my sceptical and rather unsympathetic attitude toward romanticism may carry that attitude to extreme lengths. You may develop so strong a hatred of romanticism that you will be unable to read the romantic poets without sneering and snarling. You may grow to believe that romanticism lies at the root of all the evils of modern life and must therefore be attacked without mercy whenever the slightest trace of it appears in life or letters. This is the spirit which characterizes the "new humanists." The spirit of the literary scholar is quite different, and in these last few moments I shall try to describe it in the hope that you may wish it to be yours if you do not already possess it.

Having some acquaintance with the ceaseless rise and fall of ideas, the scholar is quietly sceptical in intellectual matters. His scepticism applies even to his own opinions. His business, that of enjoying and understanding literature, entails necessarily subjective interpretations of highly complex bodies of fact or supposed fact. Naturally he prefers his own views to those of others and argues for them as adroitly as possible. He finds it difficult, however, to work himself into a lather of righteous anger about anything. When a moral principle is plainly involved he will fight for his notion of the truth, but he prefers to leave moralizing to the moralists and crusading to the crusaders. He has no reform spirit. In him the attempt to see things as they are absorbs those energies which the evangelistic person devotes to making things different. He can appreciate ideas and personalities which are good of their kind without worrying too much about the kind, can admire a fine statement of a detestable fallacy in the spirit of a surgeon who speaks of a "beautiful tumor." His thirst for clear principles of comprehension teaches him to love literary works that are perfectly representative of whatever they happen to represent. In the joy of understanding, personal disagreement is forgotten. He has been accused of lacking esthetic sensibility, but he is really a sort of poet; for, like Keats, he delights in the Iagos of his intellectual world hardly less than in the Imogens.

For the time being let those of us who are unromantic or antiromantic adopt this attitude in order to see how it may affect our study of the English romantic movement. In the first place, then, such poems as *Tintern Abbey, The Ancient Mariner, Prometheus Unbound,* and *Ode to a*

Nightingale are obviously great works of literary art. We may argue that they fall below certain rigid standards of excellence, but there is no reason why literature should consist entirely of Homeric epics and Sophoclean tragedies. If we cannot enjoy and admire romantic poetry, we had better abandon the title of critic and call ourselves new humanists. The basis of all good criticism is the ability to appreciate the adaptation of means to ends in literary creation. Whether Wordsworth is right or wrong in what he says is of less importance to the purely literary critic than the skill with which he says what he wants to say. Our personal notions are seldom important enough to justify us in condemning a great artist for not agreeing with them. We may of course dislike what we are too intelligent to condemn. Let us beware, however, of surrendering the happiness that comes from ranging freely through the realm of letters, growing in breadth and insight by sharing the thoughts of other men. The inevitable tension between esthetic admiration and intellectual disagreement is the best possible exercise for the critical faculty. An intensely unromantic student who feels that Blake was a remarkable genius and a very great man has the makings of a competent critic.

Except for pedants on the one hand and sentimental dilettanti on the other, there is no real conflict between literary criticism and historico-literary scholarship. Justly to appreciate a literary work of the past, we must become contemporaries of the author by cultivating historical imagination; and historical imagination cannot exist without historical knowledge. By historical imagination I mean the faculty of reading Shakespeare like an Elizabethan, Bunyan like a Puritan, Pope like an Augustan wit, and

Wordsworth like a romantic nature worshipper. The bookish person knows no keener pleasure than this union of learning with literary responsiveness in a reconstruction of past emotional and intellectual experience. If we run up and down the centuries measuring against our own little opinions all the ideas that we meet, we can never enjoy this pleasure which is essential to good criticism and scholarship.

The ability to enjoy great books is for some students a sufficient aim. Most scholars in our field, however, regard literature as an aspect of intellectual history as well as a fine art. This is the viewpoint which has chiefly dominated the present course, though my personal interest in the esthetic viewpoint is equally strong. Wordsworth and Shelley felt that they had important ideas to express. It is our aim not only to enjoy the expression of those ideas, but to understand them in themselves and in relation to the stream of human thought. If we really try to understand the romantic movement, we shall have no time to scold at it. What are its significant tendencies? How are they interrelated? Where do they come from? What becomes of them? How are they reflected in the minds of various writers? Regardless of our personal attitude toward romanticism, these questions are of the utmost interest and importance to anyone with a disinterested love of knowledge.

Once we learn to regard ideas from the historical viewpoint our opinions are tempered by an almost cynical charity. It becomes clear to us that literary changes are governed not by theoretical absolutes, but by specific circumstances. The distinguishing tendencies of any period could not possibly have been other than what they were.

It is idle to quarrel with the rise and fall of human thought: one might as fruitfully become indignant at some biological process observed in the laboratory. At any given time a writer says what he might be expected to say as a result of his temperamental response to his intellectual environment. That environment is an eddy of ideas and feelings circling into the present from the past, and moving on, with innumerable subtle changes, into the future. Cause and effect; stimulus and response; instinctive desire and rationalization; old, old attractions and repulsions, at work throughout the centuries. A constantly shifting pattern of eternal elements. A game of chess in which, if we can discover whether the man is a bishop or a knight, we know what general type of move he must make. No part of this spectacle deserves to be championed or attacked; every part of it deserves to be studied and understood.

Such a course as the one which is now concluding necessarily concentrates upon the romanticism of the romantic poets. The knowledge provided by this method represents only a part of what a student derives from long and thorough saturation in the literature of the 1780-1830 period. The great writers of this age were more than romantic, more than any phrase which the historiographer of ideas can devise. Although we cannot understand them without understanding romanticism, we do them great injustice, we miss much beauty and truth, if we are never able to regard them otherwise than as illustrations of a view of life which we happen not to share. Unless we are abnormally narrow-minded, our experience must have included affectionate admiration for some noble personality whose ideas were very different from our own. If we are worthy of it, we may enjoy this sort of friendship with Wordsworth.

But despite all that has been said, it is psychologically impossible to keep our instinctive prejudices and reasoned opinions from influencing our judgment of literature and our interpretation of intellectual history. Without this influence, pure criticism and pure historical scholarship would probably die of their own purity. As this course abundantly illustrates, even when we try to give a faithful account of what we think we have learned, our explanation is necessarily couched in terms dictated by our private view of life. We must not pretend that we are able to transmit the spirit of the past to our readers or students without a large amount of personal refraction. Having failed to discover *the* truth, we must be content with expressing *our* truth. Nor is this necessity to be regretted. The scholar's work, after all, demands a delicate balance between the impersonal and the personal attitudes. If his studies are to have more than merely selfish justification, he must tell others what he thinks after he has listened to the writers of the past. His mind should not be so broad that it lies perfectly flat, nor so open that it is open at both ends. The ability to enjoy good literature is precious, but the complete sacrifice of one's intellectual identity is too heavy a price to pay for it.

Our attitude toward the work of the romantic poets, then, must and should be affected by our attitude toward romanticism. The extent of the influence will vary with the individual. There are those who are so anti-Catholic that they cannot read Dante, and those who are so anti-romantic that they cannot read Shelley. Such persons are to be pitied as deficient in esthetic disinterestedness, imaginative sympathy, and historical balance; but they cannot be converted. Those of us who are less egocentric may continue to enjoy Dante and Shelley for what they have to give us without regarding them as repositories of absolute truth if we happen not to share their views.

The bitter opponent of romanticism commits the absurdity of trying to detach himself from an essential element of his own mind. No one has eradicated from his subconscious all traces of longing for the romantic illusion. Our emotions retain, though our reason may have rejected, impulses closely akin to those of the romantic poets. There is romanticism in all of us, and nothing is to be gained by denying its existence. It cannot be hunted down and killed; it must be dealt with in some humane and civilized way. We shall be the happier if we give this perfectly normal trait an outlet and a means of exercise. For this purpose nothing is better than reading in the 1780-1830 period. Our suppressed irrationality is relieved and purified through association with the ardent beauty of romantic literature. If we are as rational as we suppose ourselves to be, we need not dread contamination.

The pleasure of these emotional holidays will be tempered by our realization that it is impossible to regain the faith which for a time sustained the romanticists. Our reason will keep reminding us that their aims were misdirected, their struggle ultimately futile. We shall be amused or irritated or saddened to see so much personal greatness, so much genius, devoted to the vain attempt to preserve an immature and superstitious illusion.

Even our realization of the futility of the struggle,

however, may contribute to literary enjoyment. If we have any sense of irony, we may regard the romantic quest as a great comedy in the last act of which we ourselves are playing minor rôles. The romantic movement is an endlessly delightful comic spectacle in the highest meaning of that term.

The romantic movement may also be regarded as a tragic spectacle of the utmost beauty and pathos. Wordsworth, Coleridge, Byron, Shelley, and Keats speak lines in a tremendous spiritual drama. In their effort to preserve the illusioned view of life we recognize hopes and despairs which we had vainly tried to forget. We are moved as we watch them fighting so hard against forces to which our own deepest feelings are still unreconciled. Though we can no longer read these poets for corroboration of our personal opinions, we can read them for the more legitimately critical and literary purpose of obtaining the tragic experience through a catharsis of the emotions of pity and fear.

INDEX

INDEX

This index lists the names and the principal topics which have been considered in relation to romanticism. Under that term itself, only a reference to the definition is given, since a complete list of entries would include practically every page of the book. Students interested in nature from a general philosophical viewpoint should see: Naturalism. Those interested in nature as more or less closely related to the cult of scenery should see: Nature, external.